# Get Rich – Stay Rich

# Get Rich – Stay Rich

A practical guide to successful investment

## TERRY THORNEYCROFT

CENTURY
BUSINESS

First published in the United Kingdom by Century Ltd
Random House, 20 Vauxhall Bridge Road, London SW1V 2SA

Random House Australia (Pty) Limited
20 Alfred Street, Milsons Point,
Sydney, New South Wales 2061 Australia

Random House New Zealand Limited
18 Poland Road, Glenfield
Auckland 10, New Zealand

Random House South Africa (Pty) Limited
Endulini, 5a Jubilee Road, Parktown 2193, South Africa

Random House UK Limited Reg. No. 954009

Papers used by Random House UK Limited are natural, recyclable products made from wood grown in sustainable forests. The manufacturing processes conform to the environmental regulations of the country of origin.

ISBN 0 7126 7855 7

Typeset by Deltatype Limited, Birkenhead, Merseyside
Printed and bound in Great Britain by
Mackays of Chatham Plc, Chatham, Kent

Companies, institutions and other organizations wishing to make bulk purchases of any business books published by Random House should contact their local bookstore or Random House direct:
Special Sales Director
Random House, 20 Vauxhall Bridge Road, London SW1V 2SA
Tel 0171 840 8470    Fax 0171 828 6681

# Contents

# List of Tables

# List of Figures

# Preface

After nearly thirty years in business economics, the opportunity came for me to take early retirement. Various studies of life in retirement conclude that it is either (a) the best of times if you are financially secure; or (b) the worst of times if you are totally dependent upon the State pension.

In order to make certain that, for us, it was 'the best of times', it was necessary to ensure that our modest capital would grow to provide long-term financial security. An additional factor was that the company pension was not fully index-linked; a few years of high inflation would seriously impair our wealth.

I was in the fortunate position of having spent many years studying company finances and performance – for instance, looking at companies as both actual and potential acquisition targets. It seemed logical to put this and other knowledge to good use, to work out a long-term investment plan.

My friends and neighbours were somewhat derisory about the idea of a 'thirty-year plan' – although I think that they are all looking forward to helping to spend the accumulated capital in the thirtieth year!

Undeterred, I continued to research the subject until I was happy that I had a plan which would, indeed, remain intact for at least thirty years.

Now, in order to really understand a subject, you need to do two things: not only *research* it, but also *teach* it. Out of the blue came an invitation from the local Centre for Adult Continuing Education to present a course on Investment to a group of mature students. This experience was enormously valuable in tidying up the loose ends of the plan.

The title of that course was deliberately ambiguous – 'A Layman's Guide to Investment': it could have been either (or both) the teacher or the class who were considered 'laymen'. (We don't suffer from 'laypersons' in this part of the world!)

Experience of researching the track records of 'experts' suggested that they were a club to which one would not want to belong. Indeed, the whole perspective of the course was from the point of view of the inexpert *customer* for investment products, not the professionals or 'experts' supplying the products.

The reaction of the class to the course was also ambiguous: they all wanted to come back to repeat it the following year. I'm not sure whether that meant that they liked the course or that they couldn't understand it.

Whatever the reason, it convinced me that I should write it all up in the form of this book.

My thanks, therefore, to those students: Edna Angove, Margot Chalcroft, Pam Dunn, Ruth Evans, Barbara Nancarrow, Joan Reed, Heather Selvey-Willars, Marjorie and Harry Dunstan, Ian Nunn and David Pope. Their reactions, questions and comments proved to be tremendously valuable in refining the details of the investment plan outlined in this book.

In Lesson IX, I draw extensively on the experience of working with the world's best database of actual business experience. I am greatly indebted to Keith Roberts, Tony Clayton and their colleagues of PIMS Associates for all that they have taught me about the real factors which underlie outstanding business performance. They, of course, bear no responsibility for any misinterpretation by me of the PIMS messages.

My research has also been greatly helped by articles in, and data from, various financial magazines. Those that I have found particularly helpful are *Money Observer, Money Management* and *Investors Chronicle*. All of these are excellent sources of information. Again, I naturally take full responsibility for the way in which the data have been used in arriving at my conclusions.

I would particularly like to acknowledge permission from *Money Management* to include the data contained in Table 13.1. Chapter 13 also includes extracts from *Which? Way to Save and Invest*; these extracts are reproduced by kind permission of Which? Books Ltd.

Acknowledgements are also due to the *Financial Times*, the Association of Investment Trust Companies, Profile

Books Ltd and *The Economist* for permission to use extracts from their publications; also to Datastream for permission to reproduce stock-market graphs.

The typing of the draft was expertly carried out by Lily Chapman, who managed to cope successfully with both my writing and a new word processor at the same time.

My colleague Mike Keat kindly offered to review the draft so that the book would be – in his words –'idiot proof'. His detailed editing identified many opportunities to simplify and clarify the text.

To my wife, Jean, my thanks not only for the thorough and painstaking job of proof reading, but also for her continuing help and encouragement throughout the project.

Finally, thanks are due to the many friends and neighbours, with whom it has been a great pleasure to discuss investment topics for many years.

Oh, I nearly forgot! One thing which you must be asking is this: 'Is the plan proving to be successful in practice?' I am delighted to tell you that the answer is a resounding 'Yes!'

I hope that you will adapt the messages of the course to your own needs, and that you will be just as successful.

# Part A
# Prologue

# Chapter 1
# Introduction

Do you receive loads of junk mail advertising great invest-ment opportunities, and do you wonder if they are really any good?

Are you one of the people beguiled into putting money into a high-yielding investment, only to find a year later that the capital value of your investment has decreased by more than the interest you have received?

Have you seen those adverts for unit trusts, which proclaim their top-ranking performance for each of the last five years; and then wondered why they never seem to do so well as soon as you buy them?

Do you wonder why the stock-market always seems to go down immediately after you have bought some shares?

Do you sometimes wonder how so many people in the City seem to get annual bonuses running into millions of pounds?

Or maybe you just wonder where you should invest your hard-earned capital to provide a decent return?

Don't worry, because (a) you are not alone; and (b) help is at hand.

## Objectives

The main objective of the book is to help you work your way through the maze of opportunities for investment (or, in too many cases, opportunities for making a loss), so that *you* can decide which are the best for you.

The book is arranged like a course of lectures and, like all good courses, this means that you will be expected to do some homework. By sitting down and working out some of the answers for yourself, you will learn much more than by just relying on what I tell you.

You will also be in a much better position to bring my

analysis up to date. The inevitable lead-time in producing a book means that the last full year for which I have data is 1995; other figures (such as interest rates) are correct as of mid-1996. By doing your homework conscientiously, you will learn how to obtain and use more up-to-date information. Tax rates shown include changes introduced in the November 1996 budget.

By the end of the course you should be able to work out a personal investment plan for yourself. Moreover, it will be a very stable plan: you will find that you will be able to keep to the same general principles for many years; so you will avoid most, if not all, of the high costs involved in changing from one investment to another. You may be surprised to find out just how high are the management and administrative charges on some investments.

Your personal plan will include an adequate allocation of funds for your short-term needs and also for emergencies; in both cases, you will want investments which carry low risks and are readily converted into cash. For longer-term savings, there are higher returns to be made by taking some risk; in fact, you will learn how to achieve those higher potential returns with only a quite limited degree of additional risk.

The approach can be summed up by the expression 'Get Rich Slowly'. You will not be introduced to anything of a speculative nature. Most speculative investments are good ways of getting poor quickly. For many people, 'speculative' is synonymous with 'exciting' and, for them, that is reason enough to lose one's money. However, our approach will be much more akin to that of a recent American author who advised that all the best investments were, in fact, boring ones.

The *process* of arriving at your list of 'boring' investments will, I trust, be anything but boring.

Another criterion we shall use is that our investments will be simple to implement. Indeed, most of them involve nothing more difficult than sending off a form and a cheque in the post.

Many years ago, America's most successful investor, Warren Buffett, wrote: 'To invest successfully over a lifetime does not require a stratospheric IQ, unusual business insights or inside information. What is needed is a sound intellectual framework for making decisions and the ability to keep emotions from corroding that framework.'

The objectives of this book could not be put more succinctly.

## What is not included

We are going to look solely at purely financial investments. Specifically *excluded* are:

- Land and property (including timber)
- Collectibles and antiques
- Precious metals (other than shares in gold mining companies)
- Whisky, ostriches and similar crazes

Also, there are some purely financial investments which have been deliberately ignored, for instance:

- Home Income plans
- The Enterprise Investment Scheme
- Venture Capital Trusts

The reason for all the omissions is very simple: one of the golden rules of investment is never to risk your money on something which you don't understand. Those poor (formerly rich!) people who lost millions by becoming 'Names' in the Lloyd's insurance market learned this lesson the hard way. Indeed, we should add this to our list of deliberate omissions:

- being a 'Name' at Lloyd's.

Apart from the fact that I have not studied the investments listed above, I suggest that none of them are low-risk ways of getting rich slowly.

There are two specific features of your get-rich-slowly plan which are so important that I shall need to mention them, even though I have not studied the alternatives in detail. These are: your pension and your mortgage.

I shall outline some general principles and guidelines for you to consider, but you will need to supplement these with more specialised reading and advice. (So far as your pension is concerned you may, of course, belong to an excellent company scheme.)

You will come to see that I am very unimpressed with the general level of professional financial advice, and particularly with the high charges usually associated with it. Unfortunately, it is precisely in the areas of pensions and mortgages that professionals have, so far, been most widely criticised for giving inappropriate advice.

We can only hope that this criticism has forced pensions and mortgage advisers to 'put their house in order', if you will excuse the pun. You can improve your chances of receiving good, impartial advice by choosing an adviser who works for a fixed hourly fee, rather than one who is dependent for his income on the commissions which he receives on the products which he sells you.

I shall come back to the subject of independent advisers in a minute. First, though, I should tell you something about my own background and experience.

## About the author

I was fortunate in spending most of my working life with the English China Clays Group (ECC). I say 'fortunate' deliberately, for several reasons.

First it was (certainly up to my retirement in 1991) a wonderful company to work for. For much of the time I was Head of Corporate Planning, and this had some very specific advantages directly relevant to the course. The work required a concentration on the analysis of *facts* about the ways in which economies and companies behave: you will be doing quite a lot of work yourself to establish the *facts* about the historical performance of different investments.

One particular aspect of my analytical work with the company has left an indelible impression. We worked for a time, in the late 1980's, with the world's best database on real business performance, namely the PIMS programme. (PIMS stands for 'Profit Impact of Market Strategy'.) This experience will be very much in evidence when we come to look at direct investment in ordinary shares.

My passion for facts and figures led to the publication of my previous book, with the rather long but, I hope, self-explanatory title *Seasonal Patterns in Business and Everyday Life* (Gower Press, 1987). This original research work will be the basis of the suggestion on *when* (at what time of the year) to buy and sell shares.

Another of the advantages of working for ECC was that the head office of the company was, at that time, located in Cornwall. From a personal point of view this was, of course, very pleasant. However, it also has a distinct bearing on this course: it is, I am convinced, much easier to develop a long-term investment strategy when one is remote from the day-to-day events of the City. It can sometimes be quite amusing to watch the antics of the City at a safe distance, via Teletext. One day the share price pages will be littered with red figures (to indicate shares falling in price) because of some relatively minor snippet of news, only for the pages to be equally dominated by blue (to indicate rising prices) a few days later for no better reason. It is doubly amusing when the news item concerns some published statistic (for instance, on the level of retail sales or the state of the American economy) which is later revised, as is often the case, to something less dramatic.

As practical evidence for the benefits of being remote from the action, perhaps I can cite experience with the unit trust competition which used to be run by *The Money Programme* in conjunction with *The Times* newspaper. I was twice a prize-winner in that competition, a record which is shared by one other person to my knowledge – and he hails from the same remote town in Cornwall.

From all this, you would be correct in judging that my own investment success has been based on taking a steady, long-term view of events and on factual analysis of historical performance. This is what I intend to share with you.

Occasionally, during the course, I shall introduce you to 'Thorneycroft's Laws of Successful Investment'. These are guidelines of great significance to investment planning which are, none the less, not always fully appreciated.

## Investment Advisers

What I am *not* is an authorised financial adviser; nothing in the book is to be construed as a recommendation to invest in a specific product. (So please don't write to me for advice!)

Rather, the book presents general guidelines for successful investment and *information* on a wide range of specific investment products. It is intended primarily for people who wish to make *their own* investment decisions.

Nevertheless, you may feel it necessary to seek further and more specific guidance from an authorised financial adviser. In which case, you have a choice of three types of adviser. First, there are *tied agents* who represent one company and its products. However, you will most likely prefer the wider horizons provided by independent financial advisers, who come in two varieties:

### Commission-based

These advisers live off the commission which they receive on the products which they persuade you to buy. Details can be obtained from *Yellow Pages* (see under 'Financial Advisers' and 'Insurance Brokers') or from IFA Promotions (tel 0117 971 1177), who will give you the names and addresses of independent financial advisers in your area.

### Fee-based

Fee-based advisers will, I understand, normally give you an introductory interview free of charge, after which they charge by the hour. They should refund to you any commission which they receive on the products which you choose. They should also be much more likely to point you in the direction of products which do not carry high charges (for instance, investment trusts rather than unit trusts).

For information on such advisers in your locality, contact either The Institute of Financial Planning (tel 0117 930 4434), or The National Directory of Fee-based Advisers (tel 0117 976 9444).

For relatively small investments, the commission-based adviser is likely to be cheaper; but, clearly, the larger the amount to be invested, the more will the fee-based route be preferable.

It is perfectly in order to 'shop around' and discuss your needs with several advisers until you find one with whom you feel comfortable.

There is one publication which you should certainly study before consulting an investment adviser. This is a list of *101 Golden Rules for Investors*, published by the Investors Compensation Scheme. It is available free of charge by phoning 0171 628 8820.

The course of lessons presented in this book contains material which even an experienced financial adviser is unlikely to have come across elsewhere. Before we get down to the details, I will give you an overview of the course.

# Chapter 2
# Outline of the Course

Lecturers at my local Technical College are asked to provide a 'taster' class to precede the first formal lesson. This excellent idea offers students the opportunity to see if the course is really for them.

This chapter, then, is a taster of the full course.

If you are reading this in the hope of finding a quick-and-easy way to riches, then this course is *not* for you; our aim will be to 'get rich slowly'. The emphasis is on minimising risk and on the protection of your capital. That does not mean to say that we shall not be looking at high-risk investments – far from it – but what we *shall* be emphasising is a strategy for converting high-risk investments into a much lower-risk plan of action.

Why should we want to consider high-risk investments at all? The answer is, of course, that such investments carry the *potential* for much higher returns than their lower-risk cousins. In other words, we can draw a graph like this:

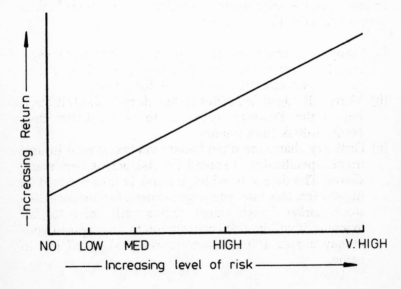

In the first full lesson we shall put some numbers onto the vertical axis of the graph, to indicate the kind of return which we might expect at each level of risk. I shall define what I mean by 'return' in the next chapter.

Subsequent lessons will deal with each category of investment in order of increasing risk: No-Risk; Low-Risk; Medium-Risk; High-Risk; Very-High Risk.

The Low-Risk category is further sub-divided into: Very-Low-Risk; Low-Risk; Fairly-Low-Risk.

In fact, we shall see that some investments which are often regarded as Low-Risk actually spill over into the Medium-Risk category.

That Medium-Risk category can itself be sub-divided, this time into two different *types* of investment:

(a) individual investments which are Medium-Risk in their own right
(b) investment products which are Medium-Risk because they are 'hybrids': they are 'packaged' from a mixture of Low, Medium and High-Risk investments

Allocating individual investments to one of five risk categories is inevitably somewhat subjective. Sometimes we shall find that we start off by putting a particular investment in one category, only to change our minds when we look at it more closely. For example:

(a) Many investments which even a highly reputable magazine like *Money Observer* describes as No-Risk will be seen, on examination, to be Low-Risk ones.
(b) Many gilt-edged securities (gilts), despite the full backing of the Treasury, turn out to be no better than Medium-Risk investments.
(c) Ordinary shares are often bought via investment in unit trusts, specifically to spread the risk across very many shares. The degree to which the risk is thus reduced is, in practice, less than you might expect: for instance, in a stock-market 'crash' most shares will tend to fall together; it will be little consolation to have spread your money across 100 different shares if they *all* fall in value.

(d) On the other hand, there *is* a very good way of spreading (or reducing) the risks involved in ordinary shares, namely by spreading the purchases over *time*. Regular monthly savings into a unit trust or investment trust converts a High-Risk investment into something no worse than a Medium-Risk one.

Example (d) exemplifies what we shall consider to be 'good' investments: it's not just that they give good rates of return on our capital; more precisely, they give better than average rates of return *for their level of risk*.

Expanding on our earlier diagram:

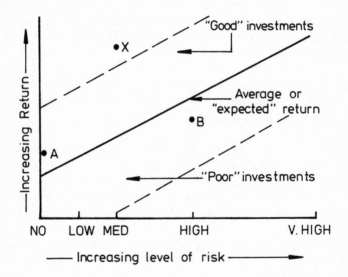

'Good' investments are those lying *above* the 'average' line; 'poor' investments lie *below* it. So, a No-Risk investment yielding A% per annum is a better one than a High-Risk investment yielding B% per annum, even though the *average* or *expected* return on the High-Risk investment is the higher of the two. (Because it *is* High-Risk, the actual return may turn out to be higher than B%, but equally it may also turn out to be very much lower.)

Of course, what we would really like is an investment which would be at, say, point X on the above diagram: a return commensurate with High-Risk investments, but with only a modest actual level of risk.

Too much to hope for? Well, no! We shall find such an investment and, because it is so outstanding, it will play a key role in our overall investment strategy.

By 'strategy' I mean a long-term plan of campaign whose general features remain the same more or less for ever.

We shall come on to that towards the end of the book, in Chapter 16.

## Summary of the course contents

As part of your taster, I should now like to summarise what we shall be covering in each lesson. The summary is given in table 2.1.

## Table 2.1  Summary of course contents

**Lesson I   RISK AND RETURN**

The Risk v Return graph

The kind of returns to expect from different investments

Inflation and tax

**Lesson II   NO-RISK INVESTMENTS**

Protecting the real value of your capital

Index-linked investments

Introduction to 'gilts' and 'annuities': the No-Risk varieties

**Lesson III   LOW-RISK INVESTMENTS – PRINCIPLES**

Investing for income

Fixed or variable capital; fixed or variable interest rates

Sub-categories of risk

Comparisons with No-Risk investments

**Lesson IV   LOW-RISK INVESTMENTS – PRODUCTS**

Banks and building societies, including TESSAs

National Savings products

Short-dated gilts

Guaranteed income and growth bonds

Strong foreign currencies

**Lesson V   MEDIUM-RISK INVESTMENTS – PRODUCTS**

Long-dated and undated gilts

Permanent interest bearing shares (PIBS)

'Conditional' investment bonds

Corporate bonds

Split-capital investment trusts – income shares

Zero dividend preference shares (zeros)

**Lesson VI   MEDIUM-RISK INVESTMENTS – HYBRID PRODUCTS**

'Managed' funds; charges

Introduction to regular savings schemes

'With-profits' endowment policies

Single-premium insurance bonds

Friendly society bonds

Pension plans

SAYE share option schemes

**Lesson VII   HIGH-RISK INVESTMENTS – INTRODUCTION TO ORDINARY SHARES**

Investing for profit

Company accounts – simplified!

Risk factors – company characteristics

Risk factors – stock-market characteristics

Spreading the risk

More about regular savings schemes

Introduction to unit trusts and investment trusts

Britain's best-kept investment secret

Personal equity plans (PEPs)

**Lesson VIII   HIGH-RISK INVESTMENTS – COLLECTIVE FUNDS**

More about unit trusts and investment trusts

Performance data: consistency of performance

Performance data: geographical regions

A key geographical region for future growth

**Lesson IX   HIGH-RISK INVESTMENTS – CHOOSING SHARES FOR LONG-TERM GROWTH**

Experts' 'tips' – historical evidence

Factors associated with good business performance

Factors associated with increasing shareholder value

Building up a short-list of candidates

When to buy

**Lesson X   VERY-HIGH-RISK INVESTMENTS**

Share 'perks'

Split-capital investment trusts – capital shares

Warrants

An intriguing investment opportunity

These various lessons will be interspersed with some homework. In some cases, this will be no more than asking you to think about the subject of the next lesson; however, the more important homework is that which will involve you in doing some calculations yourself.

## What you will need

No taster lesson would be complete without letting you know what other items you will need in order to complete the course. They are:

- A recent Saturday edition of the *Financial Times*.
- A recent monthly issue of the magazine *Money Observer* (the leading monthly magazine covering personal finance and investment topics)
- A pocket calculator

Don't be put off by the pocket calculator. The most complicated operation you will be asked to do is to divide one number by another.

You should also go along to your local Post Office and collect the following brochures:

- *Investor's Guide – Options from National Savings* (and the separate leaflet giving the current interest rates)
- *Government Stock*

You will find perhaps half-a-dozen investment magazines in good newsagents. Of these, *Money Observer* is the one which best suits our purposes. It contains some excellent and very sensible articles; more importantly, for this course, it contains very appropriate seven-year performance statistics on unit trusts and investment trusts.

If you should want to extend the historical evidence to ten years, then the magazine to choose is *Money Management*. This also has occasional and very useful statistical surveys of the performance of monthly savings plans and has some excellent articles on the charges associated with various kinds of investment.

A more specialised magazine, *Investment Trusts*, will be of interest when we come to Lesson VIII.

As you become more enthusiastic about investments, you may want to take out a regular subscription to the *Financial Times* (Saturday editions) and *Money Observer*. However, the last thing I want to do is to encourage you to spend some of your increased investment income and profits on reading matter. Don't forget to see what is available in your local library.

This will be particularly appropriate when we come to look at ordinary shares. A good reference library should have a copy of a joint *Financial Times*/Extel publication *Major UK Companies Handbook*. This is updated every six months and has a valuable five-year summary for each of almost 900 UK companies. Alternatively, rather similar information is published quarterly in the *Company Guide*. This covers the complete range of UK companies.

The same libraries should have current and back issues of the monthly *Investors Chronicle* which has a quarterly index. It's well worth looking at this magazine before investing in a particular company.

A good general guide to investment is produced by the Consumers' Association: this is the book *Which? Way to Save and Invest*. This is available to members of the Association; but if you are not a member, then again you should be able to find it in a good reference library.

You are now all set up and ready to go. Just before I give you your first exercise, I shall need to define a few terms which we shall be using throughout the course.

# Chapter 3
# Definitions

I shall need to define just a few terms now, and a few others as we go along. However, the emphasis will be very much on simplicity, for the very good reason that straightforward investments are the best ones for getting rich slowly.

The world of finance is full of all kinds of complicated jargon which is of little relevance to us. Moreover, it is also littered (I use the word deliberately) with investment products which are so complicated that it is impossible for the ordinary investor to understand them, except for one general feature: namely, that they seem to offer the opportunity for various tiers of managers and advisers to get their hands on much of the money before the investor receives his income.

In fact, this is an appropriate time to introduce my first law of investment:

---

*Thorneycroft's First Law of Successful Investment*

**If an investment looks or sounds too
clever by half, or too good to be true, it is!**

---

I know that this is not an original thought, but it is one which needs to be remembered at all times.

The first word which it is useful to define is 'Investment' itself. According to *Chambers English Dictionary*: **Investment** . . . placing of money to secure *income* or *profit* [my italics].

It is important to remind ourselves, at the outset, of the difference between the two words which I have shown in italics.

We can invest our money for *income* by *lending* it to, or

depositing it with, someone in exchange for a specified rate of interest; that 'someone' may be, amongst others, a bank, a building society, a company, a local authority, or the government. For instance, we can lend money to the government in one of two ways:

(a) by acquiring National Savings products
(b) by buying 'gilts' (which will be introduced in Lesson I).

When *lending* money, our income does not depend on how much 'profit' the borrower makes, except in the extreme case that, if the borrower should go 'bust', we may end up losing all or part of our capital and hence the future income.

The word **bond** is often used as a general term for such fixed-interest loans, and this word will frequently be used in the course in this way.

Investing-for-profit arises, not from lending money but by *owning* something – for instance, by owning shares in a company. Before we can receive our share of profits (in the form of **dividends**), the company will first of all have to *make* a profit, and then will have to pay the interest to all of the other people who have simply lent it money.

Hence, investing-for-profit is always going to be more risky than investing-for-income. So, why should we even think about ownership? The answer, of course, is that we hope to obtain a higher **return** on our money than by just lending it to someone. Much of that higher return may come, not so much from the dividends we receive, but from the **capital gain** we hope to make from an increase in the value of the shares.

It should come as no surprise to anticipate that No-Risk and Low-Risk investments are those where we *lend* money; and the High-Risk investments are those where we *own* something such as shares.

We can hence annotate our basic graph as follows:

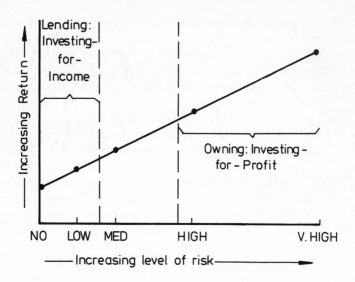

As mentioned earlier, the Medium-Risk category includes hybrids, or mixtures of the other categories of investment. It also includes some unusual investments in which, although you are really investing-for-income, you are also legally a shareholder (or owner) of a company.

A company generally raises the money it needs for running its business from a mixture of the two types of investment: both loans (or bonds) and shares. This leads us to define two particular words which you will come across frequently, namely 'equity' and 'gearing'.

**Equity** is simply the residual value (of a property or a company) after paying off all loans and any other charges. The equity of a company is hence the value of what is owned by the shareholders, and the words 'shares' and 'equities' are synonymous.

**Gearing** is a term used to describe the ratio of loan capital to share capital; that is, of debt to equity. This should become clear by considering what happens when you take out a mortgage on a house.

Suppose that you buy a house for £100,000, put down £10,000 as a deposit from your own resources, and borrow

£90,000 from a building society. Your 'balance sheet' will look like this:

| | |
|---|---|
| Your equity in the house | £ 10,000 |
| Loan from building society | £ 90,000 |
| | |
| Total capital cost of house | £100,000 |

You have a gearing ratio of 9:1; that is, your debt level is nine times the value of your own equity in the house.

Now see what happens if the house goes up or down in value by £20,000; start with an *increase* in value of that amount. Your balance sheet is now:

| | |
|---|---|
| Your equity in the house | £ 30,000 |
| Loan from building society | £ 90,000 |
| | |
| Total value of the house | £120,000 |

A 20% increase in the value of your house has resulted in a *tripling* in the value of your equity in the property. This illustrates the positive possibilities of a high level of gearing.

But what happens if the value of the house *falls* by 20%?

| | |
|---|---|
| Your equity in the house | *minus* £10,000 |
| Loan from building society | £90,000 |
| | |
| Total value of the house | £80,000 |

This is the phenomenon which has become all too common in recent years, namely 'negative equity'. Thus, high gearing can act both ways; it introduces a level of **risk** which is not shared by the lender who puts up the loan capital. Incidentally, recent history bears out the view that owning a house for profit is, like owning shares, not a low-risk investment.

This example of house purchase was a practical illustration

of the differences between the two forms of investment, 'lending' and 'owning'. Usually, there is a clear distinction between investing-for-income (lending) and investing-for-profit (owning). In one particular case, however, this distinction is very blurred. It concerns the building society which may have loaned the mortgage money for the house in the above illustration.

In order to lend you the money for your house, the building society first has to borrow the money itself, most of it coming from private individuals. These individuals have traditionally thought of themselves as *lenders*, receiving a fairly modest but low-risk return on their investments. However, building societies (unlike companies) do not separately issue shares (or equities) on which to pay out profits in the form of dividends: the *lenders* are actually the *owners* of the societies as well.

This fact has come as a very pleasant surprise in recent years to holders of several building society accounts. For instance, when Lloyds Bank acquired the Cheltenham & Gloucester Building Society, the investors in C&G received very attractive hand-outs in their capacity as owners. There has, inevitably, been a subsequent heightening of interest in building societies generally.

As lenders, investors will continue to receive a steady low-risk rate of interest; as owners, the risks are very high: there are two main possibilities:

(a)  they receive a 'bonanza' because their society is taken over or converts itself into a public company
(b)  they receive nothing because nothing happens to alter the status of the society

This illustrates what we shall define by the term **risk**: namely, the *unpredictability* of an investment in respect of its annual return and any future capital gain or loss; the more unpredictable the outcome – that is, the wider the possible range of future outcomes – the greater the risk.

Note, also, that risk should not be considered as just a negative phenomenon. We tend naturally to think of risk as the danger of *losing* one's money; but, defined as above, there is also the 'risk' of achieving a much *higher*-than-anticipated return. For many years, the high risks which, we now know, are associated with house ownership were *always* on the positive side, and a great deal of money was made.

'Risk' is sometimes also used to mean something else, which I prefer to call **volatility**. This refers to the day-to-day or month-to-month variations in the value of an investment, rather than the uncertainty in the final outcome of an investment when you come to cash it in.

Generally speaking, investments which are more volatile *are* also more risky, but this is not always the case: in particular, a one-off purchase of shares is likely to be both risky *and* volatile; whereas the same shares bought via a regular savings scheme will be equally volatile but *very* much less risky.

Finally, there is one word which I have already used quite frequently without as yet defining it. This is the word **return**. I shall also need to define the words **real** and **net** when applied to investment returns.

I can usefully illustrate all three terms by introducing a very basic formula which I want you to get into the habit of using.

We will take, as our example, the case of a simple investment in a bank account. Suppose this is advertised to yield an interest rate of 6% per annum, paid just once per year without the prior deduction of tax; assume that you have to pay tax on this income at the rate of 20%.

Let us see what this income is really worth to you, which is what I term the 'Total Net Real Return' on your investment. Having the account in a bank, rather than a building society means that we can conveniently ignore the possibility of a capital gain in this example.

The calculation is as follows:

| | |
|---|---|
| Gross Income | 6.0% |
| *minus* Tax (at 20%) | −1.2% |
| = Net Income | 4.8% |
| *plus/minus* Capital Gain/Loss | — |
| = Total Net Return | 4.8% |
| *minus* Inflation, say | −3.5% |
| **= Total Net Real Return** | **1.3% pa** |

(Note that this calculation is not strictly correct, mathematically; it is only an approximation, albeit a very close one. For the correct mathematical analysis, see the note on page 26 at the end of this chapter.)

So now we can see how the various words are used:

**Total** means the sum of net income (interest or dividends) plus capital gain, if any.

**Net** means net-of-taxation, that is, after deducting any liability to personal tax. In several cases it may additionally mean net of any charges made by the company or organisation offering the investment product. Capital gains are assumed to be tax-free – see next chapter.

**Real** means after taking into account the effects of inflation; unless you leave in the account enough of the annual interest to compensate for inflation, you will be depleting the *real* value of your investment in terms of the goods and services which it could buy.

**Return** means the annual benefit to you of the investment, taking into account both income and any capital gain (or loss) and adjusting for tax and inflation as above.

From the outset, I should like you to get used to evaluating alternative investments in terms of the **Total Net Real Return** which you will (or which you expect to) make on them, using the step-by-step calculation illustrated above.

Before we leave the subject of returns-on-investment, I need to mention something which you will often have seen in the advertisements of building societies and banks: this is the 'Compound Annual Rate' or CAR for short.

The CAR is the true rate of interest for investments paying interest more than once per year. (For investments paying out just once per year, this **true** rate is the same as the **nominal** or advertised rate of interest). Note that the word 'true' is not to be confused with the word 'real'; the true rate of interest still has to be adjusted for tax and inflation in order to calculate the real return.

Suppose that we have two alternative investments, each advertised as offering a rate of interest of 6% pa. Investment A makes interest payments once per year, starting 12 months after the investment was made; investment B pays out the annual interest in two instalments, at intervals of 6 months. We invest £100 in each. After 6 months, investment B gives us an interim payment of £3, which we can then re-invest for the next 6 months (at 6% pa): this provides additional interest of 9p at the end of the year. (6% pa interest for 6 months = 3%; which, on £3, comes to 9p.)

So, at the end of the year, the total interest received – the true rate of interest or CAR – is, for each investment:

Investment A (annual interest payment)        6   % pa
Investment B (half-yearly interest payments)  6.09% pa

This difference may not seem very much, but the effect becomes more significant at higher rates of interest and more frequent payouts. At an advertised, or 'nominal' rate of interest of 10% pa, an account paying interest quarterly would give you a true CAR of almost 10½% pa, which could be a very worthwhile bonus.

When we come to scale-up returns to allow for these mid-year payouts, we shall assume (for the purposes of tax calculations) that the interest payments are re-invested in similar securities and at the same tax rate.

Before moving on to the next chapter, you might like to re-read the last few pages to make sure that you are completely happy with the difference in the meanings of the words 'true' and 'real' when applied to investments.

### Mathematical note

This note is included for mathematical precision, but you do not need to study it.

In the example given on page 23, the inflation rate (assumed to be 3.5% pa) is simply *subtracted* from the 'Total Net Return' of 4.8% pa to give a 'Total Net *Real* Return' of 1.3% pa.

It would be more precise to calculate the Total Net Real Return as follows:

Total Net Real Return
= 100. $[ (1+ a/100) / (1+b/100) - 1]$

where

$a$ = the 'Total Net Return' (% pa)

and

$b$ = the Inflation rate (% pa)

In the example given in the text, this would give:
Total Net Real Return = 100.$[(1.048/1.035) - 1]$
= 1.26% pa

This is marginally lower than the figure of 1.3% pa given by the simple approximation used in the text. Indeed, the mathematically correct figures will *always* be slightly lower than the one which we calculate by simple subtraction, so long as all the interest rates and inflation rates are positive.

The difference need not concern us, and we shall continue to use the simple calculation shown in the text.

# Chapter 4
# Assumptions

## Your Tax Rate

Generally, the calculations illustrated in the course will assume that you pay tax at the standard rates applicable following the 1996 budget:

- 20% on investment income (interest and dividends)
- 23% on earned income

When we look at the *historic* performance of various investments, these will be based on the tax rates which existed at the time.

The calculations will often be shown, also, for someone who does not pay tax. Even if you, yourself, are a taxpayer, you may have a spouse who is not: don't miss out on the opportunity to transfer enough capital to the non-taxpayer for him or her to earn income up to the tax-free amount.

If your marginal tax rate (that is, the rate which applies to any additional income) is at the higher rate of 40 per cent, it will be necessary for you to do your own adjustments to the figures.

## Capital Gains Tax

It will be assumed that you are not, and will not be, liable for capital gains tax. If you *are* liable for such tax, then you will again need to make your own adjustments.

## Inflation

Future inflation is a major unknown in our investment planning. You will need to make some assumption (or guess) about its future level. I shall suggest (in Lesson II) how you might go about this.

The one general assumption that I make throughout the course is that inflation will not be *negative*; in other words, that prices will always go *up* and never (for any significant period of time) go down.

This has not always been the case: in the Great Depression of the 1930s, prices *did* fall, and quite dramatically. I assume that modern governments will prefer a little inflation to a lot of short-term unemployment. Indeed, at the time of writing, the government has an explicit inflation target of 1% to 4% pa; note that the target does not contemplate even the *possibility* of falling prices. This is a clear indication that the government will continue to tolerate some degree of inflation.

One would imagine (or hope) that a *Conservative* government would put sound money very high on its list of priorities. It is a sad and sobering thought that, since it came to office in 1979, the recent period of Conservative government produced a decline in the value of money of over 60 per cent!

A British economist, Roger Bootle, has argued that, in the future, prices may well fall. Whilst that is, indeed, possible, the most reasonable (and prudent) assumption at this time would be for the continuation of modest price rises. We shall see, during the course, that inflation as 'low' as 2 or 3 per cent per year still makes significant in-roads into the real returns which you can obtain on your investments.

## Age

Yes, this can make a difference to the calculations! The reason is that people over sixty-five are eligible for a higher rate of personal allowance before they start paying tax. However, above a certain income, you lose £1 of this allowance for every £2 of additional income. Within a fairly narrow band of income, this means that your marginal tax rate for investment income would increase from 20% to 30%. For someone in the appropriate age and income bands, the calculation is as follows: an additional £100 of income attracts the normal tax on investment income of 20 per cent; in addition, that tax rate is applied to £50 of tax relief that is forgone, so that a further £10 is lost in tax.

For simplicity, I have had to assume that you do *not* fall into the range in which you lose, in lost tax allowance, part of your additional income.

The relevant bands are as follows (1997/8 tax year). For a single person reaching the age of 65, the annual personal allowance is increased from the standard rate of £4,045 to £5,220; in other words, such a person could have an additional £1,175 of annual income before paying tax. However, if that same person has a total annual income in excess of £15,600, then the additional allowance is reduced by £1 for every £2 of his income above that figure. Thus, within the annual income range of £15,600 to £17,950 there is effectively a 30% tax on any additional investment income.

The age-related allowance is higher for married couples and also higher again for people over 75. If you think that you may fall within the critical range, it would be best to check on the current figures, so far as they affect you personally, with your local tax office.


## Sex

One assumption that I am *not* making is that the investor is male. I have earlier used the expression '*his* income' in which the masculine form is used in the traditional way to include both masculine and feminine, rather than using the form 'his or her income'. The modern use of the latter, rather cumbersome form, seems to be symptomatic of a society which is more interested in equality than in quality.

The reasons for not succumbing to the current fashion are not trivial: they relate directly to the attitude of mind which one needs to develop in order to be a successful investor.

First, one needs to develop a *long-term* perspective of financial trends: as with social and linguistic trends, the latest fad may not be (and very often isn't) a good guide to what will be best for the future.

Second, when we come to look at investing in different

parts of the world, we shall want to identify those countries which are 'economically correct' rather than 'politically correct' if we are to achieve long-term growth in our investments.

Third, our study of individual company shares will highlight the over-riding importance of factors such as *quality* and *differentiation* as characteristics of companies which provide long-term value for shareholders (as well as for customers).

In summary, we shall be much more successful as investors if we have an instinctive appreciation of *quality* in everything; for us, *e*quality is the antithesis of quality.

So, Ladies and Gentlemen, it is now time for you to do some work!

# Chapter 5
# Preliminary Homework

In Chapter 3, I defined what I mean by the expression 'Total Net Real Return' or 'real return' for short. For your first homework, I would like you to think what the real return might have been, over the last twenty-five years or more, on various investments.

There are many different ways of going about this task. You could, of course, just guess the answers! In one way, I would be quite happy for you to do just that: comparing your instinctive guesses with the actual answers should throw up some surprises; and these surprises should help to fix more clearly in your mind the real returns which one might expect from past experience.

For those of you who would like to consider the question more carefully, here are a few mathematical pointers to help you with your estimates.

## Rate of return v increase in capital value

Over long periods of time, relatively small differences in compound growth rates can make a huge difference to the final capital value of an investment. For instance, consider the difference between returns of 3% pa and 4% pa on an initial investment of £1,000. Now, the difference between 3% and 4% does not sound very much, but see how that difference translates into a significant difference in capital value at the end of 25 years:

| Return | Final value of initial £1,000 investment |
|--------|------------------------------------------|
| 3.0% pa | £2,094 |
| 4.0% pa | £2,666 |

In the second case, your capital gain of £1,666 is over half as much again as it would be at the slightly lower rate of return.

There are two lessons to remember from such figures:-

(a) The performance comparisons in the course are going to be given in terms of real returns; don't forget that relatively small differences in such returns (as little as $\frac{1}{2}$% pa) can make a considerable difference to your capital after many years of investment. (And we shall see that some investment products can gobble up 2% pa or more in charges.)

(b) Conversely, when answering the homework questions on pages 34 to 35, remember that some of the quite huge increases in capital values may not signify such high real returns per year as you might have thought.

**Table 5.1  Converting rates of return into changes in capital value for lump-sum investments.**

| Compound annual rate of return | £1,000 invested; all net income re-invested | | | | |
|---|---|---|---|---|---|
| | Value at end of | | | | |
| | 5 years | 10 years | 15 years | 20 years | 25 years |
| 0% | 1,000 | 1,000 | 1,000 | 1,000 | 1,000 |
| 1% | 1,051 | 1,105 | 1,161 | 1,220 | 1,282 |
| 2% | 1,104 | 1,219 | 1,346 | 1,486 | 1,641 |
| 3% | 1,159 | 1,344 | 1,558 | 1,806 | 2,094 |
| 4% | 1,217 | 1,480 | 1,801 | 2,191 | 2,666 |
| 5% | 1,276 | 1,629 | 2,079 | 2,653 | 3,386 |
| 6% | 1,338 | 1,791 | 2,397 | 3,207 | 4,292 |
| 8% | 1,469 | 2,159 | 3,172 | 4,661 | 6,848 |
| 10% | 1,611 | 2,594 | 4,177 | 6,727 | 10,835 |
| 12% | 1,762 | 3,106 | 5,474 | 9,646 | 17,000 |
| 14% | 1,925 | 3,707 | 7,138 | 13,743 | 26,462 |
| 16% | 2,100 | 4,411 | 9,266 | 19,461 | 40,872 |
| 18% | 2,288 | 5,234 | 11,974 | 27,393 | 62,669 |
| 20% | 2,488 | 6,192 | 15,407 | 38,338 | 95,396 |
| 25% | 3,052 | 9,313 | 28,422 | 86,736 | 264,700 |

Table 5.1 sets out the final value of an investment for different rates of return and different time-scales. This will be a useful reference table throughout the course, to enable you to convert annual returns into increases in capital value.

## The Rule of 72

Another way that you may like to proceed is as follows: consider how many years are likely to have elapsed before an investment has doubled in value. For example, you may think that a particular investment (with all net income re-invested) may be expected to have doubled in value in ten years. This figure can be converted into an annual rate of return using the 'rule of 72'.

Just divide the number 72 by the number of years it takes to double the value of an investment: the result is an accurate estimate of the compound annual rate of return.

So, using the above example, if our investment doubles in value in 10 years, then a good estimate of the annual rate of return is 7.2%.

The formula works equally well the other way round. Thus, if you have an investment yielding 10% pa compound rate of return, then you can estimate that it will double in value in about 7.2 years.

## The Analytical Approach

Perhaps the best and most logical way is to use the step-by-step process which was introduced in Chapter 3. In other words, for each question estimate the individual components of the Total Net Real Return:

| Gross Income (interest rate or dividend yield) | $G\%$ |
| --- | --- |
| *minus* Tax (at 20%) | . . . % |
| = Net income | . . . % |
| *plus/minus* Capital Gain/Loss | $C\%$ |
| = Total Net Return | . . . % |
| *minus* Inflation | $-I\%$ |
| **= Total Net Real Return** | **. . . % pa** |

You can, of course, use either of the earlier tips (on capital values and 'the rule of 72') in order to establish some or all of the individual components $G$, $C$ and $I$.

By tackling the questions in this way, you will at least be certain of not forgetting to include the negative effects of tax and inflation.

## Questions

The first set of questions takes a 25-year historical view. Imagine that, in each case, you invested £1,000 twenty-five years ago and re-invested all the net income. What would the real return have been over that period, if the money was invested in:

**Question 1.** A higher-rate building society account?

**Question 2.** A wide spread of ordinary UK shares?

**Question 3.** Regular monthly payments for 25 years into a 'with-profits' endowment policy (the kind of thing which, under the title 'endowment mortgage', has been a familiar method in recent years of saving to pay off a mortgage)?

**Question 4.** Adverts for a particular unit trust, the 'M&G Recovery Fund', indicate that an investment of £1,000 in May 1969 (when the trust was launched) would have grown by April 1993 (that's actually only 24 years later) to £222,538. What was the real return per year?

The next set of questions takes an even longer-term view.

**Question 5.** According to the magazine *Management Today*, anyone who invested £1,000 in the company BTR in 1965 would, by 1994, be a millionaire. What real return would convert £1,000 in 1965 into £1 million in those 29 years?

**Question 6.** Adverts for Britain's oldest investment trust, namely Foreign & Colonial Investment Trust, indicate that an investment of £1,000 in December 1945 would have grown to be worth £1,017,116 by December 1995, fifty years later. What real return do these figures indicate?

**Question 7.** An excellent *Equity-Gilt Study* is produced annually by stockbrokers BZW. The data start off at December 1918 and so provide a very long performance history for both equities (ordinary shares) and gilts (UK government bonds). What average real rates of return do you think might have been achieved since then:

(a) for equities?
(b) for gilts?

**Question 8.** If you regard nearly 80 years as being a little short-term, what about 300 years? Over that period, what real annual return do you think investors have expected to receive on what they perceive to be risk-free investments?

**Question 9.** Finally, what kind of real return would you hope to receive, on average and over a long period of time, on your investments? Write it down.

Part II
The Course

# Part B
# The Course

# Chapter 6
# Lesson I: Risk and Return

We will start the course by looking at the answers to the preliminary homework questions, although not in the same order as they were posed. From these answers, we will put some numbers onto the Risk v Reward graph:

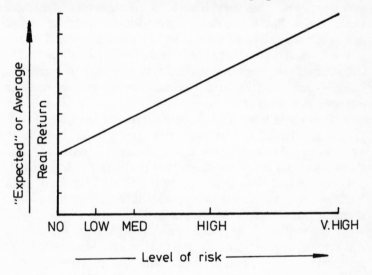

The reasons for wanting to fix this graph in your mind are as follows:

(a) It is important to have a realistic view of the likely future returns from different investments at different levels of risk.

(b) We need to bear in mind, for any level of risk, how that 'realistic view' of the likely future returns compares with the return from No-Risk investments. (In other words, is the risk worth taking for the additional rewards?)

(c) The graph provides a straightforward way of differentiating between 'good' investments (which have returns *higher* than would be indicated by the graph) and 'poor' investments (which have returns falling *below* the line).

So, let us now move on to the answers to the homework questions. We shall start with Question 8.

## Question 8. No-Risk investments

We start with the very long-term returns on investments perceived as having no risk. The No-Risk investments which are available today will be the subject of Lesson II.

We have seen that one of the principal investment risks is inflation. It is, perhaps, difficult to imagine that inflation has become a serious and persistent problem only since the Second World War.

A few years ago, *The Economist* magazine published a graph of a British consumer price index going back to the year 1661. After various ups-and-downs (with as many downs as ups) the price index was no higher in 1914 than it was in 1661. It then rose during the Great War, only to fall back again in the Great Depression of the 1930s to *below* its starting point nearly 300 years earlier.

At the outbreak of the Second World War, prices were only 13% higher than in 1661. However, from that time onwards we have seen an inexorable rise in prices; so much so that money has subsequently lost around 97% of its 1939 value.

In the eighteenth and nineteenth centuries, before the ravages of inflation (and tax), the general level of long-term interest rates on UK government bonds was around 3% pa. The exception was at and around the time of the Napoleonic Wars, when interest rates rose to around 5% pa to compensate for a temporary period of price inflation: prices roughly doubled in the twenty years from 1793 to 1813. If you recall the 'Rule of 72', you will quickly calculate that a doubling of prices in 20 years represented an inflation 'blip' of about 3.6% pa, so that real interest rates fell to around 1½% pa in that period.

At times of *falling* prices, the real interest rate would have been higher than 3% pa. However, on average over a very long period of time, it looks as if investors expected and received around 3% pa on what they perceived to be No-Risk investments.

If you are interested in looking in more detail at the histories of inflation and interest rates respectively, two fascinating sources are: 'Short History of Inflation' in *The Economist*, 22 February 1992, and *A History of Interest Rates* by Sidney Homer (2nd edition, Rutgers University Press, 1977).

Anyway, coming back to the figures, at times when inflation and tax were not perceived to be threats, the return on secure government bonds was around 3% pa or a little more.

In more recent years, the real tax-free return on index-linked National Savings certificates has varied between 2½% and 4½% pa (although currently it is at the bottom end of that range).

We can, therefore, take with some confidence a figure of 3% pa as our benchmark for the real return on No-Risk investments. This gives us the first figure for our graph:

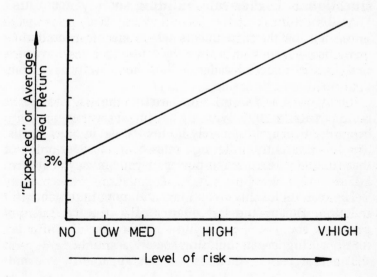

It not only gives us our first figure, it provides the basis for my second 'law':

---

*Thorneycroft's Second Law of Successful Investment*

**You cannot expect to obtain a real interest rate much in excess of 3% pa without taking some risk or receiving part of the interest out of your own real capital.**

---

If an investment appears to offer you a return substantially in excess of 3% pa, you should look carefully at the degree of risk involved and whether the *real* value of your capital will remain intact. Some recent investment products which give the impression of being Low-Risk put even the *nominal* value of your capital at risk. You should *always* consider whether you would be better off with a totally risk-free investment yielding around 3% pa over and above the inflation rate.

We turn, now, to Low-Risk investments.

## Question 1. Higher-rate building society accounts

These will be the investments which are most familiar to many people. They have been the traditional safe haven for savings for many decades – but how well have they performed, and how safe *are* they?

It may come as a surprise to learn that the real return over the 25 years to 1995, with all net income re-invested, has been *negative*: approximately *minus* 1% pa. In other words, despite apparently quite high rates of interest for much of that time, the real buying power of your money will have fallen.

The reasons for this are: (a) tax; and more importantly (b) inflation. During the last quarter of a century, inflation averaged about 9% pa, a little higher than the after-tax return on higher-rate building society accounts.

The first lesson, then, is that an apparently safe-and-secure investment such as a building society account cannot be classed as No-Risk: not only is there a theoretical risk of losing part of your capital, it has actually happened in practice in recent years.

Even if the real capital value *had* been maintained, there would still have been an element of risk, namely the risk to the rate of interest which you receive. There is no guarantee that this rate of interest, either nominal or real, will remain the same in the future; hence, you cannot know for sure just what the accumulated value of your investment will be in the future. In other words, there is a spread of possible future returns (over, say, a five or ten-year period); this is precisely what we mean by risk: namely, it is a measure of the uncertainty of future outcomes (to the value of our capital or the future level of the real interest rate).

One remote possibility which could affect your future returns is the risk of the building society going bust. This can generally be ignored as far as the larger societies are concerned; in any case, the government guarantees 90% of your nominal capital up to the first £20,000 invested with any one society.

Nevertheless, even ignoring this possibility, we have seen that even a Low-Risk investment (for such is a building society account) does exhibit specific uncertainties:

(a) there is a *range* of possible future returns on our investment

(b) that range can extend downwards into *negative* territory

We can illustrate this on our Risk v Return graph:

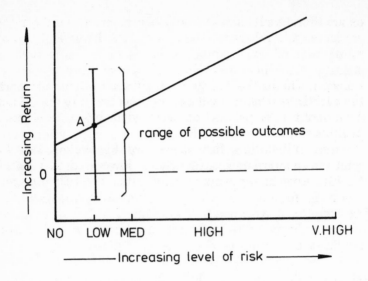

Point A on the chart is the 'expected' or average rate of return. Based on the experience of the recent 25 years, you may think that I should have shown this as a negative number, specifically –1% pa. There are two reasons for not doing this:

(a) I think (or hope!) that, in future, we might reasonably expect a modest positive real return from building society accounts

(b) there are many other Low-Risk investments, many of which *have* provided a positive return, albeit a small one; we shall see one such positive return in answer to Question 7(b).

It is appropriate, therefore, to turn next to that question, to look at the historical performance of another Low-Risk investment.

## Question 7(b). Long-term return on gilts

Gilt-edged securities (gilts) are bonds issued by the government to raise money to help fill the gap between its expenditure and its taxation revenue. So far as such UK government bonds are concerned, the risk of default can be taken as zero.

The real risk, as with other Low-Risk investments, is inflation. The BZW *Gilt-Equity Study* shows that since 1918 the average real return (with all net income re-invested) has been about +2% pa: still not very good, but at least it's a positive number.

Based on historical evidence, we would conclude that the return from a Low-Risk investment is lower than that from a No-Risk investment. This is clearly illogical, and we shall put aside, for a minute, the question of a benchmark return for Low-Risk investments.

For Medium-Risk investments, I'm going to turn next to the answer to Question 3.

## Question 3. 'With-profits' endowment policies

These policies are backed by a mixture of predominantly Low-Risk and High-Risk financial investments (plus some investments in property). It is this spread of investments which puts them into the Medium-Risk category. About 10% of the monthly premiums goes to provide life assurance.

Management and administration charges are high, but these were offset in earlier years by tax advantages. Overall, they can be taken as indicative of what to expect from Medium-Risk investments.

(Later on, we shall see that the level of risk over the life of the policy is actually considerably reduced by virtue of the regular monthly savings feature; but we can still use the average return on each individual monthly contribution to estimate our Medium-Risk benchmark.)

Over the last 25 years, the average real return on a good policy has been approximately 4½% pa. This figure would have been about ½% pa higher if part of the investment had not been pre-empted for the life assurance element. I would suggest, therefore, that 5% pa would be a realistic benchmark for Medium-Risk investments.

We can now put a second number on our graph:

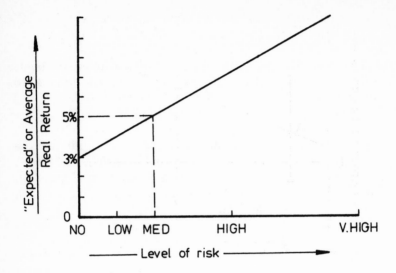

In this case, the acceptance of some degree of risk *is* reflected by an appropriately higher return on our investment.

We turn, next, to High-Risk investments and will take the ordinary shares of UK companies as being typical of that category.

## Question 2. A wide spread of ordinary UK shares

If investing-for-income in a building society account has quite a spread of possible returns, then investing-for-profit in ordinary shares (a High-Risk investment) is going to exhibit an even greater spread:

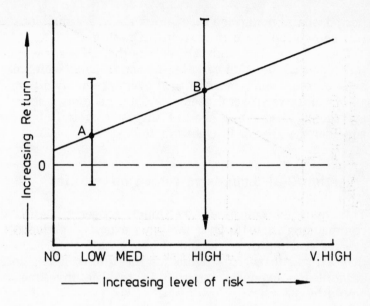

In fact, the possible down-side risk is such that the vertical 'spread' line is going to fall right off the bottom of our chart: in the extreme we could lose the whole of our investment in the shares of a particular company.

Our Risk v Reward chart is going to become too cluttered if we continue to draw in these vertical lines showing the spread of possible future returns. So, from now on, we will leave them out and just try to put in numbers for the 'expected' returns (such as the returns appropriate to points A and B on the chart) – but always remember that, the higher the risk (and the greater the 'expected' return), the wider will be the spread of possible future outcomes.

The actual average real return on a wide spread of ordinary shares over the 25 years to 1995 was about 6% pa. That's probably rather lower than you might have anticipated, but do remember that it is the *real* return after allowing for the need to rise by 9% pa just to keep pace with inflation.

Also, for the most recent 10 years of that quarter century, the real return was just about double that figure, around 12% pa. This means that, during the first 15 years of the period, shares performed very indifferently. We shall look at this sub-period again in answer to Question 6.

These figures (6% and 12% pa) are themselves one good indication of the wide variation in performance which can be expected, even when averaged over very many different shares and over several years. To obtain a good long-term average figure for our chart, I suggest that it is best to consider the answer to Question 7(a).

## Question 7(a). Long-term return on equities

This question concerned the much longer time-period commencing in 1918. Over that very extended period, the average real return works out at about 7.8% pa. I suggest that a realistic average figure for the future, taking into account the expenses incurred in real-life investments, would be 7% pa.

We can now put the third actual number on our chart:

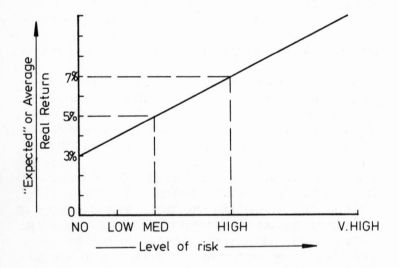

You may be disappointed to find that this figure is not much higher; however, it is essential that our investment aims are realistic rather than over-optimistic.

The wide range of future possibilities with ordinary shares can be further illustrated by the answers to some of the other questions.

## Question 4. A specific unit trust

The M&G Recovery Fund invests in a wide range of ordinary shares. It has an impressive long-term performance record: indeed, it is the top-ranking unit trust over the last 25 years.

Its average real return over that period has been about 11% pa. This compares with the average for all unit trusts which existed twenty-five years ago of no more than about 4% pa. Note that this average of 4% is some 2% below the average return from direct investment in ordinary shares over the same period. Much of this difference is due to the effects of management charges associated with funds which enable you to spread the risk over many individual shares.

I shall return again in later lessons to the subject of the charges associated with 'managed funds'.

## Question 5: A specific company

The company BTR was an outstanding performer over a long period of time. To convert £1,000 into £1 million over the 29 years to 1994 represents a real return of 17% pa. I wonder if you perhaps thought that the figure might have been even higher than this? The reason it isn't is our old enemy inflation: just to keep pace with inflation, the investment would have had to have risen ten-fold. Nevertheless, it is still a very impressive performance.

At the other end of the scale, many share investments made thirty years ago would, by today, be totally worthless.

## Question 6. A specific investment trust

We shall be looking in great detail, later on, at the differences between unit trusts and investment trusts. Both provide the means to spread one's money over a very wide range of ordinary shares. Because management charges are lower with investment trusts, we might expect them to reflect more closely the results which you might hope to obtain from direct personal investment in a range of ordinary shares.

The Foreign & Colonial Investment Trust holds shares in many companies internationally, not just in the UK. It has a very long history as its adverts demonstrate. In fact, it is the oldest general investment trust in the world, originating in 1868. If you have seen the adverts, you will see that the company usefully sub-divides its historical performance into different time-periods. The results can be summarised as follows:

|  | Average annual returns | | |
|---|---|---|---|
|  | Nominal return % | *minus* Inflation % | =Real return% |
| 1945–70 (25 years) | 14½ | 3½ | 11 |
| 1970–85 (15 years) | 13 | 11½ | 1½ |
| 1985–95 (10 years) | 18 | 5 | 13 |
| 1945–95 (50 years) | 14¾ | 6¼ | 8½ |

Using the correct mathematical calculation (see mathematical note on page 26), the real return over 50 years actually works out to be 8% pa.

You will notice that this real long-term return is just a little higher than the 7% pa which we chose earlier as our benchmark for equity investments; the difference will be due partly to the fact that the trust invests in overseas companies as well as in UK companies. When we come to look in detail at High-Risk investments, it will now come as no surprise to find that we shall not restrict ourselves to investments in *UK* companies.

You will also have noticed the huge variations in performance from one time-period to another. The figures confirm something which we noted earlier: namely that, over a recent period of 25 years, performance in the first sub-period of 15 years was very poor, whilst that in the last 10 years was very good.

One important reason for this difference now becomes clear: guess what? Yes, inflation!

The 'nominal' returns on investment (that is, before correcting for inflation) were actually not all that different from one time-period to another. What happened in the period 1970–85 was that the high rate of inflation was not compensated for by a corresponding increase in the nominal return on the investment. It was only during a subsequent catching up process that real investment returns rose to reflect the inflated values of the physical assets of companies.

To summarise the historical performance of UK equities:

- a long-term real return of 7% pa is a realistic benchmark
- we can anticipate enormous variations between the best and worst performing companies
- we can expect considerable variations from one time-period to another
- inflation is 'enemy number one'

From the figures you will, I am sure, recognise why we categorise ordinary shares as High-Risk.

## Benchmark return on Low-Risk investments

We talked earlier about Low-Risk investments but did not, at that stage, derive a benchmark figure for the expected return. Just by interpolating between the No-Risk and Medium-Risk categories it is clear that the figure *should* be about 4% pa.

Unfortunately, this is not what we have found in practice. You will recall that we looked at two specific Low-Risk investments and came up with long-term averages of:

- Building society –           – 1% pa over 25 years
  high interest accounts

- Gilt-edged stock            + 2% pa over nearly 80 years

A long way from real returns of 4% pa!

Part of the anomaly arises from the fact, which we have
already observed, that the last 25 years includes a sub-
period of very high inflation and, consequently, of dismal
real investment returns. In more recent years, these Low-
Risk investments have yielded more respectable net real
returns of around 2% pa for building societies and up to 4%
pa at times for gilts. (Incidentally, you may rightly anticipate that the slightly higher return on gilts is a reflection of
their somewhat higher risk level, when compared with
building societies.)

A reasonable excuse for some building society accounts is
that they are not just investment vehicles: they are also
convenient places to hold money for easy access. As such,
their returns will in any case be lower than for genuine long-
term investments. Having said that, this comment should
not really apply to higher-interest accounts, which usually
require 90 days notice of withdrawal, and which were the
basis for the calculation of the historical rate of return.

Many people who put their money into these accounts are
non-taxpayers, and of course that would make a significant
difference to the return: it would bring it a little nearer to
the 4% pa that we are looking for. So I am going to use the
figure of 4% pa as our benchmark, but more for good order
than out of conviction that this return may realistically be
achieved in the future on many Low-Risk investments.

We can already anticipate, from this discussion, that
many Low-Risk investments will only appeal to non-taxpayers. Quite often (and *very* often for taxpayers), we will
find that we can obtain a better return from a No-Risk
investment than from a Low-Risk one if we can leave our
money invested for several years; in which case, we shall
have no difficulty in making a choice between the two!

## Very-High-Risk investments

There is no logical way of deriving a realistic benchmark for such 'investments'. In fact, to be frank, I believe that the expected outcome of many Very-High-Risk investments is the loss of all your money. And I'm not just thinking of the National Lottery!

In the final lesson we shall look at a few of the more sensible Very-High-Risk investments; I suggest that we should look for an expected average real return of at least 10% pa if the risks are to be worth taking.

In summary, then, our basic chart of benchmark returns is as follows:

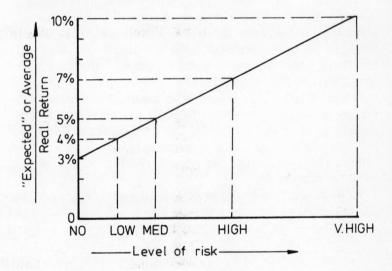

How do these figures relate to your answer to Question 9?

Unfortunately, many people have unrealistically high expectations of investment returns. In practice, a relatively unsophisticated mix of investments, across the various risk categories, should be expected to yield an average real return (after tax and inflation) of around 4% to 5% pa.

Much of the remainder of the course will aim to help you beat the averages. The effects of compound interest mean

that relatively modest outperformance will produce substantially higher capital values after several years.

## Inflation and tax

Conversely, we must always keep in mind the negative
effects of tax and, especially, inflation; both of these factors
can seriously erode the value of your capital. These investment 'enemies' have already been mentioned several times;
a third enemy was hinted at when we looked briefly at the
historical performance of unit trusts and endowment policies, namely *charges.*

We shall need to look very carefully, later, at the issue of
management and administrative charges. For the moment, I
want you to get into the habit of automatically judging
investments on an after-tax, after-inflation basis. This will
be particularly important when we look at the very wide
range of Low-Risk investments.

Suppose that we are assessing an investment which yields
a nominal rate of interest of 8% pa. It is an investment with
no risk to our nominal capital (we can always realise £100
for every £100 of initial investment). We judge future
inflation to average 4% pa. What is the *real* return on this
investment?

We will use this example to illustrate again what will be
our standard evaluation formula:

| | |
|---|---:|
| Gross Income | 8.0% |
| *minus* Tax (at 20%) | −1.6% |
| = Net Income | 6.4% |
| *plus/minus* Capital Gain/Loss | — |
| = Total Net Return | 6.4% |
| *minus* Inflation | −4.0% |
| **= Total Net Real Return** | **3.4%** |

Note that it is necessary to make a judgement or forecast
about future inflation. This is a notoriously difficult thing to
do with any accuracy. The simplest method would be to
take the current rate of inflation, which is published (and

widely publicised) monthly. In Lesson II, I'll mention a slightly more sophisticated way of judging possible future inflation levels.

In any case, future inflation is likely to have such a pronounced effect on Low-Risk investments in particular (as in the above example) that you really cannot avoid making *some* judgement, forecast, assumption, guess ... or whatever else you like to call it.

Much easier, of course, is to insert the actual tax rate applicable to yourself (but remember that, above age 65 and within fairly narrow income levels, you may have to consider the effect that any additional income might have on age-related tax allowances – see Chapter 4).

The negative effect of tax *compounds* the negative effect of inflation: I shall give you a simple calculation to do as part of your homework to illustrate this point.

By now you will have recognised that I am somewhat paranoid (for very good reasons) about the subject of inflation! Later, you will discover that I am equally paranoid (and for equally good reasons) about the levels of charges associated with many investments – but that is a subject for a later lesson.

The immediate lesson is to get into the habit of evaluating all investments on an after-tax, after-inflation basis, and then comparing the results with our benchmark returns for the appropriate levels of risk.

Many advertisements for tax-free investment products have a habit of telling you what would be the grossed-up rate of interest for a taxpayer. For instance, an investment yielding 8% pa *tax-free* is equivalent to a gross rate of 10% pa for a standard-rate taxpayer and 13.3% pa for a higher-rate taxpayer. Now, whilst these figures may be *true*, they are not very *useful*! It's much better to approach investment calculations the other way round: instead of showing what the equivalent grossed-up rate would be for a taxpayer, *always* deduct whatever tax is applicable in your case and compare all investments on an after-tax (and after-inflation) basis.

The first homework question will help to fix in your mind the step-by-step formula for calculating this *real* return on investment.

# Homework I

## Exercise 1

You might expect that there would be little to choose between the following two scenarios; in both cases, the interest rate is 3% above the inflation rate:

   *A*. 8% pa interest rate and 5% pa inflation

   *B*. 18% pa interest rate and 15% pa inflation

Using our step-by-step process, calculate the Total Net Real Return for each scenario. (Assume a 20% taxpayer and no capital gain or loss.)

## Exercise 2

Towards the end of your copy of *Money Observer* you will find a table headed 'Check out the best buys among these 15 leading risk-free investments'.

Which of these investments do you think are really risk-free?

(Several of the investments are National Savings products. It will be helpful for you to refer to the booklet which you should already have obtained from your local Post Office, namely *Investment Guide – Options from National Savings*, together with the separate leaflet giving the current interest rates.)

## Exercise 3

Try to think of as many *genuinely* risk-free investments as you can. (I should mention that there are actually very few of them.)

# Chapter 7
# Lesson II: No-Risk Investments

In the first lesson, we saw how the returns on our investments can be eroded by tax and by inflation. At the end of that lesson, I implied that the *combined* effect of the two together is especially damaging. We also went through a step-by-step process to evaluate these effects.

The first homework question will have given you practice in using this process; and it should have confirmed the compounding effect of tax *plus* inflation. This is what your answers should have looked like:

|  | Scenario A | Scenario B |
|---|---|---|
| Gross Income | 8.0% | 18.0% |
| *minus* Tax (at 20%) | −1.6% | −3.6% |
| = Net Income | 6.4% | 14.4% |
| *plus/minus* Capital Gain/Loss | — | — |
| = Total Net Return | 6.4% | 14.4% |
| *minus* Inflation | −5.0% | −15.0% |
| **= Total Net Real Return** | **1.4% pa** | **−0.6% pa** |

In both cases, the apparent yield on the investment is 3% above the inflation rate. Unfortunately, the tax system makes no allowance for the fact that you need to earn interest at the inflation rate just to stand still in real terms (that is, in terms of the goods and services your money will buy). At high rates of inflation – as in scenario B – you can effectively be taxed at 100% or more on your real interest rate. It is not our task to consider the morality of such penal tax rates; our task is to make sure that *we* are not paying them!

In both scenarios the investment was one in which there was no risk of a capital gain or loss; hence, the nominal value of our investment remains intact: for each £100 we invested initially, we can always draw out £100 in cash at some future date.

This is what many (probably most) people regard as a No-Risk investment. However, in scenario B the real value of our capital is being eroded; even if we re-invest *all* the net income, the real value of our savings is going down by 0.6% pa. You will recall that we should really expect No-Risk investments to give us a *positive* return of around 3% pa.

Hence, so far as *we* are concerned, just keeping the *nominal* value of our capital intact does *not* qualify an investment for our No-Risk category.

So, what answer did you come up with for homework Exercise 2?

*Money Observer* has (up to now, at least) used 'Risk-Free' in the conventional sense, namely as applying to the *nominal* value of your capital. In fact, on our more rigorous definition, hardly any of their 'Leading Risk-Free Investments' would qualify as having no risk: only one, in fact, namely index-linked National Savings certificates. These are savings whose value rises in line with inflation as measured by the retail price index.

Indeed, *only* index-linked investments are truly No-Risk ones.

Please do not think that I am 'knocking' the magazine *Money Observer*, which I think is excellent. Our homework exercise does emphasise, though, how careful one has to be not to misinterpret even the most reputable of sources.

I wonder just how many genuinely risk-free (inflation-linked) investments you thought of in Exercise 3? What we shall do now is to look at the most important of them in detail, starting with the one which *is* included in the *Money Observer* list, namely National Savings index-linked certificates.

## National Savings index-linked certificates

These certificates provide a safe home for lump-sums which can be set aside for five years. The advantages are:

(a) the value of the certificates goes up in line with the retail price index

(b) additionally, if held for the full 5 years, interest is added at the rate (currently) of $2\frac{1}{2}\%$ pa, which also goes up in line with inflation
(c) they are tax-free

These certificates *can* be cashed in before the five years are up, but in that case you would lose some of the interest. As long as you do not cash them in within the first year, the capital sum will be completely protected against inflation.

To buy these certificates, just go along to the Post Office for an application form and send this off with your cheque to the address shown on the form.

The National Savings literature will tell you the current limits to the amount which any one person can invest in these certificates. Additionally, husbands and wives can both hold certificates in trust for each other.

## Index-linked gilts (held to maturity)

Gilt-edged securities (or gilts) are bonds issued by the British government. They are very easy to buy (and sell if necessary): again, you go along to the Post Office and, in this case, request the booklet: *Government Stock*. This contains an application form which, again, you just fill in and send off with your cheque.

The booklet contains a list of various gilts which you can buy; the list is sub-divided into three sections: Conventional Gilts, Undated Gilts and Index-linked Gilts.

It is only the index-linked ones which concern us at the moment, but the following discussion will also be a useful introduction to conventional and undated gilts – which are included in subsequent lessons – so we will look at these investments in some detail.

The section in the National Savings booklet on index-linked gilts lists several different stocks, each with a different 'maturity' year. Let's have a look at two of the rows of the table in the booklet:

| 2½ % | Index-Linked Treasury Stock 2003 | 20 May | 20 Nov |
|------|----------------------------------|--------|--------|
| 4⅜ % | Index-Linked Treasury Stock 2004 | 21 Apr | 21 Oct |

The first column of figures (2½ % and 4⅜ %) is called the 'coupon': it indicates the annual rate of interest which the government pays (in two half-yearly instalments) on the particular stock. This is followed by the title of the stock, of which the only part of interest is the year at the end. This is the year in which the government repays the capital sum (adjusted for inflation). Finally, two dates are given: these are the dates on which the interest is paid.

When issuing a new index-linked gilt, in tranches of £100 of stock, the government makes two promises:

(a) during the lifetime of the stock it will pay the specified interest rate, inflated each year in line with the retail price index

(b) at the maturity date, it will repay the original nominal capital of £100, also inflated in line with the retail price index

In practice, the inflation figures used are the retail price indices eight months earlier, but this need not concern us.

In between times (that is, between the first issue of the stock and its maturity) you are able to buy and sell the stock, but the government has no direct say in the price at which the stock will change hands: this price is dictated, day by day, by market forces – that is, the balance between buyers and sellers on the stock-market. Since there is no guarantee as to what that price will be until final maturity, we cannot consider these stocks to be No-Risk *unless* they are held until maturity (at which time, the government's promise of a specified repayment value comes into force).

We can illustrate this by an artificial example, see figure 7.1

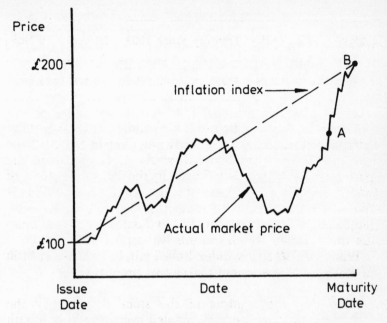

*Fig 7.1* Illustration of movement of index-linked gilts (assuming a doubling of the retail price index)

Suppose that, between the date of issue and the date of maturity, consumer prices (as measured by the retail price index) double. The government would then pay, on maturity, the sum of £200 for every £100 of stock; it would also provide an (index-linked) rate of interest, paid twice a year.

What happens between issue and maturity depends on the prices at which individual holders are prepared to buy and sell. So, the actual price might follow a zig-zag pattern as shown by the solid line in the diagram; there is no pre-determined selling price until the final maturity date. As that date approaches, of course, the market value of the stock will approach close to the price implied by the government's inflation-proofing promise.

It also follows from this that the actual interest rate you receive, if you buy the stock somewhere in the middle of its life, will not necessarily be the same as the nominal interest rate given in the title of the stock: it could be higher or lower.

So, if we wish to buy a particular stock in mid-life, how

do we discover what this current rate of interest will be?

For the answer, turn to the appropriate page of your *Financial Times* (or, indeed, of many other newspapers). The *FT* publishes daily a list of 'UK Gilts Prices'; it is, of course, the section headed 'Index-Linked' which interests us.

Let us take two artificial but realistic examples corresponding to those which we extracted earlier from the National Savings booklet. A daily entry might be:

| | | Yield | | | | | |
|---|---|---|---|---|---|---|---|
| | (b) | (1) | (2) | Price £ | + or – | High | Low |
| 2½% '03 | (78.8) | 3.30 | 3.65 | 167¾ | +½ | 167¾ | 161½ |
| 4⅜% '04 | (135.6) | 3.31 | 3.63 | 112¼ | +½ | 112½ | 108¼ |

You will see, first of all, that the names of the stocks have been abbreviated. Then, in a column designated (b), is given the base figure for the retail price index (rpi) applicable to the date at which the stock was first issued. Continuing from left to right, two figures are given for the yield, based on different assumptions about future inflation. The next figure is the market price, at the close of yesterday's trading, for £100 of nominal stock; this is followed by a fractional number indicating the change in price on that previous day. Finally, the last two columns show the highest and lowest prices reached this year.

The first thing to notice is that the original 'nominal' interest rate set for the two stocks has become irrelevant: although these nominal rates differed widely between the two stocks illustrated, the market has adjusted the current prices of these stocks so that they now have almost identical yields.

The 2½ % stock now yields an *increased* rate of interest; for this to be so, the *price* of the stock must have fallen below what it would have been on an exact inflation-linked calculation; conversely, the current yield on the 4⅜ % stock has *fallen*, indicating that its price has risen above its inflation-linked value.

Before we proceed, make sure that you are happy with this description of how these stocks work. If not, I suggest that you go over the description again until you fully understand it.

Coming back to the examples, the $2\frac{1}{2}$ % stock is below its 'correct' (inflation-linked) value, but the government still guarantees to repay its inflation-linked value on maturity. Referring to figure 7.1, its current price might therefore be at point A in the diagram, whilst we know that the government will finally repay the amount indicated by point B. I trust that you can see, from this, that the 'real redemption yield' of 3.30% or 3.65% (depending on the future inflation assumption*) is made up of two separate components:

(a) the interest payments
(b) a real capital gain, over and above the increase in capital value necessary to keep pace with inflation

In the case of the $4\frac{3}{8}$% stock, the higher interest payments will be offset, to some extent, by a capital *loss* if the stock is held to maturity, thus bringing the projected real redemption yield *down* to the range 3.31% to 3.63%.

The importance of this to taxpayers is that the interest component is taxable, whereas any capital gain is not. So, the total after-tax return to taxpayers will be slightly higher by choosing a stock in which the *current* yield (as read from the newspaper) is higher than the nominal yield, or 'coupon', indicated in the name of the stock. We know that, in this case, part of the total return will be in the form of a (tax-free) capital gain.

## When are index-linked investments worth buying?

At various times in the past the government has issued

* It may seem odd that the real return on an index-linked investment depends on the future level of inflation. This apparent paradox is due to the fact that these stocks are valued on the basis of the rpi eight months before the issue and maturity dates respectively. Hence, very high inflation in the last eight months of the life of the stock will not be reflected in its final maturity price.

index-linked gilts with 'coupons' (initial yields) ranging from 2% pa to 4⅜% pa. Similarly, the yield on index-linked National Savings has varied, from time to time, from 2½% to as high as 4½% pa.

How can you judge whether it is a good time to add some index-linked investments to your portfolio?

You will recall that, over a long period of time, the typical expectation for the real return on a No-Risk investment is around 3% pa or a little more. I suggest that you might use the following guidelines to decide whether or not this is an appropriate time to buy:

| Yield on index-linked investment | Guidelines |
|---|---|
| above 4% | Buy! |
| 3½% – 4% | Good return; likely to be better than most Low-Risk investments |
| 3% – 3½% | Average return; worth considering |
| 2½% – 3% | Poor return; buy only if no better alternative |
| below 2½% | Don't buy! |

Notice what the guidelines would have suggested in respect of the examples mentioned earlier. You would not have bought the 2½% stock when it was first issued, nor the current issue of index-linked National Savings; you *would* have bought the 4⅜% stock and an earlier issue of index-linked National Savings yielding 4½% above inflation.

Not surprisingly, since it was issued the 2½% stock has fallen in real value (that is, its price increase has not kept pace with inflation) whilst the 4⅜% stock has appreciated at a faster rate than inflation.

If you follow the guidelines given above you should, from time to time, make some useful No-Risk investments which will add a measure of long-term stability to your portfolio.

## Buying (and selling) index-linked gilts

I've put 'and selling' in brackets because you will not normally sell these securities before they mature (at which time the government will send you the appropriate maturity value). You will normally buy index-linked gilts because of their No-Risk quality: and they are only such if held to maturity. Nevertheless, if you *do* have to sell, the process is very simple and is explained in the National Savings brochure: *Government Stock.*

It is one of the criteria of this course that all your investments should be easy to carry out. This is true of index-linked gilts, when bought via the National Savings Stock Register (that is, through the Post Office), so please do not be put off if you have not invested in them before.

The brochure, *Government Stock*, also obtainable from the Post Office, gives all the details and includes an application form. Just fill this in, as directed, and send it off with your cheque.

If you wish to receive interest more frequently than twice a year, you can spread your investment across, say, three different stocks with different interest payment dates.

There are some small charges involved (which is not the case with savings certificates). These charges, for either buying or selling, are 0.7% for the first £5,000 and 0.375% thereafter. For large sums (in excess of £10,000) you could obtain a better deal through a stockbroker, but you would then receive interest payments with standard-rate tax already deducted.

There is one other, less obvious charge. The daily price quoted in your newspaper is what is called the 'middle-market' price: that is, it is the average of the price paid by a buyer and the slightly lower price received by a seller of the stock. In other words, there is a small spread between the two prices.

In total, however, the charges are quite small. Buying via the National Savings Stock Register also means that your half-yearly interest is paid to you gross (that is, without prior deduction of tax), although you do have to pay tax later if your total income brings you into the tax net. If you buy through a stockbroker, the interest will be paid after deduction of standard-rate tax, so non-taxpayers will then need to reclaim this tax from the Inland Revenue.

It is when you come to fill in your tax return that my aim of keeping things simple tends to fall down. This is due to a technical factor called 'accrued interest', which is explained in the National Savings booklet. Interest on gilts is added on a daily basis and accumulates for six months before it is paid to you as your half-yearly interest. This means that, if you buy a gilt in-between interest payment dates, the price you pay will include the value of the interest accumulated up to that date. Your first interest payment, being a full six months interest, will therefore include the repayment to you of a little bit of your capital outlay. The Inland Revenue recognises that this receipt of 'accrued interest' is really a repayment to you of your own capital, and it is accordingly free of tax so long as you identify it with your tax return – see Inland Revenue leaflet IR 68. There is a corresponding adjustment to be made if you sell the stock before maturity.

I'm sorry about this complication. The good news is that it is only applicable to the tax year in which you receive your first interest payment! The amount of accrued interest is shown on the stock certificate which you will receive shortly after sending off your cheque.

## Future inflation expectations

Whether or not the present is a good time to buy them, you should always be aware of the current redemption yield on index-linked gilts. One reason is that it provides a valuable benchmark for evaluating other investments, particularly the Low-Risk variety. When you come to do your sums on Low-Risk investments, by adjusting the yields for tax and inflation, you may be surprised how often they fail to match up to the real returns available from index-linked products.

In order to make the comparison, you need to make some estimate of the possible future course of inflation. You could, of course, assume that inflation will continue at its current level.

There is a slightly more sophisticated approach. Look back at the *Financial Times* and see what the current yield is on index-linked gilts. Now look earlier in the table at the conventional gilts in the sub-section headed 'Five to Fifteen Years' (that is the number of years until the maturity of these stocks). Note the general level of *their* redemption yields; these figures are found in the column headed 'Yield-Red'.

The difference between the redemption yields on conventional and index-linked stocks is one measure of future inflation expectations. So, for example, suppose that the redemption yields are, on average:

- Conventional gilts        7½%
- Index-linked gilts        3½%

then you can reasonably use this 'inflation premium' of 4% (the difference between the two figures) as an estimate of future inflation expectations. The reason for this is that it indicates the yield premium which large tax-exempt buyers of gilts, such as pension funds, require to compensate them for their expectation of future inflation.

Unfortunately, as we shall see in a later lesson, expert opinion on financial and economic matters is somewhat unreliable, so we cannot place too much confidence in this projection of future inflation rates. Even more unfortunately, there aren't any more reliable forecasting methods.

It actually makes sense to let your personal circumstances affect your inflation assumption. If you are a young man, in a secure job, with a future pension linked to your final salary, you probably do not need to concern yourself too much with inflation; in which case, you could realistically assume a relatively low figure for future price inflation.

At the other end of the scale, if you are retired and largely dependent upon a company pension which does not have full index-linking, then you would rightly be very concerned lest the real buying power of your pension were to be seriously eroded by inflation. In that case, you would be advised to make your judgements on the basis that future inflation could be quite high.

What we *can* confidently assume is that *some* level of price inflation will continue for the foreseeable future; in which case, it is a sensible plan to include some index-linked investments in one's portfolio.

So far we have actually identified only two such investments ... and there really aren't many more! There is, though, one important class of investment which we now need to consider, namely annuities.

## Index-linked annuities

For those of you who are not familiar with annuities, I shall first describe the concept.

You assign a lump-sum to an insurance company; they, in turn, guarantee to pay you a fixed income for the rest of your life. When you die, that income ceases, of course, and there is normally no repayment of your capital; hence, the money which you invested in an annuity is lost to the beneficiaries of your estate. (There are some variations on this, which need not concern us here.)

In exchange for surrendering your capital, the lifetime income you receive is much higher than it would be from other investments. You will recall 'Thorneycroft's Second Law of Successful Investment' (page 42); in the case of an annuity, you are *deliberately* receiving an enhanced income out of your own capital.

The advantage to you is that you can enjoy a considerably enhanced income so long as you live.

To put this into perspective, at a recent time when interest rates generally (for instance, on conventional gilts with five or ten years to maturity) were around 7½%, the following rates could be obtained from a £10,000 lump-sum invested in an annuity:

- Male aged 65:        11%
- Female aged 65:      10%
- Male aged 70:        12½%
- Female aged 70:      11%

The higher rates for men arise from their shorter life expectancy: the insurance company is able to pay them back their capital at a faster rate than it can prudently do for women.

As far as the tax-man is concerned, the income from an annuity acquired with your own capital (not from a pension plan) consists of two components:

(a) interest, which is taxable
(b) repayment of capital, which is tax-free

The split between the two depends on age, sex and the general level of interest rates.

Taking out an annuity would appear to offer a very attractive deal: you don't have to worry about living for a very long time; you can continue to receive an enhanced income 'for ever'.

Of course there is a snag, and it is again inflation. If you do live to be a ripe old age, how much is that enhanced income really going to be worth to you in later life? For that reason, annuities have traditionally been considered seriously only by people aged, say, 75 or over; a 60-year-old would naturally be very concerned about the long-term effects of inflation.

The advent of index-linked gilts, described above, has radically altered that perception. Using these gilts, insurance companies can now offer *index-linked* annuities, so removing a major fear. What happens is that the initial income level is lower than it would be with a conventional annuity, but the income rises in line with inflation. Hence, the buying power of that income will remain intact.

As a result it is now perfectly feasible for someone as young as 60 to consider an annuity for part of their capital. This would apply if an enhanced income were more important than leaving a large legacy.

Recently, at a time when index-linked gilts were yielding around $3\frac{3}{4}$%pa, the following inflation-proofed incomes were available via index-linked annuities:

- Male aged 60:            about 7% pa
- Female aged 60:          about 6% pa
- Male aged 70:            about 9% pa
- Female aged 70:          about 8% pa

Certainly by the age of 70, these look very attractive rates when set against the benchmark figure of 3% pa for the other index-linked investments, in which your capital remains in your own hands.

Annuity rates differ widely from one insurance company to another, so it is advisable to shop around and obtain several quotes; alternatively, and more simply, you could look at the Annuity pages of Ceefax, updated each weekend. Another method is to approach one of the specialist brokers, such as The Annuity Bureau at Enterprise House, 59/65 Upper Ground, London SE1 9PQ.

## Annuity-type investments

There is one final class of index-linked investments; they have the *characteristics* of annuities (inasmuch as capital is surrendered irrevocably in exchange for a higher income), but they are not usually appreciated in this light.

The main one by far is the deferral of your State pension.

The great thing about this pension is that it is indexed to the retail price index. At one time, it was indexed to average earnings, which was even better: on average, earnings tend to rise by about 2% pa faster than prices as a result of increased productivity in the economy.

Because it is index-linked, wouldn't it be nice if we could have more of it! Well, in fact we can, if we defer taking it for a time.

If you decide to forgo your State pension for one year, then you will thereafter receive an extra 7.5% more than would otherwise have been the case. Perhaps you can see why I refer to this as an annuity-type investment? You are irrevocably surrendering the money which you would otherwise have received in one year; in exchange, you will receive a future income enhanced by 7.5%. The whole of the enhanced future pension, including the extra 7.5% will be index-linked. For a woman aged 60 that rate of annuity of 7.5% pa is a particularly good deal.

You can forgo your pension for up to five years at the most. For each year that you do so, a further 7.5% is added to your subsequent pension.

The longer you defer, however, the lower is the effective

'annuity' rate: this is because you are forgoing not only the pension income, but also the interest which you could otherwise have received on that pension income.

Whether or not you should defer and, if so, for how long, is a very personal matter. In general, if you are not desperate for additional current income and you can't think of some better way of investing your pension, then it might be worth considering a deferral period of one or two years.

If you do consider this possibility, you are advised to read National Insurance leaflet NI 92, available from your local office of the Department of Social Security.

There is one other group of annuity-type investments which you might wish to consider, although the sums of money which you can 'invest' in them are rather small. I am referring to life memberships of your favourite charities and other organisations.

In exchange for a single lump-sum donation, you save yourself the future annual payments, which would generally rise more-or-less in line with inflation. As with a normal annuity, the lump-sum is irrevocably lost, but your future income is increased (by virtue of the saving on the annual subscription). You would need to work out the effective annuity rate based on figures which each organisation would be happy to provide.

To do so, just divide the current annual membership subscription by the cost of life membership and multiply by 100. For example, in recent years the annuity rates for a couple, both aged 60, for two particular organisations were:

- National Trust:        a little over 6% pa
- English Heritage:      a little over 7% pa

## Summary

In setting you the homework exercises, I mentioned that there are very few genuine No-Risk investments. In fact, we have identified only four:

- Index-linked National Savings certificates
- Index-linked gilts

- Index-linked annuities
- Annuity-type investments, in particular the deferral of the State pension

The common characteristic of all of these investments is that the returns increase in line with inflation, so that the real value of your interest income remains intact whatever happens to prices.

We shall find a very much wider range of choice when we turn next to look at Low-Risk investments.

# Homework II

We are going to look next at Low-Risk investments. This homework is intended to encourage you to start thinking about these products.

In many cases, there is no risk to your *nominal* capital – your £100 invested will always be worth £100. The capital risk is that the *real* value of your money will be eroded due to the effects of inflation. In other cases, even the nominal capital is not guaranteed.

Thus, we can categorise Low-Risk investments according to whether they have a fixed or variable nominal capital.

We can also sub-divide them according to whether their interest rates are fixed or variable.

Thus, we can set up a simple 2 x 2 table to help us categorise the various investments:

| Interest rate | Nominal capital | |
|---|---|---|
| | Fixed | Variable |
| Fixed | A | C |
| Variable | B | D |

Any Low-Risk investment can be placed into one of the boxes A, B, C or D; at least, this will suffice for now: we shall see in Lesson III that there are a few cases for which it is not obvious which category is appropriate.

Before setting you your homework, let me illustrate this categorisation with some specific examples.

## A. Fixed nominal capital; fixed interest rate

Example: National Savings pensioners guaranteed income bonds. Your nominal capital remains fixed and the rate of interest is fixed for five years.

## B. Fixed nominal capital; variable interest rate

Example: a bank or building society account. Your nominal capital is again fixed, but the bank or building society can (and often does) vary the rate of interest.

## C. Variable nominal capital; fixed interest rate

Example: conventional gilts not held until maturity. The interest rate to you is fixed at the time you buy them; but the capital value goes up and down daily according to the balance of supply and demand between buyers and sellers on the Stock Exchange.

Think about the difference between:

(a) a gilt which matures in 1 or 2 years time
(b) an undated gilt – one which never matures, but continues to pay a fixed rate of interest for ever

## D. Variable nominal capital; variable interest rate

There are not many of these. It has been suggested that the government might introduce variable-rate gilts; these would fit into category D.

The one important example of a D-type investment which already exists is a foreign currency account. Overseas banks vary their interest rates from time to time, just like their UK counterparts; in addition, your capital is variable because of the variations in the rate at which the foreign currency can be exchanged into pounds.

I hope this has given you a feel for the types of investment which fall into each category. Now for your homework.

## Exercise 1

Think of as many examples of Low-Risk investments as you can, and assign each to one of the categories A, B or C. (Don't worry about category D.)

**Tip 1:** you should look again at the guide to National Savings products which you should have picked up already from the Post Office; make sure that you include most of these in your answer.

**Tip 2:** refer back to the *Money Observer* table on what they define as Risk-Free Investments but which we, in general, do not.

You can use the table 7.1 to list your answers.

**Table 7.1    Blank table for homework exercise on Low-Risk investments**

| Interest rate | Nominal Capital | |
|---|---|---|
| | Fixed | Variable |
| Fixed | | |
| Variable | | |

## Exercise 2

Whilst all the categories A, B, C and D may be Low-Risk, some are likely to be of lower risk than others. For each of the boxes (including box D this time) consider how you would more precisely describe each category from this list:

- Very-Low-Risk
- Low-Risk
- Fairly-Low-Risk
- Not such a low risk (in other words, more akin to Medium-Risk)

# Chapter 8
# Lesson III: Low-Risk Investments – Principles

You will recall, from Chapter 3, that No-Risk and Low-Risk investments share an important characteristic: the primary object is investing-for-income rather than investing-for-profit. There may sometimes be the prospect of a capital gain (or loss), but this is generally very much a secondary consideration.

In another respect, Low-Risk investments differ markedly from No-Risk ones: namely, there are very many of them! It will help, therefore, if we can first categorise them into various sub-groups, which we can then cover (in the next lesson) one at a time.

In this lesson, therefore, we need to discuss a number of general principles concerning Low-Risk products. As a result of that discussion, we shall then be able to do two things:

(a) correctly allocate each product to its appropriate sub-group
(b) assign realistic levels of risk and benchmark returns to the various sub-groups

Only then shall we really be able to assess whether each individual investment product may be of interest to us.

This discussion may not sound terribly exciting, but I think that it will throw up some surprises. If you work your way conscientiously through this lesson, you will be in a much better position to assess the value to you of the various Low-Risk products.

To start with, you will have seen from the homework that we can sub-divide the products into four sub-groups:

A – fixed nominal capital; fixed interest rate
B – fixed nominal capital; variable interest rate

C – variable nominal capital; fixed interest rate
D – variable nominal capital; variable interest rate

That probably seemed like a quite logical way in which to classify the investments. As often happens, unfortunately, real life is not quite so simple! It is not always obvious which category applies to a particular investment; so I shall first need to clear up such ambiguities.

The first possible confusion is the word 'fixed' as applied to interest rates. This does *not* necessarily mean that the future interest rate remains constant; rather, that the future pattern of interest rates is *predetermined* at the time that you invest your capital. Two examples will illustrate this point:

### (a) Building Society 'escalator' bonds

These provide an annual rate of interest which *increases* each year, usually for five years. The interest rate is clearly not constant, but it *is* predetermined at the start of the five-year period. This will classify it as a 'fixed-interest' opportunity.

### (b) National Savings fixed-interest certificates

These again provide an *increasing* annual rate of interest which, in this case, is added to the value of the certificates and can be withdrawn as a predetermined lump-sum at the end of five years. As the National Savings booklet says: 'You know at the beginning what you'll get at the end'; so, this again is a 'fixed-interest' investment.

This second example also illustrates another point of possible confusion. When you encash your National Savings certificate at the end of five years, you receive what probably feels more like a *capital gain* than accumulated interest; nevertheless, what you are really receiving is the accrued *interest* on your capital. We shall see other examples in which, what appears to be a capital gain is really accrued interest. This difference is often immaterial, but not always so because of the separate tax treatments of interest and capital gains.

rk, the 'fixed capital, fixed interest' exam-
that of another National Savings product,
ners guaranteed income bonds. These pro-
interest which is fixed (and also, in this case,
r five years. However, are you really 'tied in' to
thi.       f interest for five years?

Suppose that the rate of interest when you bought these
bonds was 6½% per annum. Now let us suppose that, for
whatever reason, the interest rate on *new* pensioners bonds
shoots up – say, to 8% pa. Are you stuck with the lower rate
of interest for the remaining period of your five-year
contract?

The answer is No. There will always be a penalty for early
encashment of any five-year investment, but it may actually
be worthwhile to incur that penalty. In the case of pensioners bonds, the penalty is the loss of 60 days' interest. At
an annual interest rate of 6½%, this means that you would
lose interest of a little over 1% by early repayment. It would
clearly pay you to cash in your original pensioners bond,
with no loss of nominal capital but with the loss of 60 days'
interest, to be able to start another contract at the new,
higher rate of 8% pa.

We can see, therefore, that pensioners bonds are not quite
such 'fixed-interest' securities as they may have at first
appeared. Now, I could introduce another category of Low-
Risk investment to cover this kind of situation; it would be
called something like 'semi-variable interest'. However, this
is likely to introduce unnecessary confusion. What I shall
do, therefore, is to redefine as 'variable interest' any such
apparently fixed-interest securities for which the penalties
for early encashment are very small.

Fixed-interest securities which will *remain* in the fixed-
interest category will include those for which either or both
of the following apply:

(a) a high penalty (in terms of loss of interest or capital)
    for early repayment
(b) an escalating structure of future interest rates, with
    much higher rates of interest being added in the later
    years

We have seen, so far in this lesson, that it is not always obvious whether the interest rate should be categorised as 'fixed' or 'variable'. We shall now see that the same can apply to the nominal capital.

Of particular relevance, in this respect, is the case of conventional gilts.

We discussed index-linked gilts at length in the previous lesson, so I don't think that I need to describe conventional gilts in any great detail, other than to point out the main differences compared with the index-linked variety.

You will recall that one of the government's promises to buyers of index-linked gilts was to repay (at some defined 'maturity' date) the original capital *inflated in line with the retail price index*. In the case of conventional gilts, the promise is simply to repay £100 for every £100 of the stock which was originally issued; there is no index-linking. As compensation for the risk to one's real capital, the interest rate (or 'coupon') attached to conventional gilts is, of course, quite a lot higher than for the index-linked ones.

In between the original issue of the conventional gilt and its repayment at maturity, the buying and selling prices are determined on the Stock Exchange: on any particular day, the price may be more or less than the £100 which will definitely be paid on maturity. So it looks as if the capital value of gilts is going to be 'variable'.

There is a particular class of gilts which do not, in fact, have a maturity date: these are called, appropriately, 'undated' stocks. The only promise which the government makes is to continue to pay a fixed rate of interest for ever. Clearly, the capital values of these stocks are *always* going to be variable, fluctuating according to the whims of the Stock Exchange. But what about a gilt which matures in, say, one year's time?

I suggest that it would be much more appropriate to regard this as an investment with a *fixed* nominal capital: you know, when you buy the stock, precisely what you are going to receive from the government in a year's time.

The question, then, is: where do we draw the line (in terms of the number of years to maturity) between gilts which we shall regard as 'fixed' capital and those we shall regard as 'variable' capital?

The choice is rather arbitrary. I shall choose to regard a gilt with a maturity date less than five years hence as having a fixed nominal capital (as well as a fixed interest rate). If interest rates were to rise, then the stock-market value of all gilts would fall; but we do have the security, with these 'short-dated' stocks, of knowing that we can recover a pre-determined capital sum by hanging on for a few years at the most.

There is just one final area of possible confusion which I should like to address. A few minutes ago I mentioned that some interest-bearing securities actually roll up the interest and pay it out as a lump-sum at the end of five years; nevertheless the return to you is still *interest* and not capital gain. In some cases, however, the total return to you *might* include an element of capital gain: for instance, a conventional gilt bought at a unit price below £100 will, on maturity, produce a capital gain.

Indeed, all of the 'variable-capital' investments *may* produce a capital gain (or loss).

## Lump-sums v regular savings schemes

Some Low-Risk investments are specifically tailored to encourage regular savings: for instance, there used to be a popular 'Save-as-you-earn' scheme for monthly contributions. Also, the National Savings 'Yearly Plan' is a halfway house to regular savings: you contribute monthly for one year and then the accumulated capital is held for a further four years before the repayment of capital and accumulated interest.

I shall deliberately ignore all Low-Risk regular savings schemes. We shall see, later in the course, that a regular savings policy is ideally suited to High-Risk investments; meanwhile, Low-Risk (and No-Risk) investments are especially suitable for lump-sums.

## Tax considerations

Low-Risk investments are usually most appropriate for non-taxpayers; taxpayers will often (but not always) find that they would get a better return from one of the No-Risk investments described in Lesson II.

Because the tax implications are so important with Low-Risk products, the calculations given in the next lesson will be presented for both non-taxpayers and standard-rate taxpayers (20% tax on investment income).

It should be relatively easy for higher-rate taxpayers to adapt the calculations to meet their personal circumstances.

Don't forget to make use of your tax allowances. At budget time each year, the Chancellor announces the level of tax-free personal allowances; also, the enhanced allowances for people aged 65 or over. You may find that you or your spouse have an unused tax allowance. It will very often be worth transferring capital to one's spouse so that it can be invested (largely in Low-Risk products) to earn a good tax-free return.

## Just how low a risk?

We saw, earlier in the lesson, that there could be some ambiguity in assigning a particular investment product into 'fixed' or 'variable' categories, along both dimensions of nominal capital and interest rate. As a result of that earlier discussion, we can now proceed to place each investment into its appropriate category.

A key reason for this categorisation is that each 'box' in the 2 x 2 table will have rather different risk characteristics. In practice, I sub-divide the Low-Risk category into four sub-categories:

- Very-Low-Risk
- Low-Risk
- Fairly-Low-Risk
- Not such a low risk (ie really Medium-Risk)

In homework Exercise 2 you were asked to consider the sub-category of risk appropriate to each 'box' in our table. Let me describe the method which I shall use for assigning these sub-categories of risk.

In each case, we start off with a 'base' scenario in which the interest rate is 8% pa and inflation is 4% pa. We then look at what happens if there is a sudden external 'shock', namely a change in inflation . . . or in inflation expectations, it does not really matter. Let us suppose that inflation (or the expectation of future inflation) rises to, say, 6% pa. There will be a consequent increase in the general level of interest rates, let us suppose to 10% pa, although the actual amount of the increase is not critical to the calculations.

Now, let us take each sub-category in turn, and see how the real return is affected by these changes. The lower the risk level of an investment, the lower will be the effects of such an economic shock on the value of our investment.

## A. Fixed nominal capital; fixed interest rate

|  | Base Scenario | 'Shock' Scenario |
|---|---|---|
| Gross Income | 8.0% | 8.0% |
| *minus* Tax (at 20%) | –1.6% | –1.6% |
| = Net Income | 6.4% | 6.4% |
| *plus/minus* Capital Gain/Loss | — | — |
| = Total Net Return | 6.4% | 6.4% |
| *minus* Inflation | –4.0% | –6.0% |
| **= Total Net Real Return** | **2.4% pa** | **0.4% pa** |

By definition, the interest rate is fixed, so it remains at 8% pa; and the nominal capital is fixed, so there is no capital gain or loss in either scenario. The increase in inflation has caused a commensurate fall in our real return. I class such investments as normal **Low-Risk** ones.

## B. Fixed nominal capital; variable interest rate

Now let us carry out the same calculations, but with the interest rate variable:

| | Base Scenario | 'Shock' Scenario |
|---|---|---|
| Gross Income | 8.0% | 10.0% |
| *minus* Tax (at 20%) | −1.6% | −2.0% |
| = Net Income | 6.4% | 8.0% |
| *plus/minus* Capital Gain/Loss | — | — |
| = Total Net Return | 6.4% | 8.0% |
| *minus* Inflation | −4.0% | −6.0% |
| = Total Net Real Return | 2.4% pa | 2.0% pa |

In this case, the interest rate offered on the security rises to offset, to a large extent at least, the rise in inflation; by definition, there is again no capital gain or loss.

For non-taxpayers, on the assumed figures there would actually have been *no* decrease in the real return. You might think, therefore, that this is a No-Risk investment if held by a non-taxpayer. This isn't actually the case, since the change in interest rate may not, in practice, exactly match the change in inflation rate; and, anyway, it will probably be implemented only after some time delay.

Nevertheless, it is reasonable to designate this class of investment products as **Very-Low-Risk** ones.

## C. Variable nominal capital; fixed interest rate

The archetypal investment in this category would be a long-dated (or undated) gilt. The price is set by the Stock Exchange; imagine what happens to that price when interest rates rise. For simplicity, we will take the example of an undated gilt, so there is no 'safety net' of an eventual guaranteed repayment at 'par'.

Suppose you paid £100 for your gilt when interest rates were at 8% pa. If interest rates rise to 10% pa, what price would you expect to get if you were to sell this stock? The *buyer* of the stock is going to pay you a price which gives *him* a yield of 10% pa; in other words, he will only pay £80 for each £100 of stock. So, the market price of your stock is likely to fall from around £100 to around £80, thus presenting you with an actual or potential capital loss. For that particular year, the figures will be:

|                                  | Base Scenario | 'Shock' Scenario |
|----------------------------------|:-------------:|:----------------:|
| Gross Income                     | 8.0%          | 8.0%             |
| *minus* Tax (at 20%)             | −1.6%         | −1.6%            |
| = Net Income                     | 6.4%          | 6.4%             |
| *plus/minus* Capital Gain/Loss   | —             | −20.0%           |
| = Total Net Return               | 6.4%          | −13.6%           |
| *minus* Inflation                | −4.0%         | −6.0%            |
| **= Total Net Real Return**      | **2.4% pa**   | **−19.6% pa**    |

By definition, the gross income has remained the same as our original investment; but the total net real return has plummeted. Incidentally, these figures are quite realistic; it is not uncommon for the price of long-dated and undated gilts to change (up or down) by 20% in a year or so.

Frankly, this doesn't really look like a Low-Risk investment at all, does it?

I would actually categorise such an investment as a **Medium-Risk** one, and it will not be considered further until the appropriate lesson.

The price variation will be lower in the case of short-dated stocks. Indeed, with such short-dated stocks (maturing within five years) we were able to consider them to be in the fixed-capital category because of the relatively short time remaining before receiving a guaranteed repayment sum. Stocks maturing in the 5–10 year period can, I suggest, be considered as **Fairly-Low-Risk**, but anything not maturing for ten years or more should be considered as no better than Medium-Risk: it is quite impossible to make even an intelligent guess as to what inflation will be ten years from now, and consequently how it will have eroded the value of such investments.

To summarise the risk characteristics of gilts and other variable-capital, fixed-interest investments:

| Time to Maturity | Risk Level |
|---|---|
| Up to 5 years | Low-Risk |
| 5–10 years | Fairly-Low-Risk |
| Over 10 years and undated | Medium-Risk |

Accordingly, longer dated and undated gilts will be left until Lesson V, which is on the subject of Medium-Risk investment products.

## D. Variable nominal capital; variable interest rate

There are few investments in this sub-category. In fact, there is only one of interest at the moment, namely a foreign currency account. Different foreign currencies will have different degrees of risk; we are concerned only with strong currencies, notably the German mark, Swiss franc and Japanese yen.

What matters this time is not inflation in the UK, but inflation in the relevant foreign country. Germany, Switzerland and Japan all have long track records of keeping inflation in check, so that the real values of their currencies are eroded only very slowly by inflation.

Roughly, a difference in inflation rates between two countries would be compensated for by a corresponding change in the exchange rate. So, if UK inflation were 4% higher than that in Germany then, all other things being equal, the pound sterling would be expected to fall in value by 4% each year against the German mark. Conversely, if you hold money in Deutschmarks, then this would be worth 4% more each year when converted back into pounds.

Life is never quite as simple as this, but this description will suffice for the moment.

These 'safe' currencies will offer commensurately lower yields, so we shall need to use slightly different numbers in our calculations. We will assume *their* inflation to be constant at 2% pa and that the investments typically have a gross yield of 4% pa.

|  | Base Scenario | UK 'Shock' Scenario |
|---|---|---|
| Gross Income | 4.0% | 4.0% |
| *minus* Tax (at 20%) | –0.8% | –0.8% |
| = Net Income | 3.2% | 3.2% |
| *plus/minus* Capital Gain/Loss | +2.0% | +4.0% |
| = Total Net Return | 5.2% | 7.2% |
| *minus* Inflation | –4.0% | –6.0% |
| **= Total Net Real Return** | **1.2% pa** | **1.2% pa** |

The capital gain occurs on converting the foreign currency into sterling and (as described earlier) is assumed to equal the difference between the two inflation rates.

In practice, a sudden deterioration of inflation expectations in the UK of, say, an extra 2% per year, is likely to have a much more dramatic and immediate effect on the exchange rate: rather than having a total 10% effect over five years, it is more likely that the total effect would be felt within a few weeks (or even a few days).

This means that these investments are only **Fairly-Low-Risk** in the short term but, over a long period of time (which is the way I shall suggest using them) they can be classed as **Very-Low-Risk**.

Depending on how long you keep them for, I would judge the risk levels of these strong foreign currency accounts to be:

- Held for up to 5 years       Fairly-Low-Risk
- Held for 5–10 years         Low-Risk
- Held for more than 10 years   Very-Low-Risk

The longer you plan to keep these investments, the lower the risk (because any short-term exchange-rate effects will be ironed out). This contrasts with the variable-capital, fixed-interest investments, such as gilts, for which the risk level *rises* as the period to maturity increases.

This feature of our 'D' sub-group makes them particularly suitable for an emergency fund: money which you may, one day, need in a hurry, but which you don't *expect* to need for very many years.

## Summary of risk levels

We can now put together all of the above analysis into one summary table – Table 8.1. This indicates the general level of risk for each 'box' in the table. Having seen that a variable interest rate is less risky than a fixed one, it seems appropriate to rearrange the table slightly and put 'variable' above 'fixed' on the interest rate axis.

**Table 8.1   Summary of risk levels for different classes of Low-Risk investments**

| INTEREST RATE | NOMINAL CAPITAL | |
|---|---|---|
| | Fixed | Variable |
| **Variable** | Very Low Risk | *(a) held for up to 5 years* Fairly-Low-Risk<br><br>*(b) held for 5–10 years* Low-Risk<br><br>*(c) held for more than 10 years* Very-Low-Risk |
| **Fixed** | Low Risk | *(a) maturing in less than 5 years* Treat as fixed-capital ie Low-Risk |
| | | *(b) maturing in 5–10 years* Fairly-Low-Risk |
| | | *(c) not maturing within 10 years* See under 'Medium Risk' |

At this point, it is worth reminding ourselves that the word 'risk' is not always an abbreviation for 'downside risk'; it can also mean the 'risk' (or chance) of making a *gain*.

We have seen that the long-dated and undated gilts (and similar investments) are, in fact, quite risky. That also means that, if inflation rates (and hence interest rates) were to *fall*, there would then be the opportunity to make a capital gain.

If you are really convinced that interest rates have peaked – and that the next move in such rates is downwards – then it would make sense to invest in variable-capital, fixed-interest securities. However, I should warn you that trying to predict the future course of inflation and interest rates is a hazardous business: the track records of 'experts' do not offer much encouragement.

## Risk v Reward for Low-Risk investments

If different sub-categories of these investments have, as we have seen, different risk levels, then they will also have different benchmark returns.

In figure 8.1, I suggest appropriate levels of these benchmark returns which we can subsequently use to assess the value of each individual investment. For instance, a Very-Low-Risk investment yielding a real return of 4% pa should be regarded as a better bet than a Fairly-Low-Risk investment yielding 4 $\frac{1}{2}$% pa: the former lies *above* the Risk v Return line; the latter lies *on* the line.

When we analysed the risk levels of the various sub-categories, we implied that the only significant risk was that of future inflation; we did not consider any possibility of losing our capital due to the failure or default of the organisation to which we have lent our money.

In the case of loans to the government (whether in the form of National Savings or gilts) we can rest assured on this point. The risk of failure of a *major* bank, building society or insurance company can also be confidently ignored. Smaller ones both can and do fail, albeit very infrequently – witness, for instance, the collapse of Baring's Bank (which was actually not all that small!).

Security is enhanced by a government investor protection scheme. For building societies and banks, the government guarantees the security of 90% of each account, up to the first £20,000 in the account. For joint accounts, the limit is doubled to £40,000. A Policy-holders Protection Act guarantees 90% of money in insurance funds, with no maximum.

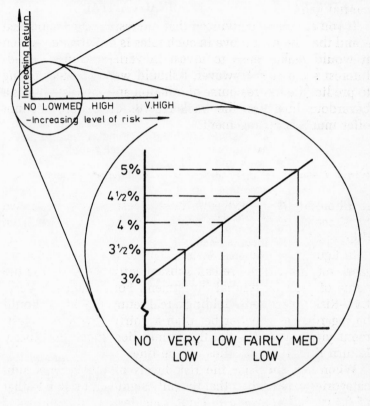

*Fig 8.1* Expected or 'target' real returns for sub-categories of Low-Rich investments

We cannot be so complacent about money lent to companies in exchange for 'Corporate Bonds' – fixed-interest securities such as debentures and preference shares. (Strictly, preference shares – as their name implies – are shares not bonds, but they have more of the characteristics of bonds, and will be regarded as such.) I would class these as Medium-Risk; they therefore appear in Lesson V.

**Table 8.2   Summary of relevant Low-Risk investments**

| INTEREST RATE | NOMINAL CAPITAL | |
|---|---|---|
| | **Fixed** | **Variable** |
| **Variable** | *Very-Low-Risk* | *Very-Low-Risk* |
| | • Bank and building society instant-access and cheque accounts<br>• Bank and building society notice accounts<br>• Variable-rate TESSAs<br>• National Savings income bonds<br>• National Savings pensioners guaranteed income bonds*<br>• National Savings FIRST option bonds* | • Foreign currency accounts (strong currencies, held for several years) |
| **Fixed** | *Low-Risk* | *Fairly-Low-Risk* |
| | • Building society term accounts<br>• Fixed-rate TESSAs<br>• Building society 'stepped' or 'escalator' bonds<br>• National Savings – savings certificates<br>• National Savings – capital bonds<br>• Short-dated gilts (maturing within 5 years)<br>• Guaranteed income and growth bonds | • Medium-dated gilts (maturing in 5–10 years)<br><br><br>(for other variable-capital, fixed-interest products see Medium-Risk Investments) |

\* Interest rate really 'semi-variable' – see text

We are now in a position to move on to look at specific investment products, or, at least, the most interesting and relevant ones: table 8.2 summarises the opportunities which feature in the next lesson. We shall start with the Very-Low-Risk category and then move up the risk scale, leaving Medium-Risk investments until Lessons V and VI.

Before leaving this chapter, however, I must introduce you to my third law.

---

*Thorneycroft's Third Law of Successful Investment*
**Never invest-for-income without first considering whether the product offers an adequate additional real return over that on index-linked gilts.**

---

In the next three chapters, we shall be looking in detail at many specific products in the Low-Risk and Medium-Risk categories. I think that, when you carry out the Total Net Real Return calculations, you may be surprised how few of them are really better than index-linked gilts.

# Homework III

I suggest that you work out, for several of the investments listed in Table 8.2, the Total Net Real Return for:

(a) non-taxpayers
(b) standard-rate taxpayers

Also, if it is relevant to yourself

(c) higher-rate taxpayers

Information on current rates of interest can be obtained from the following sources:

*National Savings products* – the details are contained in the leaflets which you should have collected already from the Post Office.

*Bank and building society products, including TESSAs* – *Money Observer* carries regular quarterly reviews of these investments.

*Government bonds (gilts)* – see the table in the *Financial Times* headed 'UK Gilts Prices'.

Don't worry, at this stage, about foreign currency accounts; nor about 'guaranteed income and growth bonds'.

See how many investment products you can find which meet our benchmark real returns.

When interest is paid out monthly, remember that the true interest rate is slightly higher than the 'nominal' rate: look back to page 24 to revise the meaning of Compound Annual Rate (CAR).

We can anticipate from Lesson II that many Low-Risk investments will give a lower real return than perfectly safe No-Risk ones; can you think of reasons why investors may still want to put some of their money into the Low-Risk products?

# Chapter 9
## Lesson IV: Low-Risk Investments – Products

We are going to look, in turn, at each of the investment products mentioned in table 8.2.

Illustrative calculations are based on figures (for interest rates, tax rates and inflation) appropriate at mid-1996. Many products have a five-year life to maturity, and we need to 'guesstimate' a figure for the inflation rate over that period. The relevant figures are:

| | |
|---|---|
| Redemption yield on 5-year gilts | 7.7% pa |
| Redemption yield on index-linked gilts | 3.7% pa |
| Implied future inflation | 4.0% pa |
| (Current inflation rate, about | $2\frac{1}{2}$ % pa) |

On the basis of these figures, it would be logical to use two different inflation assumptions:

(a) a figure of $2\frac{1}{2}$% pa when evaluating investments which do not have to be kept for more than two years
(b) to err on the side of caution, a figure of 4% pa for investments where you are 'locked in' for a longer period of time, usually five years

It won't always be the case that the short-term inflation assumption is lower than the longer-term one. You will need to rework these figures for yourself, based on up-to-date figures at the time you make your investment decisions – and, of course, you will need to check on the current rates of interest offered on each product.

Always keep in mind Thorneycroft's Third Law, which you learned in the previous lesson (page 93). As you work your way through the Low-Risk investment products, you will be surprised to find how difficult it is to beat an index-linked investment.

We shall end the lesson by going over the (very easy) mechanisms for investing in each of these Low-Risk products.

## Very-Low-Risk investments

General characteristics:

- **Fixed or variable nominal capital**
- **Variable interest rate**
- **Target real return 3½% pa**

*Banks and building societies: cheque accounts and other instant-access accounts*
These are what I refer to as 'working' accounts. You will need one or more of them for your day-to-day and month-to-month transactions: somewhere to pay in all your income and receipts; and from which to draw cash and pay cheques. Their function is not to provide a home for long-term investments (although, of course, it's nice to be able to earn *some* interest on them).

There are three general types of instant-access accounts:

(a) Current accounts on which you can draw cheques; these tend to pay negligible rates of interest.

(b) Instant-access accounts which do not have a cheque-book facility themselves, but which allow instant transfer of cash to your current account; these pay a reasonable rate of interest.

(c) Instant-access accounts which pay a reasonable rate of interest *and* offer a cheque-book facility.

You will need either (a) + (b) operating in tandem; or an account of type (c).

An excellent review of currently available instant-access accounts (showing the interest rates offered by each) is given quarterly in *Money Observer*. In practice, it is not unreasonable to choose, for your current account, a bank or building society which happens to be geographically convenient for you; you will not be keeping much money in this account, so that the rate of interest isn't crucial. What *is* important is never to overdraw, otherwise you will find yourself paying charges at a penal rate.

Some of the best interest rates for the type (b) accounts are with postal accounts. Money can be readily transferred to a current account to meet short-term needs, and transferred from the current account to the postal account to earn some useful interest on cash not immediately required.

You can never expect to obtain the benchmark return on instant-access accounts; that, as we have seen, is not their role in life.

Nor is their role that of providing an 'emergency' fund. By this, I mean the money which you *may* need to use at a few days' notice, but which you *hope* that you won't. For instance, you might suddenly need a fairly substantial sum to buy a new car if your present one 'dies' on you; or you may have an unexpected hospital bill to meet. With any luck, you won't need to touch your emergency fund for many years but, when the emergency does arise, you need to have almost instant access.

We saw in Lesson I that, over a long period of time, the real value of your capital can be eroded even with higher-rate building society accounts. I would certainly be very reluctant to think of leaving 'emergency' money permanently in a UK financial institution, even in a Very-Low-Risk product.

One very appropriate way of providing for future emergencies is by means of a foreign currency instant-access scheme.

*Foreign currency accounts*
With capital freely transferable around much of the globe, there is no need these days to restrict yourself to having your accounts denominated in pounds sterling. A good alternative for part of your money is to keep it in the currency of one of the countries with strong anti-inflation credentials, of which Germany, Switzerland and Japan are pre-eminent. This is actually quite easy to do. A straightforward route, with low charges, is via Rothschild Asset

Management's 'Five Arrows' funds. I'll tell you how to go about this at the end of the lesson.

In this case, you don't actually have a personal foreign currency bank account as such; your money acquires 'shares' in a particular currency fund which, in turn, is invested in short-dated deposits with banks and other financial institutions, with a great emphasis on safety.

If and when the emergency arises, you can withdraw the money you need very quickly, and have it paid (in pounds of course) into your current account.

There are actually two groups of funds available:

(a) *International Reserves.* Interest earned in this fund rolls up until the money is remitted to the UK, at which stage any gain (interest plus any exchange-rate gain) is all treated as income for tax purposes.
(b) *Currency Fund.* Interest is paid out every six months; any exchange-rate gain is treated for tax purposes as a capital gain.

The latter is more suitable for your emergency fund: you don't want to be faced with a possibly substantial income tax bill on top of whatever emergency has arisen. With the 'Currency Funds', capital gains tax can be avoided by occasionally selling the shares and immediately reinvesting in them, thereby establishing a higher base cost for calculating future gains.

It is possible (and, indeed, very easy) with these funds to switch from one currency to another at any time, although the sensible approach for an emergency fund is simply to leave it in one of the strong currencies. As to which one, I personally favour Swiss francs for the following reasons:

(a) uncertainty as to what might happen to the German mark as we move towards a single European currency
(b) uncertainty as to what will happen in Japan, now that the number of older, non-working people is rising quickly

These funds carry the risk that, in the short term, the strong currency might actually go *down* in value against the pound (for instance, if UK interest rates were to be raised), so they are really most appropriate for longer-term savings, but still offer instant access.

It should also be mentioned that these overseas funds are not covered by the UK government's protection scheme. Also, if you unfortunately die, it is not quite so straight-forward for your executors to get the money back to the UK.

There is an alternative approach for your 'emergency' fund which does not have these drawbacks, but which does expose you to the uncertainties of the future real value of your pounds. This is to place it in a UK account which requires, say, 90 days' notice of withdrawal, and then accept the penalty for withdrawing early if necessary. Withdrawal could be either because a personal emergency has arisen; or because UK inflation looks set to 'take off'.

This would mean investing in one of the bank or building society notice accounts.

## Banks and building societies: notice accounts

These offer higher rates of return than instant-access accounts in exchange for requiring (usually) 90 days' notice of withdrawal. You *can* withdraw at shorter notice in an emergency, but then you are likely to lose 90 days' interest. Some notice accounts do allow you to withdraw some cash without penalty, so long as you retain a specified minimum sum in the account.

Interest is usually paid quarterly or half-yearly. Details of what is on offer at any time are available from the regular reviews in *Money Observer*. If you decide, on the basis of those reviews, on a short-list of suitable products, do then get the full details from the chosen banks and building societies; study the details carefully, especially in respect of the penalties for early withdrawal (including any penalty-free withdrawal options) and any bonuses which are sometimes added if you make no withdrawals for twelve months.

These accounts are mainly suitable for non-taxpayers; in which case it is advisable to register as such with the bank or building society, so that you receive the interest gross; otherwise, the interest will be paid (or added to the account) after deduction of 20% tax, and you will then have the hassle of obtaining a refund from the Inland Revenue.

The bank, building society or your local tax office will be happy to supply a form R85, so that you can register as a non-taxpayer. (This also applies to the UK instant-access accounts mentioned earlier and to the building society Term Shares mentioned later.)

*Variable-rate TESSAs*

These 'Tax-Exempt Special Savings Accounts' offer the opportunity to invest up to £9,000 over a period of five years.

Current rates of interest are again given in the *Money Observer* databank. Typically, the larger banks and building societies offer rates of $6\frac{1}{4}$% to $7\frac{1}{4}$% pa tax-free, which means $2\frac{1}{4}$% to $3\frac{1}{4}$% over-and-above our five-year inflation assumption. Whilst not quite reaching our target return, this yield could be of interest to higher-rate taxpayers especially.

A TESSA offers a sensible way of accumulating a lump-sum for something which you may need in five years' time. That 'something' may, for instance, be a new car, kitchen, bathroom . . . or anything else like that for which you need to save. It could also be a very good way of building up the lump-sum which will, later, become your emergency fund.

The full tax advantages are only realised if the investment is kept up for the full five years. You are allowed to withdraw 80% of the interest without jeopardising the tax benefit.

The main disadvantage of TESSAs, to my mind, is that they are designed for regular (monthly or annual) savings. We shall see later that, if you don't expect to need the money in five years' time, then it is best to apply such regular savings to High-Risk investments, and to reserve Low-Risk investments for lump-sums.

If you happen to have built up a TESSA already over the previous five years, and have no plans to spend it, then you *are* in the position of having a lump-sum to reinvest; at that stage, one option is clearly to leave up to £9,000 capital in a 'follow-on' TESSA.

For non-taxpayers, especially those requiring a regular monthly income, the following two National Savings products are possibly the most appropriate Very-Low-Risk investments.

## National Savings Income Bonds
The key features of these bonds are:

- minimum investment of £2,000
- interest paid monthly
- interest paid gross (ie without deduction of tax), but the interest is taxable for taxpayers
- need to keep for one year to obtain full interest
- interest rate variable – the government gives notice of any changes
- 3 months' notice for withdrawals (no earlier repayment possible, even by forgoing interest)
- interest rates (mid-1996):
  - below £25,000: 6¼% pa
  - £25,000 or over: 6½% pa

The following calculations are based on the higher of these two rates of interest.

This is where I test to see whether you have revised the meaning of CAR, as I suggested on page 94 . . . it stands for 'Compound Annual Rate'. Because the interest is paid monthly, the true yield is actually slightly higher than the 'nominal' yield of 6.5% pa; in fact, it is about 6.7% pa. The tax calculation assumes that you reinvest the income at the same interest rate.

|  | Non-taxpayer | Standard-rate taxpayer |
|---|---|---|
| Gross Income | 6.7% | 6.7% |
| *minus* Tax (at 20%) | — | −1.34% |
| = Net Income | 6.7% | 5.36% |
| *plus/minus* Capital Gain/Loss | — | — |
| = Total Net Return | 6.7% | 5.36% |
| *minus* Inflation | −2.5% | −2.5% |
| **= Total Net Real Return** | **4.2% pa** | **2.86% pa** |

Clearly, for taxpayers the return falls below our target, but these bonds *are* of interest to non-taxpayers.

Non-taxpayers over the age of 60 (for both men and

women – no sex discrimination here) can receive a higher monthly income with:

*National Savings Pensioners Guaranteed Income Bonds*

- only available to people aged 60 or over
- minimum investment £500
- interest paid monthly
- interest paid gross (but still taxable)
- interest rate fixed for five years, but you can withdraw early by giving 60 days' notice (and losing 60 days' interest)
- current interest rate 7% pa

Because interest is paid monthly, the CAR is slightly higher than the nominal yield; about 7.2%, in fact.

Thus the calculations are:

|  | Non-taxpayer | Standard-rate taxpayer |
|---|---|---|
| Gross Income | 7.2% | 7.2% |
| *minus* Tax (at 20%) | — | −1.44% |
| = Net Income | 7.2% | 5.76% |
| *plus/minus* Capital Gain/Loss | — | — |
| = Total Net Return | 7.2% | 5.76% |
| *minus* Inflation | −2.5% | −2.5% |
| **= Total Net Real Return** | **4.7% pa** | **3.26% pa** |

What have we here! We have found a Very-Low-Risk investment which (for non-taxpayers) easily beats our target real rate of return! What a pity that many of you will have to wait a long time to be able to make use of it.

*National Savings FIRST Option Bonds*

- Minimum investment £1,000
- Interest added (less standard-rate tax)
- Option to withdraw, without penalty, at each anniversary of purchase

FIRST is an abbreviation for 'Fixed Interest Rate Savings

Tax-Paid', so what is it doing in our 'variable interest' category? The reason is that the interest rate is fixed for only 12 months; on each anniversary, you can cash in your bond or reinvest the proceeds in a new bond at whatever is the rate of interest at the time.

At mid-1996, they offered a rate of interest of 6.25%. Holdings of £20,000 or more attract a small bonus of 0.25% pa. At that rate, these could well be of interest as a short-term haven for lump-sums.

The bonds can be cashed in before the anniversary date, but some interest will be lost.

## Low-Risk investments

The general characteristics of these are:

- **Fixed nominal capital**
- **Fixed (predetermined) interest rate**
- **Target real return of 4% pa**

*Building society term accounts*
These differ from notice accounts in several ways:

- they offer a slightly higher rate of interest
- in exchange for this, the interest rate is usually (but not always) fixed for a number of years; and . . .
- you are usually (but not always) not allowed to withdraw money before the end of this fixed-term contract
- interest is generally added once per year

As with notice accounts, you will find details in the regular reviews presented by *Money Observer*.

*Fixed-rate TESSAs*
In this case the fixed interest rate has the advantage of being tax-free.

These have the same advantages and disadvantages as variable-rate TESSAs.

I suggested that, for your homework, you should have looked at the various bank and building society accounts (including TESSAs), to see for yourself just how they match up to our benchmark returns. You should, by now, have no difficulty in applying our step-by-step process to calculate the real returns!

*Building Society – 'stepped' or 'escalator' bonds*
These usually tie up your cash for five years. As the name implies, the interest rate rises each year in predetermined steps. For instance, a top-of-the-range interest-rate profile might be:

| | |
|---|---|
| year 1 | 6.25% |
| year 2 | 6.5% |
| year 3 | 6.75% |
| year 4 | 7.00% |
| year 5 | 10.25% |

In this case, you must accept that you are 'locked in' for the full term of the contract: the penalty (in terms of loss of future high levels of interest) is usually too great to consider early withdrawal, unless interest rates rise dramatically.

If you calculate a simple average of the five annual interest rates, you will find that it comes to 7.35% pa. This sounds very good: but is it really so good? Well, actually it is: the true average annual compound yield (if all interest is reinvested) works out to be very close to the simple average of 7.35% pa. Interest is paid (or added to the account) annually. Don't forget that we shall have to use our higher (five-year) inflation assumption in this case:

| | Non-taxpayer | Standard-rate taxpayer |
|---|---|---|
| Gross Income | 7.35% | 7.35% |
| *minus* Tax (at 20%) | — | −1.47% |
| = Net Income | 7.35% | 5.88% |
| *plus/minus* Capital Gain/Loss | — | — |
| = Total Net Return | 7.35% | 5.88% |
| *minus* Inflation | −4.0% | −4.0% |
| **= Total Net Real Return** | **3.35% pa** | **1.88% pa** |

These figures fall short of our target, based on figures

current at the time of writing. However, there have been occasions, quite recently, when you could have obtained a real return as high as 5% pa on such an escalator bond.

It is well worth keeping a check on what is on offer from the building societies, making use of the regular reviews in *Money Observer*.

To obtain the full benefit of these escalator bonds, you should allow the interest to roll up in the account. In that way, the high rates of interest earned in the last year or two will be applied to the accumulated interest as well as to the original capital.

Investments such as these, for which the interest rate escalates each year for five years, are rarely worth cashing in early; this is why they are firmly in our 'fixed-interest' category. The following two National Savings products also fall into this category for the same reason. They are aimed, respectively, at two different classes of investor: Savings Certificates are aimed at taxpayers and Capital Bonds at non-taxpayers. In both cases, interest rolls up in the fund and is paid out along with the original capital at the end of five years.

*National Savings – fixed-interest Savings Certificates*
Interest is added tax-free in amounts which increase year by year for five years. The current profile of escalating interest rates works out as being equivalent to an annual tax-free yield of 5.35% pa over the full five years. On our inflation assumption, this represents a real return of 1.35% pa.

If you *do* have to cash in your certificates early, you should receive the cash within a few days. The same applies to . . .

*National Savings – Capital Bonds*
In this case, the escalating rate of interest is taxable; what is more, taxpayers have to declare the interest each year, even though the accumulated interest is not received until the end of five years.

The current rate of interest, for a bond held for the full five years, is equivalent to 6.65%.

|                              | Non-taxpayer | Standard-rate taxpayer |
|------------------------------|--------------|------------------------|
| Gross Income                 | 6.65%        | 6.65%                  |
| minus Tax (at 20%)           | —            | –1.33%                 |
| = Net Income                 | 6.65%        | 5.32%                  |
| plus/minus Capital Gain/Loss | —            | —                      |
| = Total Net Return           | 6.65%        | 5.32%                  |
| minus Inflation              | –4.0%        | –4.0%                  |
| **= Total Net Real Return**  | **2.65% pa** | **1.32% pa**           |

These are not very exciting returns.

*Short-dated gilts (maturing within five years) and held to maturity*

Government bonds, or 'gilts', currently available are listed daily in the *Financial Times* and in several other newspapers.

Remember that, at some predetermined maturity date, the government promises to pay you £100 for each £100 of nominal stock which was originally issued. At any point in time, the market value of the stock may be above or below £100. If it is below £100 when you buy them, then – as well as receiving half-yearly interest – you will enjoy a capital gain when the government pays you £100 on maturity. If the current price is *above* £100 when you buy, you will of course suffer a capital loss on maturity.

Consequently, the tables in the financial press quote two yields:

(a) the current interest rate (the column headed 'Int' in the *Financial Times* table and 'Flat' in some other newspapers), which represents the annual interest rate at today's price for the stock

(b) the redemption yield (the column headed 'Red' in the *FT*) which represents the combined effect of the interest payments together with the capital gain or loss on maturity

It is the redemption yield which is the more important figure. You will see from the *FT* table that, whatever the original yields (or 'coupons') on gilts when they were first

issued, the market subsequently adjusts the prices so that
the redemption yields are all very much in line with each
other – at least for gilts maturing at or around the same
future date.

Depending on whether or not the redemption yield
includes an element of capital gain, our calculation will be
slightly different, as shown by the following examples. In
each case, the gross redemption yield is 7% pa, but in one
case it includes a small element of capital gain and in the
other case a small capital loss.

|  | Redemption Yield includes Capital Gain | Redemption Yield includes Capital Loss |
| --- | --- | --- |
| Gross Income | 6.0% | 8.0% |
| *minus* Tax (at 20%) | −1.2% | −1.6% |
| = Net Income | 4.8% | 6.4% |
| *plus/minus* Capital Gain/Loss | +1.0% | −1.0% |
| = Total Net Return | 5.8% | 5.4% |
| *minus* Inflation | 4.0% | 4.0% |
| **= Total Net Real Return** | **1.8% pa** | **1.4% pa** |

There is a small benefit to taxpayers by choosing a gilt
whose redemption yield includes an element of capital gain;
in other words, a gilt whose current market price is below
its maturity value of £100.

Note, also, that for *very* short-dated gilts (maturing within
the next two years), we would use our lower (short-term)
inflation assumption.

You should familiarise yourself with the table of gilts
prices in your newspaper. From time to time, you will find
that the redemption yield, less your inflation projection,
will give you a real return which matches or exceeds our
benchmark rate for Low-Risk investments. When it does,
then these short-dated gilts are well worth thinking about.

*Guaranteed income and growth bonds*
Up to now, our Low-Risk investment products have been
issued by banks, building societies and the government (the
latter in the form of both National Savings and gilts).

We now introduce a new group of players, namely insurance companies. The difference between their 'income' and 'growth' bonds is simply what happens to the interest which you earn on them: income bonds make a regular (usually annual) payment of interest; with growth bonds, the interest accumulates within the fund and is paid out as a lump-sum at the end of the term of the contract; this term is usually, but not always, five years.

Because the insurance company has already paid tax, the interest is tax-free to standard-rate taxpayers. However, the tax cannot be reclaimed, so that these bonds tend not to be suitable for non-taxpayers.

More importantly, they are not suitable for anyone who cannot leave the money untouched for the full term of the contract: there are usually significant penalties for early withdrawal.

These bonds can offer attractive returns to taxpayers, for instance because the insurance company can make use of certain tax concessions. Changes in the tax rules can cause insurance companies to alter the way in which they structure their bonds. This is only of significance to the investor if the company alters its guarantee part-way through the life of a bond, because of such a tax change.

For example, a recent change removed the tax advantages of something called 'gilt options'. Even though this may affect the cash flow of the insurance company, it really shouldn't affect the investor: a guarantee is a guarantee. If you decide to look at these bonds, it is best to seek the advice of an independent financial adviser. You should make sure from him that the recommended insurance company has never resorted to using the 'small print' of the contract to alter the guarantee in any way.

A good source of information on available guaranteed income and growth bonds is the magazine *Money Management*.

Genuine guaranteed growth bonds should not be confused with those which offer a *conditional* guarantee, usually based on the future performance of some stock-market index. These will be discussed later under the 'Medium-Risk' heading.

## Fairly-Low-Risk investments

These are characterised by:

- **Fixed interest rate**
- **Variable nominal capital**
- **No guaranteed 'escape route' within five years**; if you need to withdraw your money before the investment matures, then there is no guarantee of keeping intact your original nominal capital
- **Target real return of 4½% pa**

There is really only one significant product in this category, namely . . .

*Medium-dated gilts (maturing in five to ten years)*
We have discussed the other UK government bonds (gilts) before, and we shall deal with long-dated and undated gilts in the next lesson. Hence, there is really little to add at this stage.

Data on these gilts are to be found in the usual *Financial Times* table on 'UK Gilts Prices'. Note, however, that the *FT* – in line with other sources of information – has a subcategory of gilts which mature in anything from five to fifteen years. Personally, I suggest that anything over *ten* years should be regarded as 'long-dated' and hence Medium-Risk. I certainly wouldn't wish to be a buyer of any fixed-interest bond not maturing in less than ten years, without having the compensation of the slightly higher rate of return which one would hope to receive from a Medium-Risk investment.

## Buying and selling Low-Risk investments

As you know, one of my objectives is to help make it easy for you to buy (and sell, if necessary) your chosen investment products. It is generally not difficult to achieve this with Low-Risk investments.

*Bank and building society accounts*
These financial institutions will be only too happy for you to call in personally and ask for an application form!

You will have decided, with the help of the *Money Observer* tables, just which accounts are of interest to you. Study the leaflets which describe each one; in particular, look for answers to the following questions:

- What is the current rate of interest?
- Is interest paid monthly, quarterly or annually? (Remember that the true rate of interest is slightly higher for accounts paying interest monthly or quarterly.)
- Is there a minimum amount which can be invested?
- What are the restrictions on, and penalties for, withdrawing your money early on?
- Are there bonuses for not making any withdrawals?
- Can interest be rolled up in the account (this is especially important for 'escalator' bonds)?

If you are a non-taxpayer, ask for a form R85 so that you can receive the full interest free of tax.

In the case of TESSAs, also look to see what, if any, are the costs of withdrawing your money and reinvesting it in someone else's TESSA. You may wish to do this if your chosen bank or building society falls behind the competition in terms of the interest rate which it offers; the government allows you to move a TESSA from one financial institution to another without any loss of the tax advantages, but there may be penalty charges imposed by the institution from which you are moving your account.

*National Savings products*
You should, by now, be familiar with the mechanism. From the Post Office you can obtain:

- *Investment Guide – Options for National Savings*
- *Interest Rates*: a leaflet showing the current rates applicable to each product
- A more detailed brochure on whichever product or products you wish to consider

The detailed explanatory brochure will contain an application form. Just send off this form, with your cheque. To make life really easy, the Post Office will even give you an addressed envelope.

*Gilts*
Again, use the Post Office. In this case, ask for the leaflet: *Government Stock*; this also includes an application form, and lists all the available stocks.

Remember that, in this case, there are some small charges involved: about 0.7% of the first £5,000 invested in each stock and 0.375% thereafter, plus a little for the spread between the buying and selling prices.

You would not normally invest less than £1,000 in any one stock. There is an upper limit of £25,000 in any one stock in one day; so, larger amounts would need to be spread over a number of days.

A better approach is to spread the money between a number of different stocks with different dates for paying interest. These dates are given in the brochure. For instance, you could choose three different stocks paying interest as follows:

| Stock A: | January and July |
| Stock B: | March and September |
| Stock C: | May and November |

In this way you would receive a regular income every two months.

*Foreign currency accounts*
There are several possibilities here. Avoid anything which incurs significant charges (more than 1% a year).

A straightforward approach is provided by Rothschild Asset Management. Details are to be found in the *Financial Times*; look for the pages headed 'FT Managed Funds Service', the sub-section headed 'Offshore and Overseas' and then look under 'Guernsey'. This will give you an address and phone number to contact for details.

You will find that this is a very straightforward way to

hold your money in foreign currency with easy withdrawal (in pounds sterling) when you need it.

*Guaranteed income and growth bonds*
The magazine *Money Management* lists current rates of interest available from various insurance companies. If they appear to be of interest to you, you will be able to obtain more information from your bank. Alternatively, you can contact an independent financial adviser (see Chapter 1).

We shall now move on, in Lessons V and VI, to the next of our risk categories, namely Medium-Risk investments. Many of these are quite similar in principle to the 'Fairly-Low-Risk' medium-dated gilts, but with some additional measure of uncertainty; hence we shall be looking for a somewhat higher real rate of return.

## Homework IV

### Exercise 1

If you look through your National Savings *Investment Guide*, you will see that I have not mentioned three of their products:

- Ordinary Account
- Investment Account
- Childrens' Bonus Bonds

I should like you to have a look at these products, as a means of revising what you have learned about Low-Risk investments.

**Question 1.** What sub-category of risk applies to each of these products: Very-Low, Low or Fairly-Low?

**Question 2.** How do they compare (as regards real return) with other products in the same sub-categories of risk?

**Question 3.** What kind of investor (if any) would find each product to be of interest?

I shall leave you to look at these products for yourself; I shall not comment on them further.

### Exercise 2

Most of the products discussed in the next lesson are still in the 'investing-for-income' category. One of them, however, is rather different: it would be more accurately described as 'investing-for-capital-gain'. What you get at a specific future date is a predetermined capital sum which represents a guaranteed *capital gain* on your investment (subject to certain provisos). For tax purposes, the accumulated 'income' which you receive is treated as a capital gain.

These products are called 'zero-dividend preference shares' and are issued by many investment trusts.

You will find occasional articles on these shares in magazines such as *Money Observer* and *Investors Chronicle*. What I should like you to do is to look through the indexes of these and other investment journals, so as to locate any recent articles on these 'zeros' as they are called for short. I think that it will help you to have read up a little about them before we discuss them in the next lesson.

At the same time, you will find it useful to try to track down articles on two other investment opportunities:

- Building Society Permanent Interest Bearing Shares (PIBS)
- Split-capital investment trusts

# Chapter 10
## Lesson V: Medium-Risk Investments – Products

When we looked at Low-Risk investments, we found it useful to sub-divide the range of products into sub-categories, ranging from Very-Low-Risk to Fairly-Low-Risk; indeed, some products which we may have intuitively thought to be Low-Risk turned out to be Medium-Risk ones.

Now that we have moved on to look at these Medium-Risk investments, we shall again find it useful to sub-divide them. This time, however, it will not be on the basis of varying degrees of 'Medium-Risk-ness', but on the fundamental nature of the products.

We shall, in fact, consider two sub-categories.

(a) The first sub-category (which is the subject of this lesson) is that of straightforward investments such as long-dated gilts. They are generally variable-capital, fixed-interest products, although one of them is rather unusual in being variable-capital and variable-interest. They fail to get into our Low-Risk section because of either or both:

● a long time-span to maturity
● some risk that, because they are not government-backed, the issuer may not be able to maintain the interest payments or repay the capital

(b) The second sub-category acquires its Medium-Risk tag for a completely different reason: these are investment products which are put together for you from a *mixture* of various individual investments, ranging from No-Risk to Very-High-Risk (although predominantly a mix of Low-, Medium- and High-Risk investments). I call these 'hybrid' investments; they form the subject of Lesson VI.

So, for now, we will go on to look in detail at the more interesting of the straightforward Medium-Risk investment products. What we shall do is to look in turn at products offered by the government, by building societies, by insurance companies and by other companies. The last group will also provide our first introduction to the ways in which companies raise money to finance their operations; also, to a special type of company called an investment trust which will feature prominently in later lessons.

You will notice that National Savings products are not mentioned. This is because they all fit into our No-Risk and Low-Risk categories. (I hope that your answers to the first homework exercise *did* put them into the Low-Risk sub-categories!)

A list of those investments which *are* included in this lesson is as follows:

- Government bonds (gilts) – long-dated and undated
- Building society permanent interest bearing shares (PIBS)
- Insurance companies – 'conditional' investment bonds
- Industrial and commercial companies, 'corporate bonds' – preference shares, debentures and convertibles
- Investment trusts – income shares of 'split-capital' trusts and zero dividend preference shares (zeros)

Don't be put off if some of these sound a little daunting! I shall try to explain each one fairly simply.

Most of the lesson is devoted to PIBS and to the two investment trust products. This is because:

(a) they are potentially of considerable interest to both non-taxpayers and (in the case of zeros) to taxpayers
(b) they may be new to you and they do require a little bit of explanation

I think that you will find that it is well worth spending the time and effort required to learn about them.

Keep in mind the target real return which we established in the very first lesson: for Medium-Risk investments we are aiming for a Total Net Real Return of 5% pa; at or above that level of return, these investments will be worth considering for inclusion in our portfolios.

## Long-dated government bonds, or 'gilts'

By 'long-dated', I mean that it is at least ten years before these gilts are due to mature. At some time in the future, ten or more years hence, the government guarantees to pay you back £100 for each £100 of nominal stock which you have bought.

The principles are the same as for the short-dated and medium-dated gilts which we discussed in the last lesson. You may have actually paid more or less than £100 for each £100 of nominal stock: the price you pay will be the market price on the day you buy. If the market price is *less* than £100, you will make a tax-free capital gain on maturity; if it is *more* than £100, then you will make a capital loss.

Because of this, the interest rate which really matters to you is the one called the redemption yield: this represents the combined effect of the half-yearly interest payments, plus or minus the effects of any capital gain or loss on maturity.

With such a long time to go before maturity, the effect of any future capital gain or loss is actually quite small. You will see what I mean if you turn once again to the 'UK Gilts Prices' table in the *Financial Times*. For 'shorts' (no more than five years to maturity) there can be substantial differences between the interest yield (the column headed 'Int') and the redemption yield (the column headed 'Red'): the forthcoming capital gain or loss can be a significant factor in the overall return.

If you now move down the table to the 'Over Fifteen Years' category, you will see that the interest yields and the redemption yields are much the same as each other: any capital gain or loss, being spread over a long time-period, has only a small effect on the overall yield.

One consequence of this is as follows. If there is a change in the general level of interest rates, then the prices of the long-dated stocks will be affected much more than those of the shorts, because they do not have the same cushion of an early guaranteed lump-sum repayment. This is, of course, precisely why we have had to put them in a higher risk category than shorts.

You will also recall, from the previous lesson, that I would personally treat anything over 10 years to maturity, rather than 15 years, as 'long-dated'.

Generally, the slightly higher rate of interest (as measured by the redemption yield) which you would get on a long-dated gilt does not compensate for the higher level of risk. On the other hand, if you really felt sure that interest rates were going to come down, then the longer-dated stocks would be expected to increase in value more than the shorter-dated ones.

Trying to guess the future movements of interest rates is really incompatible with a 'get-rich-slowly' philosophy. By all means look at these long-dated gilts from time to time, using our Total Net Real Return formula, but most of the time it is unlikely that they will match up to our target return for Medium-Risk investments.

You may wonder, therefore, who on earth buys all these long-dated gilts. They are really more suitable for pension funds and insurance companies, who need to match their investments to known or projected commitments stretching well into the future.

## Undated government bonds

These gilts differ from those which we have discussed thus far inasmuch as there is no maturity date: there is no time in the future at which the government has committed itself to repay each £100 of nominal capital; instead, it has simply committed itself to paying the half-yearly interest payments for ever. Consequently, there is no such thing as a 'redemption yield'.

All of my above comments on the relevance of long-dated gilts apply to these products, only more so.

If you do decide to buy either long-dated or undated gilts, remember that it is easy to do so through the Post Office.

## Building society PIBS

Permanent interest bearing shares are to building societies what undated gilts are to the government: they offer a permanent, fixed rate of interest, but no eventual repayment of capital.

They do differ from gilts, however, in several important respects. First, there is, in principle, a risk to the future security of your money. In the event of the building society getting into financial trouble, the PIBS are last in line for a payout from the residual assets of the society.

Second, they are not quite so easy to buy and sell. You do not obtain them through the Post Office, nor even from the building society itself. Instead, you have to go through a stockbroker (which your bank can arrange).

Third, some PIBS can be bought only in rather large amounts: in several cases, the minimum investment is £10,000 or even £50,000, although there are several PIBS which can be acquired in multiples of £1,000.

Fourth, remember that investors in a building society have an unusual position: whilst they are ostensibly investing-for-income rather than investing-for-profit, they are in fact also the *owners* of their society. Hence, in the event of a takeover of the society, or its conversion into a quoted company, the PIBS investors would benefit from a windfall 'hand-out'.

PIBS *are* similar to gilts inasmuch as neither is subject to tax on any capital gain which is made, if and when you come to sell them.

You will find occasional articles on PIBS in *Money Observer*, *Investors Chronicle* and other financial journals. Your Saturday copy of the *Financial Times* gives you the current yields. Generally, these yields will be 1 to 2% pa higher than you would obtain on undated gilts, because of the slight perceived risk involved (the first of the four points listed above). The larger and more secure the building society, the smaller the 'risk premium' over gilts. For instance, the yield on PIBS issued by the Halifax, which was Britain's largest building society prior to becoming a bank (in conjunction with the Leeds Building Society) would typically be at the lower end of the range – namely, about

1% pa above the yield on undated gilts.

It is not unknown for a building society to fail. In the past, such a society would have been rescued by being taken over by another, larger society. However, the chances of failure of any of the largest five or ten building societies must be very low, and shouldn't cause any loss of sleep. For our illustrative calculations, we will take one of the larger societies, but not *the* largest, and work on a 'risk premium' over undated gilts of $1\frac{1}{4}$% pa.

Let us see how the numbers stack up. The calculations below were carried out when undated gilts yielded about $8\frac{1}{2}$% pa and inflation was below 3% pa, but expected to increase; we shall take 4% pa again as our inflation 'guesstimate'. If interest is paid half-yearly, the true rate of interest rises from $9\frac{3}{4}$% to about 10% pa.

|  | **Tax rate** | |
| --- | --- | --- |
|  | Nil | 20% |
| Gross Income | 10.0% | 10.0% |
| *minus* Tax (at 20%) | — | 2.0% |
| = Net Income | 10.0% | 8.0% |
| *plus/minus* Capital Gain/Loss | ? | ? |
| = Total Net Return | 10.0±? | 8.0±? |
| *minus* Inflation | −4.0% | −4.0% |
| **= Total Net Real Return** | **6.0±? pa** | **4.0±? pa** |

Being undated (and hence having no maturity date to look forward to) it is quite possible that you would want to sell the PIBS at some time in the future. In that case, there will be some unpredictable average annual capital gain or loss indicated by '±?' in the calculations.

You will need to rework the calculations for yourself using current figures for yield, tax and inflation expectations. In any case, it is likely that the same general conclusions will apply, namely that an investment in PIBS could be of some interest if *both* the following apply to you:

(a) you are a non-taxpayer; *and*
(b) you are confident that interest rates are not going to rise significantly in the future (which, if they did,

would result in a fall in the market value of your PIBS)

I have to repeat that I consider it unwise to try to anticipate the future direction of interest rates. Nevertheless, I would also consider the 'bonus' of, say, 1¼% pa over undated gilts to be more than a fair compensation for any minor risks attached to a *major* building society.

There is no simple postal method of acquiring PIBS; you would need to contact your bank, who, in turn, would use the services of a stockbroker.

## Insurance companies – 'conditional' investment bonds

In Lesson IV, we looked at guaranteed income bonds and guaranteed growth bonds issued by insurance companies. The annual rate of interest and the final capital repayment, respectively, are guaranteed at the time you subscribe; hence (especially being for a limited period of five years), these products fall firmly into our Low-Risk category.

Many insurance companies, these days, also produce 'high income bonds' for which the ultimate payout (at the end of five years) is *conditional* upon the performance of a price index of ordinary shares – usually the FT-SE 100 index (of which, more later).

These bonds are not actually backed by holdings of ordinary shares but, rather, by a complicated arrangement of exotic things called 'options'. This need not concern you, the investor; all you need to consider is whether you think the payout conditions make the products worth considering.

The first thing you need to be aware of is the nature of the 'guarantee'. You will invariably see, in the brochure, some phrase such as 'guaranteed return of capital' or 'the total return will never be less than 100% of your investment'.

At first sight, this will often seem to you to be *in addition* to an annual income of perhaps 10% pa tax-free. However, on closer scrutiny, you will see that this is not so: in certain circumstances, if you have taken £1,000 pa in 'interest' for five years on a £10,000 bond, your final capital repayment may be only £5,000.

Whilst you have, indeed, ended up in total with your £10,000 back, it is only because you have been withdrawing your own *capital* during the life of the plan.

This worst-case scenario would typically occur if the FT-SE 100 share index, after five years, was somewhat lower than it was when you made the investment. You would clearly have been better off, if that proved to be the case, to have invested in something like conventional five-year gilts.

Conversely, if the stock-market were to power ahead during those five years, you would not receive the full benefits of such a rise.

There is a rather narrow range of future stock-market performance over which the bonds would prove, in retrospect, to have been good investments: this is around the point at which you receive the maximum return from the bond, without forgoing any significant gain from any *additional* rise in the share index.

Don't forget, also, that there will usually be a significant penalty if you decide that you need to cash in the bonds in the early years.

I have found, in presenting very many examples of these bonds to mature students, that they were unanimously unimpressed by them, a feeling which I share. We shall certainly want to link *some* of our capital to the future performance of shares, but we shall want to do so in a way which takes full advantage of the possibilities of capital gains if the stock-market rises strongly. We shall also see later that stock-market-related investments are better made via regular savings schemes rather than by means of lump-sums. And we don't want to pay unnecessary charges!

These comments also apply to a new breed of TESSAs for which part of the return is linked to stock-market performance; also, I suspect, to so-called 'protected' stock-market investment schemes.

## Corporate bonds

It is not only the government and building societies which issue long-dated fixed-interest securities. Such bonds are also issued by industrial and commercial companies.

Like the gilts and PIBS discussed above, they have relatively high rates of interest commensurate with their Medium-Risk character. Again, therefore, they would be expected to appeal mainly to non-taxpayers.

Until recently, this was so. All that changed when the government announced that corporate bonds would henceforth be eligible for inclusion in personal equity plans ('PEPs') and could hence be sheltered from tax. Consequently, there are now very many 'corporate bond PEPs' available, in which virtually all of the invested cash is placed in such bonds.

Incidentally, an investment manager offering a corporate bond PEP can also include some building society PIBS and gilts in the portfolio – something which you can't do directly for yourself in a 'self-select' PEP.

'Wait a minute!' I can hear you say. 'You've started to talk about PEPs as if we already know all about them!' Well, you are quite right, of course: we don't cover PEPs until we come on to ordinary shares. It is in relation to 'equities' (or ordinary shares) that PEPs will most likely have a place in your investment plan.

Nevertheless, because corporate bonds are very much in the Medium-Risk category (and corporate bond PEPs are very much in the news), I would like to mention them at this stage, just so that you know what they are when you come across the term.

There are basically three kinds of corporate bonds. They are all, essentially, fixed-interest loans raised by companies to help finance their operations. The investors lending money to companies in this way are investing-for-income rather than investing-for-profit: they do not *own* the company nor share in its future profits. They do rank ahead of the owners (the shareholders) to get their money back in the event of the company going bust.

The three main categories of relevance to the UK investor are:

*Preference shares*
Although these are, strictly speaking, *shares* in the company, they are more usefully considered as loans. They pay

a fixed rate of interest in the form of (usually) half-yearly dividends.

### Debentures and other loan stock

These are basically IOUs issued by the company. They carry a (usually) fixed rate of annual interest. They have a 'redemption date' at which the company pays back the lump-sum of the IOU.

### Convertibles

These are loans which carry the additional right to convert into the ordinary shares of the company at predetermined future dates and at a predetermined price (or into a predetermined number of shares, which amounts to the same thing). Alternatively, they can be redeemed for cash rather than converted into shares if the investor so desires; this would occur if the company's share price fails to reach the conversion price.

Even with the advent of corporate bond PEPs, I don't believe that these bonds are of great interest to most private investors. My reason for saying that will become clear when we look at the historical performance statistics of collective funds: those based on components of corporate bonds have a very modest track record.

I'm very keen on PEPs, as you will see later. However, I shall suggest that you reserve your annual PEP allowance for investments in ordinary shares. If you take out a corporate bond PEP, you are denying yourself an opportunity to invest in a (better) alternative. They only really become interesting late in life – see Chapter 16.

There are two particular Medium-Risk collective fund investments which *are* of general interest, the first to non-taxpayers and the second to taxpayers. For that reason, I am devoting the remainder of this lesson to them.

## Investment trust income shares

The two main types of collective funds which I shall deal with in detail in Lessons VII and VIII are unit trusts and investment trusts. Essentially, both of these provide mechanisms for spreading relatively small amounts of money across a wide range of ordinary shares. Despite this spread, the basic unit trusts and investment trusts are still generally High-Risk investments.

There are, however, two specialised categories of investment trust shares which provide Medium-Risk opportunities, and so need to be introduced here. The first one goes under the formidable title of 'Income shares of split-capital investment trusts'. It is well worth learning about them: for non-taxpayers in particular they can form a very useful part of an investment plan, and I am going to describe them in some detail.

With an investment in a straightforward investment trust, your money is 'pooled' with that of thousands of other investors; the managers of the trust then invest this pool of money in the ordinary shares of perhaps a hundred or so individual companies.

The investment trust, itself, is a company quoted on the Stock Exchange; you will find a list of investment trusts in the share price pages of the *Financial Times*.

The shareholders of a conventional investment trust are entitled to the 'profits' of the trust; that is, to the dividends which the trust receives from its shareholdings, less the amount required to service any loan capital and to pay the management's expenses. The shareholders also gain the full benefit of any appreciation in the capital value of the underlying shares, at least to the extent that that value is reflected in the stock-market price of the shares of the trust.

If all this sounds a little complicated, I hope that it will become clearer when we look in more detail at collective funds in Lesson VII.

Now for the really complicated bit. This is where I have to introduce the concept of split-capital investment trusts.

We mentioned, earlier, the way in which some Medium-Risk investments were constructed as *hybrids* of individual investments which themselves carry different levels of risk. A split-capital trust does just the opposite: it *de*-constructs (or sub-divides) itself into two different classes of shares, each with vastly different risk characteristics. In a simple (!) case, these are:

(a) *Capital Shares* – which receive none of the income accruing to the trust, but all of the capital gain; *and*
(b) *Income Shares* – which receive all the income (after paying off loans and other expenses) but none of the capital gain

Thus, what started out as a collection of ordinary shares (a High-Risk investment) is de-constructed into:

(a) *Capital Shares* – Very-High-Risk; *and*
(b) *Income shares* – Medium-Risk

Each class of shares then acquires its own stock-market quotation, and each can hence be bought and sold separately. The *Financial Times* share pages include a separate section, after 'Investment Trusts', headed 'Inv Trusts Split Capital'.

The class of shares which interests us in this lesson is the Medium-Risk one of income shares.

Another feature of split-capital trusts is that they have a limited life: at some predetermined future date, subject to shareholder approval, the trust will be wound up. Thus, they have a 'maturity' date in the same way as conventional gilts. At that maturity date, the holders of income shares will receive a predetermined amount per share; all of the remaining value of the assets (after paying off any loans) goes to the holders of the capital shares.

Thus, as income shareholders, we know just what we will get back (or, at least, hope to get back) as a lump-sum at some future date. This price often (but not always) equates to the price at which the shares were first issued. If we buy the shares part-way through their life, it is likely that we will pay more than the issue price; hence, on maturity (when the trust is wound up) we shall get back *less* than we actually paid for the shares.

We know this when we buy the shares – just as we know with an annuity that we will never get back the lump-sum which we have placed with an insurance company. Just as with an annuity, the *quid pro quo* for this loss of capital is a higher-than-normal interest rate during the lifetime of the investment.

In the case of income shares, the investment goes on until the *trust* dies, not until *we* die. So, we do expect to see *some* of our capital back again, but not all of it.

If we continue to regard the investment as similar to an annuity, then it is most akin to one in which the return from the annuity *escalates* over time. Because we, the owners of the income shares, are entitled to *all* of the net income of the trust, we can expect our dividend to increase year-by-year in line with (we hope) increasing dividends paid *to* the trust by the companies in which its money is invested.

This means that, in order to work out the value to us of the income shares, we shall need to make some estimate of the rate at which our future dividends may increase. We shall see in a minute how we might go about this.

To start with, though, let us take a simple example in which we do *not* expect any growth in dividends. Suppose that the income shares of a particular split-capital investment trust were issued at 100p five years ago and that they will be repaid at 100p in five years' time. At present, the price of the shares is, say, 200p; so we know that in five years' time we shall only get back half of our capital outlay – a rate of capital *loss* of about 13%pa.

Suppose, further, that we receive a single gross dividend payment of 50p each year for each share (an initial gross yield of 25% pa on our 200p per share investment).

Our standard calculation is as follows:

|  | Tax Rate | |
|---|---|---|
|  | **Nil** | **20%** |
| Gross Income | 25% | 25% |
| minus Tax (at 20%) | — | −5% |
| = Net Income | 25% | 20% |
| *minus* Capital Loss | −13% | −13% |
| = Total Net Return | 12% | 7% |
| *minus* Inflation, say | −4% | −4% |
| = **Total Net Real Return** | **8% pa** | **3% pa** |

You will immediately see how the structure of these investments penalises taxpayers, but it is quite beneficial to non-taxpayers. Indeed, this was the very purpose of introducing split-capital investment trusts in the first place: the income shares would appeal particularly to non-taxpayers and the capital shares to taxpayers.

Now, this example was a very simple one, inasmuch as the gross interest was assumed to be constant. In real life, we would hope that the interest rate, paid half-yearly or quarterly, would increase over time; the *amount* by which it increases is going to depend on many factors, one of which is the size of the assets attributable to the *capital* shareholders – because we are going to receive all of the income from *their* stake in the trust, as well as our own.

Clearly, if we are to have any chance of sorting out the relative value of each income share, we should need a great deal of information on each split-capital trust and a relevant computer program! In practice, there is no need to rush off to buy a computer as the task is already done for us by the Association of Investment Trust Companies*

Each month AITC produces a report which includes a table on split-capital investment trust income shares. The trusts which are included are just those which are members of the Association, but these cover a high proportion of all those which are quoted on the Stock Exchange.

Table 10.1   Examples of typical information available on split-capital investment trusts, income shares

| Share Price | Gross Yield | Years/ Months to wind-up | Redemption Price | Company | Gross Redemption Yield (% pa) assuming annual growth rates of | | | |
|---|---|---|---|---|---|---|---|---|
| | | | | | 0% | 5% | 7.5% | 10% |
| 105.5 | 11.1 | 4-8 | 100p | A | 11.2 | 12.3 | 13.0 | 13.6 |
| 98.5 | 13.9 | 5-4 | 50p | B | 6.0 | 8.3 | 9.6 | 10.9 |
| 83.5 | 13.0 | 11-2 | 10p | C | 9.0 | 14.1 | 16.2 | 19.3 |
| 67.0 | 19.3 | 8-3 | 1p | D | 12.7 | 18.0 | 20.7 | 23.4 |

(*Source*: AITC)

* For a specimen of their *Monthly Information Service*, contact AITC Services Ltd, Park House (6th Floor), 16 Finsbury Circus, London EC2M 7JJ, or phone 0171 588 5347. Another good source of information is the River & Mercantile *Guide to Split Capital Investment Trusts* (0171 405 7722).

Their table shows the projected 'gross redemption yield' on different assumptions regarding the annual growth rate of the total income of each trust. My table 10.1 illustrates the kind of information produced in these monthly reports. I would suggest that, in practice, you assume an annual growth rate of 5% per annum. All you have to do, as a non-taxpayer, to obtain good estimates of the likely Total Net Real Returns, is to deduct your inflation assumption from the figures in the tables.

You should also read up what the report says about 'asset cover' and 'hurdle rate'. I shall talk about these concepts when I come on to introduce zero dividend preference shares.

In table 10.1 I have chosen four real-life companies to illustrate four different levels of redemption price. In the case of Company A, the lump-sum received on winding-up would almost repay the price paid for the shares. As you go down the table, the other trusts have decreasing 'redemption prices' and hence have increasing capital losses on maturity. One effect of this is that there is also an increase in the degree of uncertainty about the final redemption yield.

Company D is an illustration of an investment which is almost a pure 'annuity'. At the end of its life, a little over eight years hence, there is virtually no repayment of capital. When we come to put together an investment plan (Chapter 16) we shall see that an annuity-type investment can form a useful part of the plan; if this is so in your circumstances, then one of these split-capital investment trust income shares could well fit the bill.

You will need to go to your bank or to a stockbroker in order to acquire the shares. This is actually no bad thing: I have found, in practice, that you can obtain some good advice as to just *which* trust's income shares meet your needs.

You should indicate to your bank or stockbroker:

- Your 'time horizon' – roughly the number of years over which you wish to receive an income before the trust is wound up.

- Any strong personal views you may have about the future growth of company dividends.
- The level of risk which you are prepared to take (namely, very little!).
- The specific type of split-capital trust which is of interest; in particular, I suggest that you specify a 'conventional' split-capital trust with only two classes of shares – income shares and capital shares (with no zero dividend preference shares). There are other, more complicated and more risky types of split-capital trusts, which I suggest you ignore.

None of this discussion on income shares will have been of much practical interest to you if you pay income tax (although you will anticipate that the discussion on capital shares in Lesson X *could* be of interest). Meanwhile, the good news is that the next investment to be discussed is very much tailored to your needs.

## Zero dividend preference shares (zeros)

These shares are also issued by several split-capital investment trusts. They pay no dividend (hence the name) but repay a fixed capital sum at some predetermined maturity date. Hence, there is no income tax to pay; all of the return comes in the form of capital appreciation.

At the maturity date, the trust is wound up (unless the shareholders vote otherwise) and the trust's holding of shares is liquidated. The resultant 'pool' of cash is shared out amongst the various categories of shareholders, based on a formula which is set out when the trust is first established. So far as the zeros are concerned, this formula – as I say – means that they receive a fixed, predetermined capital repayment.

Let us consider some imaginary (but realistic) figures. Suppose, when the trust was first set up, its share capital included zeros issued at 100p per share; and that, at the end of a fixed lifetime of ten years, these zeros are to be repaid at 310p. This would represent a compound annual interest rate of 12% over the ten years, all paid in the form of a final capital repayment at the end.

That's how it would look to someone buying the shares when they were first issued and holding on to them for the full ten years.

You don't *have* to keep them for the full term; in between times, these zeros can be bought and sold on the stock-market just like any other shares.

At the time when most zeros were issued, interest rates were rather high; since then, they (interest rates) have fallen substantially, resulting in a commensurate *rise* in the value of all fixed-interest investments. If you were buying zeros now through the stock-market, the price will have risen to a level at which the total return, from now until maturity, would be rather less than when they were first issued. Let's look again at the same numerical example, and see what the position might be half-way through the ten-year term.

First, what would the price be today if the general level of interest rates had *not* changed? The answer is that, at the end of the fifth year, the market price would be expected to be about 176p. The original holder of the shares, selling after five years, would have made a capital gain of 76p per share (a compound annual interest rate of 12% pa); similarly, the *buyer* would know that, in five years' time, he was going to receive 310p per share, giving him a similar capital gain of 76% (310 ÷ 176 = 1.76) or 12% pa.

In practice, the market price of the shares at the end of five years might have risen to, say, 200p. The initial holder, selling at this point, now makes a capital gain of 100% (an annual return to him of about 15% pa); meanwhile, the new buyer will have a predetermined growth over the remaining five years of only 55% (310 ÷ 200 = 1.55) or just over 9% pa.

For the new buyer (intending to retain the shares to maturity), the Total Return formula would read like this:

| | |
|---|---|
| Gross Income | 0.0% |
| *minus* Tax (at 20%) | — |
| = Net Income | 0.0% |
| *plus* Capital Gain | +9.0% |
| = Total Net Return | 9.0% |
| *minus* Inflation, say | −4% |
| **= Total Net Real Return** | **5%** pa |

You will generally find that the Total Net Real Return on these zeros is, indeed, very much in line with our target for Medium-Risk investments, namely 5% pa.

We'll look now briefly at two specific features of these zeros: (a) just what the risks are; and (b) where you can go to find out information on them.

The first and most obvious risk is that future inflation may not be as we project: it may be higher or lower, but it is unlikely to be precisely what we have assumed. In this respect, of course, zeros are no different from government bonds or, indeed, any other investment which is not actually in the No-Risk category.

Where they *do* differ from government bonds is in the confidence we can place in the promise to repay a fixed sum on maturity. The problem is not that the managers may abscond with the money. It is that the total assets of the trust, when it is wound up, may be insufficient to keep the initial 'promise'; even though zeros rank first in line for payment on maturity.

To help you judge this risk, for any particular investment trust, tables are produced which indicate two useful guides. These are:

(a) *Asset Cover (at winding up).* This is the number of times the promised redemption value of the zeros is currently covered by the value of the assets on which the zeros have first call. So, an asset cover of 2.0 means that (at present, at least) there is enough value in the shareholdings of the investment trust to cover the maturity payment on zeros twice over; whereas a cover of less than 1.0 means that the shares will not be repaid in full on maturity unless the trust's portfolio of investments rises between now and the maturity date.

(b) *Hurdle Rate.* This is the future annual compound growth rate in the assets of the trust, which would be necessary in order to repay the zeros in full, at the pre-determined price. A hurdle rate of 5% pa means that the trust's assets must grow at that rate until maturity for the promise to be kept; conversely, a figure of –5% pa means that the assets can actually *decline* at that rate and still leave enough cash on maturity to repay the zeros in full.

You will appreciate that a current asset cover in excess of 1.0 means that the hurdle rate will currently be negative, and vice versa.

A zero with an asset cover below 1.0 (and hence a positive hurdle rate) clearly carries a higher level of risk than one with an asset cover in excess of 1.0. This higher risk should be reflected in a redemption yield which is somewhat higher than average for Medium-Risk investments.

So, where do we find all this information on yields, asset covers and hurdle rates?

The current market prices of zeros are given daily in the 'London Share Service' pages of the *Financial Times*, under 'Inv Trusts Split-Capital'. Unfortunately, this table does not give the current redemption yield to maturity of the zeros.

An excellent source of information is the *Monthly Information Service on Investment Trusts* published by the Association of Investment Trust Companies. (See footnote to page 129.)

As well as giving the current prices of the shares, the AITC table on zero dividend preference shares also indicates:

- years/months to wind-up
- redemption price
- gross redemption yield (based on full repayment at maturity)
- asset cover
- hurdle rate

When you look at an example from this publication, you will see that the zeros with the lowest asset covers and highest hurdle rates have the highest redemption yields; this is to compensate for the higher risks involved, as we have just discussed.

To recap: these zero dividend preference shares are likely to be of most interest to taxpayers, especially to those paying tax at the higher rate. If you find them to be of interest, then you could choose to invest in a series of zeros, each maturing at different dates in the future, so that you can plan for a steady stream of capital repayments. One purpose of spreading your capital gains in this way would be to avoid the risk of falling into the capital gains tax net in any one year.

Although zeros produce their return in the form of a capital gain, it is still appropriate to consider them as 'investing-for-income' products, rather than ones in which you are 'investing-for-profit'. So (along with all the other Medium-Risk investments introduced in this lesson), do not forget to apply Thorneycroft's Third Law of Successful Investment (page 93)! You may well find that some of the Medium-Risk investments are less attractive to you than index-linked gilts.

Nevertheless, you may also find some of these investments to be quite attractive, depending on your tax position. The strictures about remembering Thorneycroft's Third Law apply, even more so, to some of the other group of Medium-Risk investments which are the subject of the next lesson.

# Homework V

In the next lesson, we look at the class of Medium-Risk investment products which I call 'hybrids'. They are Medium-Risk because they are a *mixture* of different investments, each with different risk characteristics, but averaging out somewhere around our Medium-Risk level. For instance, such a product could, typically, be a blend of Low-Risk short-dated gilts, Medium-Risk long-dated gilts and corporate bonds, together with High-Risk equities; often, there will also be some property in the portfolio. A very few contain a significant proportion of No-Risk index-linked gilts.

Because of the wide variation in the make-up of these products, they will have different degrees of 'Medium-Riskness', which will often be very difficult to estimate.

Some of the products are tailored for lump-sum investment; others for regular saving over many years.

With some of them, you are effectively 'locked-in' for several years; with others, there is not such a high penalty for early encashment.

With all this variety, you may wonder whether there is *any* common theme which links these investments together as a class.

There is just one such feature – namely *charges*.

Being hybrids, created from several distinct individual investments, they clearly have to have managers and administrators; and this means that you have to pay for their services.

This feature is not confined to hybrid Medium-Risk products: the same is true also of unit trusts, investment trusts and managed personal equity plans, all of which we shall consider when we come to look at High-Risk investments. The difference is that, in *these* cases, the manager puts together for you a package of investments (predominantly in ordinary shares) which are *themselves* all High-Risk; and, as we shall see, pooling together several High-

Risk investments does not actually reduce the risk all that much.

This contrasts with our Medium-Risk hybrid products which might, for instance, typically combine Low-, Medium- and High-Risk investments.

Generally, a 'managed fund', such as our Medium-Risk hybrids, will have two layers of charges:

(a) an *initial* charge of, perhaps, 5% of your investment
(b) an *annual* charge, which might be about 1% to 1½% each year, based on the current value of the fund

For such an investment product, the combined effect of these charges would be to reduce the return to you by about 2% to 2½% pa if the investment is held for five years; and 1½% to 2% pa if it is held for ten years before being cashed in.

What I should like you to do for your homework is to think seriously about the impact of these management charges. To help you to do so, I will pose some questions for you to answer:

## Question 1

Consider a typical 'managed fund' issued by an insurance company in which the effect of charges is to reduce the return, to you, by: (a) 2% pa; and (b) 2½% pa.

Suppose that the fund manager earns a total net return (after-tax income plus capital gain) of 10% pa on the investments which he makes on your behalf. Inflation is assumed to be 4% pa.

The question is this: from the *real* profits which the manager makes on the investments, what is the percentage which is swallowed up in charges?

## Question 2

What do you consider to be a fair and reasonable level of charges to pay for professional management?

## Question 3

Can you think of reasons why it might sometimes be worthwhile paying over-the-odds; in other words, paying more in charges than indicated by your answer to Question 2?

From the next lesson onwards, we shall be focusing on investments which can be accumulated over several years by means of regular savings plans. So I need to introduce a table of figures to show you how different rates of return affect the final capital value of a long-term savings plan.

You will recall that, in the preliminary homework (Chapter 5), I gave you a table which provided the equivalent information for lump-sum investments (see page 32).

In practice, most regular savings plans will involve monthly instalments. For simplicity, however, the table is based on *annual* instalments, with interest added at the end of each 12-month period.

**Table 10.2   Capital sum (in £) accumulated at the end of a regular savings plan, for different rates of return** (Based on an investment of £100 per annum)

| Compound annual rate of return | Length of savings plan (years) | | | | |
|---|---|---|---|---|---|
| | 5 | 10 | 15 | 20 | 25 |
| 0% | 500 | 1,000 | 1,500 | 2,000 | 2,500 |
| 1% | 515 | 1,057 | 1,626 | 2,224 | 2,853 |
| 2% | 531 | 1,117 | 1,764 | 2,478 | 3,267 |
| 3% | 547 | 1,181 | 1,916 | 2,768 | 3,755 |
| 4% | 563 | 1,249 | 2,082 | 3,097 | 4,331 |
| 5% | 580 | 1,321 | 2,266 | 3,472 | 5,011 |
| 6% | 598 | 1,397 | 2,467 | 3,899 | 5,816 |
| 8% | 634 | 1,565 | 2,932 | 4,942 | 7,895 |
| 10% | 672 | 1,753 | 3,495 | 6,300 | 10,818 |
| 12% | 712 | 1,965 | 4,175 | 8,070 | 14,933 |
| 14% | 754 | 2,204 | 4,998 | 10,377 | 20,737 |
| 16% | 798 | 2,473 | 5,993 | 13,384 | 28,909 |
| 18% | 844 | 2,776 | 7,194 | 17,302 | 40,427 |
| 20% | 893 | 3,115 | 8,644 | 22,403 | 56,638 |
| 25% | 1,026 | 4,157 | 13,711 | 42,868 | 131,849 |

To take a specific example, suppose that we invest £100 per year for 15 years (a total outlay of £1,500); and that, at the end of that 15 years, our investment has grown to £3,495. Table 10.2 tells us that the average annual return (net income plus capital gain) over the life of the plan would have been 10% pa.

This is the total return, but not the total *real* return: in order to calculate the real return, we would need to deduct the average level of inflation over the same period.

**Table 10.3    Approximate average UK inflation for different time-periods up to 1995**

| | | |
|---|---|---|
| 5  years | 1990–95 | 4% pa |
| 10  years | 1985–95 | 5% pa |
| 15  years | 1980–95 | 6% pa |
| 20  years | 1975–95 | 8% pa |
| 25  years | 1970–95 | 9% pa |
| 50  years | 1945–95 | 6% pa |
| 100  years | 1895–1995 | 4% pa |

Table 10.3 summarises the average rate of UK inflation (as measured by the retail price index) for various time-periods up to 1995.

So, if our 15-year investment, yielding a total return of 10% pa, had been started in 1980, then 6% pa of that yield would have been due to inflation: the *real* return on our investment would have been 4% pa.

Now, I don't expect you to learn by heart all of the figures in table 10.2; all you need to remember is the page number for later reference.

What I *would* like you to do is to use the tables to work out a practical example.

The example concerns a 'with-profits' endowment policy, which will be featured in the next lesson. The figures are based on a non-smoking male aged 29 at the outset of the policy in 1970. The policy is a savings plan to which he contributes £20 per month for 25 years; it includes an element of life assurance (of around £6,000) to be paid in the event of his death before the policy matures. In fact, we assume that he survives the full term of the policy, at the end of which he receives a lump-sum.

The amount which he receives will depend on which insurance company he had chosen in the first place.

Fortunately, he chose one of the best policies and received a payout of around £42,000.

## Question 4 is in two parts:

(a) What was the average return on his savings over the 25 years?
(b) What was the *real* return, after correcting for the effects of inflation?

# Chapter 11
# Lesson VI: Medium-Risk Investments – Hybrid Products

Let's start straight away by considering the contentious question of charges.

The sales literature, for products which we shall discuss in this lesson, has to include the approximate effect of management charges on the potential returns from the investments. In the homework example, we considered a product (which might, for instance, be offered by an insurance company) for which the charges reduce the return to the investor by either 2% pa or 2½% pa. Take, first, the lower average level of charges, and let us see how our standard formula will need to be modified.

*As seen by the insurance company*

|  | | |
|---|---|---|
| Gross Income, *less* Tax, *plus/minus* Capital Gain/Loss | | |
| = Total Net Return | 10.0% | |
| *minus* Inflation, say | −4.0% | |
| **= Total Net Real Return** | **6.0%** | |

*As seen by the investor*

|  | |
|---|---|
| *minus* Charges | −2.0% |
| **= Total Net Real Return** | **4.0% pa** |

Incidentally, you will see that the total net real return to the insurance company, in this example, is rather good by the standards of our Medium-Risk investment benchmark. You will also see that the charges take *one-third* of the real return on this hypothetical investment: they reduce the real return from 6% pa to 4% pa. Although this is a hypothetical example, the figures are actually quite realistic.

If charges cause a loss of potential income of 2½% pa

then, out of a real return to the insurance company of 6% pa, this would mean that *over 40%* of the real return from the investment would be swallowed up in charges!

You might like to see for yourself what would happen if the company achieves only an 8% net return on its investments.

The figure of 2% pa, for the effect of charges on our returns, is deceptively small. We have seen that it can represent a huge slice of our real potential return.

Naturally, the insurance company *has* to make charges. Also, even if we ourselves invested directly in the same mixture of, say, gilts and equities, then *we* would still incur some charges. Over the lifetime of our investment, those charges might well reduce the total return to us by perhaps ½% to 1% pa.

Perhaps the insurance company can compensate for its charges by producing an annual return higher than we might achieve on our own? This, unfortunately, is very unlikely: we shall see, when we look at collective funds, that the track records of professionals is, in general, very uninspiring.

Perhaps, rather, the company can offer additional benefits which we could not provide for ourselves? In this case, I am happy to say that the answer is often Yes; we shall look in a minute at cases in which it *is* worthwhile paying the management charges.

Where there are no such benefits, what would be a reasonable level of charges to make it worthwhile considering entrusting our money to the professionals? What was your answer to homework Question 2?

The answer to this question must be a very personal one, although I very much doubt whether your answer was as high as the 30 to 40% of the real return which we saw in the numerical examples. I would guess that, more likely, you came up with a figure of around 10 to 15%. This would mean, for the underlying investment performance of our example, a maximum of about 1% pa for the effect of charges on the rate of return from the investment.

In real life the insurance company's charges (as a percentage of your potential real return) will depend on its investment performance and on the future level of inflation.

In general, I suggest that you work on the following simple guideline:

---

*Thorneycroft's Fourth Law of Successful Investment*

**Unless there are specific, quantifiable advantages, don't pay charges of more than 1% pa on managed investment funds, averaged over the life of the investment.**

---

We haven't yet finished with the matter of charges; there is more to come!

So far, we have looked at the obvious (and declared) charges which pay for the management and administration of the investment product. The process of 'management' involves, amongst other things, the *switching* of investments within the fund. Some degree of switching is unavoidable: from time to time, there *will* be external events or new company information which dictate that a change of investments is appropriate.

Don't forget that, every time the managers change an investment, this is going to cost *you* some money! For instance, there are likely to be stockbrokers' fees and stamp duty to pay, as well as a loss from the spread between the buying and selling price of a particular stock or share.

When the list of sales and purchases is published by the managers (as, for instance, with unit trusts and pension funds), it seems that a typical fund switches at least *half* of its investments *each year*. This is, to me, a staggeringly high figure: at this level, sensible switching becomes better described as 'churning' of the portfolios.

This churning is often euphemistically described by the fund managers as 'active management' . . . as if this was a good thing. I know of no evidence (although I am happy to be persuaded otherwise) that 'actively managed' funds perform any better than those with a low switching rate. Unless and until firm evidence is provided to the contrary, I suggest that you avoid such funds.

*Thorneycroft's Fifth Law of Successful Investment*

**Avoid investment products which are
advertised as being 'actively managed'.**

It must be great fun for the managers to do all this buying
and selling; but I don't think *we* should be contributing to
the lifestyle to which such managers and their stockbrokers
aspire. It has been estimated that active management can
typically reduce investment returns by anything between
$\frac{1}{2}$% and 2% pa.

A famous American economist characterised public servants as 'doing good with other people's money'. An additional problem for the private investor is that of fund
managers having fun with other people's money!

So, how can fund managers and advisers earn their keep
*and* keep us happy at the same time?

Well, there *are* ways, as I hinted earlier, by which the
manager can provide 'added value' to his product. We shall
look at these now.

There is one apparent added value factor which is usually
not worth considering: this is the incorporation into the
product of an element of life assurance. It is almost always
better to separate your life assurance needs from your
investment needs. For a good discussion of this, you could
refer to the Consumers' Association publication *Which?*.
Their 'best buys' for life assurance are policies which are
quite separate from any form of investment (see, for
instance, *Which?*, September 1994, p20). The simplest and
most straightforward (and also reasonably priced) life assurance policies are those which are known as 'term assurance'
policies.

Where you really *can* recoup all and more of the
management charges is where there are substantial tax
advantages. The most important example is that of pension
funds; these are extremely important and we shall take a
look at them towards the end of this lesson.

The other added value feature, which may make the charges worth bearing, occurs when the investment product is so structured that it significantly reduces the risk level, for a certain level of reward. There are two ways in which this can occur:

(a) when the ups-and-downs in the value of the investment fund are smoothed out for you, by a method in which annual bonuses are added to your capital
(b) when the investment provides an opportunity to make relatively small, regular savings contributions over a long period of time

Up to this point in the course, the investment products which have been described have been most suitable for lump-sums, rather than for regular (monthly) savings schemes.

From now on, we shall place very great emphasis on regular savings schemes.

Suppose that we invest a fixed sum each month, every month for ten years. Each individual monthly 'premium' or contribution buys units in some Medium-Risk fund. Sometimes, the final outcome of that month's investment will be better than expected, sometimes worse. Now, by averaging out the individual risks of the separate monthly payments, we *very substantially* reduce the average level of risk.

This is far more important, as a means of reducing risk, than spreading an investment across a large number of ordinary shares.

This is an extremely important point for you to recognise.

---

*Thorneycroft's Sixth Law of Successful Investment*

**Regular savings schemes reduce the level of risk substantially, without much – if any – reduction in the real rate of return on your capital.**

---

In fact, we shall see later that you can actually *increase* your average returns by investing on a regular basis.

We have reached a very important watershed in the course. When we come to put together a complete investment plan, we shall sub-divide it into two separate sections:

(a) *Lump-sums* invested in products chosen from those described in Lessons II to V.

(b) *Regular savings* invested in products chosen from those described in Lessons VI to X.

Regular savings can be made either monthly or annually; and they can be for any length of time. So, it is not possible to be precise about their effect on risk reduction. However, as a general guide, I would suggest that for regular savings plans of at least five years' duration, made by monthly instalments:

(1) A Medium-Risk investment, when made by regular savings, becomes a Low-Risk investment.
(2) A High-Risk investment, when made by regular savings, becomes a Medium-Risk investment.
(3) A Very-High-Risk investment, when made by regular savings, becomes a High-Risk investment.

We can visualise the effects by looking once again at our Risk v Reward graph:

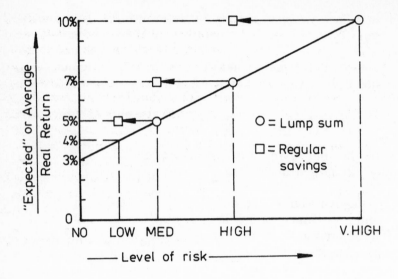

*Fig 11.1* Effect of regular savings on risk levels

Investments which started out at our benchmark rates-of-return for their risk levels are now, as a result of regular savings, well into positive territory (above the line), which we regard as the area of 'good' investments.

Even if a specific investment starts off (as a lump-sum) *below* the line (perhaps because of high charges), it can still end up as a good investment if we build up a stake in it over several years by regular contributions. This might apply, for instance, to regular savings into an endowment policy.

We shall look, now, at the individual 'hybrid' managed investment products which may offer us some or all of the possible advantages which we have identified.

## With-profits endowment policies

With these plans, you pay a fixed monthly premium for a period ranging from (usually) ten to twenty-five years. At the end of that time (or on your death if you do not survive the term of the policy), the company pays out a tax-free lump-sum representing the accumulated value of your investment.

Endowment policies are really the archetypal regular savings products. At one time, they had certain tax advantages, which have now disappeared. Even so, very many people still take out 'endowment mortgages' with the specific intention of accumulating a lump-sum with which to pay off a mortgage after, say, 25 years. There is no need, in fact, to link such a policy to house purchase.

 They have certain *dis*-advantages:

(a) fairly high charges (although this becomes less of a problem over a 25-year term of savings)
(b) *extremely* high charges if the investment is cashed-in early on
(c) about 10% of the monthly premiums is siphoned off to provide life assurance

They have, to some extent, been superseded as popular regular savings vehicles by other products, such as unit trusts and personal equity plans. They do, however, have one advantage not shared by those alternatives: they reduce risk still further by the way in which the increase in the value of the fund is smoothed out during the lifetime of the savings plan.

An endowment policy provides you with a stake in a 'hybrid' fund, comprising investments in fixed-interest bonds, ordinary shares and property. The actual value of this fund will go up or down daily, depending on the vagaries of the various markets for gilts, shares and property. However, the investor is shielded from these short-term variations.

Instead, each year the insurance company declares a bonus, based on its recent investment performance – not just for the year in question. These bonuses are added to the value of the policy and cannot subsequently be taken away; hence the title 'with-profits'. When the policy eventually matures, a further 'terminal bonus' is added, which reflects the investment performance of the fund over the whole life of the policy.

These policies are most appropriately (but not necessarily) used as a means of building up a capital sum to repay a mortgage after, say, 25 years. This is because:

(a) a long time-period is necessary in order to reduce the effects of very high initial charges down to something reasonable

(b) the life assurance feature (for which you are paying in your monthly premiums) is actually relevant to anyone committed to expensive house purchase

Do remember, though, that you should not start such a policy unless you are confident that you can keep up the payments for the full term. Make sure that, if and when you move house, the building society will let you continue to use the same endowment policy to repay the new mortgage.

*So long as you keep the policy going for the full term*, then you should be well rewarded when the policy matures, with a substantial cash sum several times that which you need to pay off the mortgage*; and you will have had no sleepless nights worrying about how your investment is performing.

How do we choose an insurance company from the large number which offer with-profits endowment policies? This is one of the few cases when it *is* best to look at the track records of each company, going back over the *previous* 25 years; the figures can be found in magazines such as *Money Management*.

When we look at collective funds, investing in ordinary shares on your behalf, we shall see that historical track records are really very little use as a guide to future performance. In the case of endowment policies, on the other hand, there *are* some insurance companies which seem to be consistently in the top ten for performance.

I suspect that this has as much to do with consistent differences in their levels of charges as with any consistent differences in investment performance.

That being the case, there is a very good chance that

---

* This will not be the case with 'low-cost endowment mortgages'; indeed, the value of such a policy on maturity may fall short of the amount needed to repay the mortgage. This kind of policy is not relevant to us.

historical performance *will* have a bearing on future investment returns; so choose one of the companies whose
endowment policies consistently appear high up in the
performance tables.

We can illustrate the possible returns from a with-profits
endowment policy by reference to the homework question.
You will remember that an investment of £20 per month for
25 years yielded a final payout of £42,000.

In this example, the annual contribution was £240. Our
homework table 10.2 (on page 139) gives results based on an
annual investment of £100, rather than £240; so we shall
need to divide the final payout figure of £42,000 by 2.4. This
tells us that, per £100 of annual payments, the payout
would have been £17,500.

We now turn to table 10.2 and look down the column
headed '25 years'. We see that the figure of £17,500 comes
between the final capital sums for returns of 12% pa and
14% pa; in fact, the investment has yielded an average total
return over the 25 years of 13% pa.

This sounds excellent, but what about inflation? From
table 10.3 (on page 140), we see that inflation accounted for
9% pa of that return. So the real return is more like 4% pa.

This is still a very realistic return from an investment
which has become a Low-Risk one on account of the regular
savings feature; and it does have life assurance thrown in.
Excluding the cost of that life assurance, the pure 'investment' money yielded a real return of about 4½% pa.

Many endowment policies would have produced a significantly lower return over the same period. It is important,
therefore, to make sure that you choose one with a good
track record, as noted above.

We should note that the 25 years to 1995 included several
which were quite traumatic for the investor (as well as some
very good ones): there was a major stock-market decline in
1972–4 and again in 1987; and the 1970s were the years of
OPEC oil crises. It would be quite realistic to imagine the
top with-profits policies in the future averaging a real return
of around 4½% pa over a long period.

If you would like to read more about with-profits endowment policies, there is a quite excellent chapter in the book

*Which? Way to Save and Invest*, published by the Consumers' Association.

## Non-profit endowment policies

You will have noticed that we have been talking specifically about 'with-profits' endowment policies; that suggests that there are other variations called 'without-profits' or 'non-profit'. Indeed, this is the case. They provide a fixed sum on maturity (or earlier death) and do not have the bonuses added each year. They are not relevant to us, any more than are 'low-cost endowment mortgages'.

## Single-premium insurance bonds

Most insurance companies now offer managed investments in the form of lump-sum bonds. Many of these fall into our Medium-Risk 'hybrid' category, being made up of investments in gilts, equities, corporate bonds and perhaps property. They are the lump-sum equivalents of endowment policies.

They are widely advocated by the financial services industry, which immediately draws attention to the level of charges. There is generally a 5% initial charge, followed by an annual charge of around 1% pa of the value of the fund.

Another disadvantage, for us, is that the bonds are – by definition – designed for lump-sum investments and not regular savings.

They used to have an advantage to higher rate taxpayers. You could take a tax-free income of up to 5% pa for 20 years; but impending changes to the tax laws look set to reduce this tax benefit. They should still be tax-free in the hands of standard-rate tax payers. Retaining a bond for 20 years will reduce the average annual charge to something reasonable, but the annual income may not be worth much in real terms after that length of time.

The investment is not really tax-free, of course, as the

insurance company will have paid both income tax and capital gains tax at a 23% rate.


## Friendly society bonds

Everyone is entitled to invest a rather small sum each year into a friendly society savings plan, with considerable tax advantages (but high charges). It is rather like a small-scale endowment policy, but with additional tax benefits.

As with endowment policies, there is no tax to pay if the bonds are held until maturity (ten years). The additional benefit is that the friendly society itself pays no tax on its investment fund, neither income nor capital gains tax.

The limit to your annual investment is currently £270, normally paid by regular monthly instalments for ten years. You can imagine that it is quite expensive for the friendly societies to administer these rather small policies; consequently, the charges are very high. Averaged over the ten years of the policy, the charges would typically reduce the potential return to the investor by 3% pa or even more. This is a very long way above our criterion, so are they really worth considering?

Before answering that, it is necessary to consider the options open to you at the end of the ten years. You can, of course, simply take the tax-free lump-sum. Alternatively, you can continue to pay contributions for a further ten years. Thirdly, you can stop making contributions but allow the investment to roll up tax-free for a further period of time. If you retain your money in the fund in this way, the subsequent annual charges are quite modest.

These savings plans are, I suggest, quite useful if you start young and let them roll up for a few *decades* (well, I did say that our aim is to get rich slowly!).

When you are young, the low monthly premiums may be all that you can afford. Well before the end of ten years, you should be in a position to consider something more substantial. On maturity of the policy, at the end of ten years, just leave the money in the fund to grow tax-free for a further 10, 20, 30 or even more years: you will find that you have a very useful lump-sum when you do eventually cash in the policy.

Something else which you should, ideally, start to think about whilst still young is your retirement pension.

## Pension plans

These are the most important of all 'hybrid' products; indeed, a pension plan may prove to be just about the best investment you ever make. You may well belong to an employee pension plan already. Nevertheless, you can still make additional voluntary contributions (AVCs) up to a certain proportion of your income.

If you are self-employed – or if you have additional earnings not covered by your company scheme – then you will need to consider a personal pension plan. You may even be retired and drawing a company pension but still doing some part-time work. It is still well worthwhile putting some of these earnings into a personal pension plan, to produce an additional pension income from, perhaps, age 70.

The great advantage of saving via pension plans is their *very* favourable tax treatment. There are three specific tax 'breaks'.

First, you are not taxed on the contributions which you make to your pension fund. If you are a standard-rate taxpayer, your spendable income will be reduced by only £770 for each £1,000 which goes into your pension plan. (If, instead, you had taken the same £1,000 of gross salary to spend or to invest elsewhere, then you will have first paid £230 in income tax.)

This particular tax benefit is even more valuable to higher-rate taxpayers. If you are liable for tax at 40%, then the options for a tranche of £1,000 of gross salary would be either:

(a) use the after-tax sum of £600 to spend or to invest elsewhere; *or*

(b) invest the whole £1,000, tax-free, into a pension plan

The second tax advantage is that (like friendly society investments) the fund into which you have invested pays neither income tax nor capital gains tax.

Finally, when you come to draw your pension, you can take part of the accumulated capital as a tax-free lump-sum. (The remainder of the capital from a personal pension would then be used to fund an annuity, which will pay you a *taxable* income for the rest of your life.)

You will see that the tax advantages are likely to far outweigh the management charges which you will pay.

The limits to the proportion of your income which you can allocate to a pension plan are quite generous.

For an employee in a company scheme, the limit is 15% of your pensionable earnings. You perhaps already pay 5% of your salary into your company pension scheme, so there is plenty of leeway for additional contributions. There is, however, a limit to the company pension which you will ultimately be allowed to draw, namely two-thirds of your final pay after a minimum of 20 years' service with the company; there is also an upper limit to the amount of your pension, namely £56,000 pa (1997/8 figures).

Even if you expect to receive the full company pension of two-thirds of your final salary, there is still scope to earn *some* additional retirement income: the Inland Revenue includes, in 'net relevant earnings', some items which the company does not, namely the value of fringe benefits such as a company car. Your company pensions adviser will be happy to take you through the possibilities.

For personal pension plans (for instance, for the self-employed), the contribution limits are:

| | |
|---|---|
| Up to age 35 | 17.5% |
| 36–45 | 20% |
| 46–50 | 25% |
| 51–55 | 30% |
| 56–60 | 35% |
| 61–64 | 40% |
| 75 and over | Nil |

These limits apply up to an earnings limit of £84,000 pa (1997/8).

The benefits which you receive on retirement, in this case, depend on the accumulated value of the fund which you have built up, rather than on the number of years that you have worked. You can take 25% of the accumulated fund as a tax-free lump-sum; the remainder of the fund (however large it has grown to be) has to be used to set up an annuity, the income from which is all taxable.

So, what kind of funds can we invest in?

Traditionally, pension funds were of the 'hybrid' type, similar to with-profits endowment policies (but with the additional tax advantages). There is now a much wider choice: funds based on unit trusts, for instance, are now commonplace; also, 'unitised' funds created by insurance companies, which act in the same way as unit trusts.

Which type to choose?

The newer schemes may well produce a rather higher return on your investment: they fall mainly into our High-Risk category (which becomes equivalent to Medium-Risk when the payments are made by regular monthly or annual instalments). Meanwhile, as we have seen, the traditional 'with-profits' policies are Medium-Risk investments which become Low-Risk as regular savings plans.

Ultimately, you will have to make your own decision, but I should like to offer the following suggestions.

Our whole strategy is based on getting rich slowly. It would seem inappropriate to commit your post-retirement income to a fund whose final value could be greatly affected by the state of the stock-market at the time you retire. In practice, with unitised plans, you can usually switch between funds, for instance out of an equity-based fund into a cash fund. Such a switch, as you approach retirement, could be used to 'lock in' your gains so far, and hence help avoid the worry of a possible stock-market crash. However, I suspect that you would be equally upset if, having switched into a cash fund for the last few years, you find that you have missed out on a further substantial rise in the equity-based units.

Taken in isolation, the unit-linked policies may well prove to give better returns in the long term (commensurate with their higher risk levels). But, in practice, no investment can be taken in isolation from the rest of your portfolio. If, as

I suggest, you opt for the lower risk route of a with-profits endowment-type pension plan, then you are going to be much more free to direct *additional* savings into the higher-risk, higher-return investments.

If, on the other hand, your pension plan is one which does carry some additional risk, then you may be (or, I must say, you *should* be) more reluctant to invest additional savings into some of the very good high-risk, high-reward opportunities which we are going to introduce in the next few lessons.

The 'with-profits' type of pension plan has become a little unfashionable in recent years, compared to more 'sexy' (and higher risk) alternatives. I suggest that this is another very good reason for sticking to the traditional 'with-profits' policies!

Finally, how do you go about setting up a personal pension plan?

Normally, I am reluctant to suggest using the services of professional financial advisers, for the simple reason that they are usually dealing with products which carry high charges.

However, if you are going to start a personal pension plan, you *know* that you are prepared to incur some charges because of the tax benefits and because of the peace of mind offered by with-profits policies. An adviser will also be able to help you work out things like the level of your 'net relevant earnings' and all the other technicalities involved in setting up a pension plan.

So, when it comes to personal pension plans, we should be happy to contribute to the lifestyle to which our financial adviser would like to remain accustomed! At this point, you may wish to refer again to the comments on financial advisers in the Introduction, especially the notes on fee-based advisers on pages 8–9.

Your chosen adviser should suggest an insurance company whose performance has been excellent for very many years (because, for instance, although its charges may seem high, they are not as high as the competitors).

It would be useful to arm yourself, beforehand, with the latest performance tables on with-profits pension plans (to be found, for instance, in *Money Management*). As part of your background reading, I would again suggest the book *Which? Way to Save and Invest*; this contains a chapter devoted specifically to personal pension plans.

If you belong to a company pension scheme, you are quite probably also fortunate in another way: in the ability to invest in something which is really a Low-Risk product, which it has not been appropriate to mention earlier, namely . . .

## Save-as-you-earn share option schemes

With these, you save a fixed monthly sum for a minimum of three years; the money is usually invested on your behalf in a building society account. At the end of three years (with an option to allow the money to roll up in the account for up to seven years), you can either take the lump-sum in cash or use the money to acquire shares in your company at a discount of 20% on *the market price at the time you started the plan.*

If such a scheme is available to you, it is generally well worth considering. It is *certainly* worth considering if your company fulfils most of the criteria, which we shall look at later, for choosing a share for long-term sustainable growth.

The risk you take is not that the share price of your company might languish or fall (because you have the fall-back of being able to take the accumulated value of the fund in cash); it is that you might be missing out on an opportunity to invest those monthly savings into something better.

One of the 'something better' opportunities, for instance, might be that of making additional pension contributions.

Now that we have, I hope, arranged for a comfortable retirement, we can turn our attention to the next level of risk, namely the High-Risk world of ordinary shares.

## Homework VI

You should now have your mind clearly focused on the benefits of regular savings schemes.

What I would like you to do, for your homework, is to compare two different approaches to regular savings. To make the example a simple but tangible one, we can think of it as an annual purchase of units in a unit trust. For even greater simplicity, we shall ignore the difference between the buying and selling prices of units.

Consider the following alternatives:

(a) We buy 1,000 units each year
(b) We invest £1,000 each year

In the first case, the number of units which we buy is fixed, but the amount we invest each year will be higher or lower depending on the unit price. Meanwhile, in the second case, what will vary each year is the number of units we acquire; the amount of money we invest remains constant.

We are going to look at two different patterns of price movements in the units: these are illustrated in figure 11.2. By the time we make the fifth instalment, the unit price is back to where it was when we started the plan; but in the meantime the price has first risen, then fallen, and finally recovered to its starting value of 100p, at which it stays for a further year after we have made our fifth and final contribution.

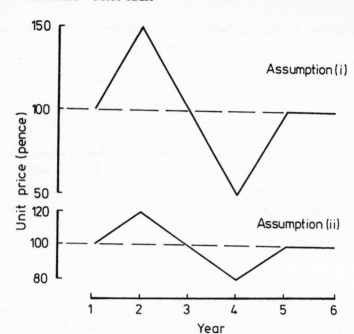

*Fig 11.2* Price movements of a unit trust assumed for examples of regular savings plans

Had we just acquired 5,000 units for £5,000 on day one, then we would of course end up with the same 5,000 units and our initial £5,000 would remain intact.

I should like you to calculate the value of your holding of units in the four cases of regular savings shown in table 11.1. Fill in the blanks.

**Table 11.1   Blank table for homework exercise on unit trust savings plans**

|  | Volatility of units | |
|---|---|---|
|  | **Assumption (i)**<br>**Price ± 50p** | **Assumption (ii)**<br>**Price ± 20p** |
| **(a) Fixed no of** | No of units 5,000 | No of units 5,000 |
| **units – 1,000** | Cost        - - - - | Cost        - - - - |
| **per annum** | Ave cost | Ave cost |
|  |   per unit  - - - - |   per unit  - - - - |
| **(b) Fixed annual** | No of units - - - - | No of units - - - - |
| **outlay of** | Cost       £5,000 | Cost       £5,000 |
| **£1,000** | Ave cost | Ave cost |
|  |   per unit  - - - - |   per unit  - - - - |

In the case of a single lump-sum investment, the corresponding figures are, of course:

No of units             =   5,000
Cost                        = £5,000
Average cost per unit   =   100p

When you have worked out all the numerical answers, consider the following questions:

# Question 1

Which is the better way of regular saving: a fixed regular payment or a fixed regular number of units?

## Question 2

What do the calculations tell you about 'volatility' in respect of regular savings schemes? (What I mean by volatility is probably obvious from the examples; if not, refer again to the definition on page 23.)

## Question 3

Compare the best of these regular savings plans with the alternative of a single lump-sum investment: what *additional* benefits do you think the regular savings plans offer over a lump-sum investment?

## Question 4

Under what circumstances do you think that a lump-sum investment would be preferable to a regular savings plan?

# Chapter 12
# Lesson VII: High-Risk Investments –
# Introduction to Ordinary Shares

It's probably helpful, at the outset, to set out a brief agenda of the subject matter of this lesson.

1. The factors which put shares into the High-Risk category
   1.1 Company characteristics
   1.2 Stock-market characteristics

2. Reducing the level of risk – general principles
   2.1 Spreading the risk across several shares
   2.2 Regular savings schemes – quantifying the benefits

3. Reducing the level of risk – choice of specific investment plans
   3.1 Collective funds: unit trusts and investment trusts
   3.2 Personal equity plans

As well as reducing the level of risk, the other side of the coin is to increase the likely returns from our investments. This will be the subject of Lesson VIII (collective funds) and Lesson IX (direct investment in ordinary shares).

## Company characteristics

We are going to start by taking a brief look at the way in which company accounts are presented. Don't worry! We shall not spend too much time on this subject for a very good reason: some of the most important factors which influence the future performance of a company are not to be found in its accounts. We shall see what these other factors are in Lesson IX.

If you are interested in a particular company, you can often obtain a copy of its latest annual Report and Accounts through the *Financial Times*. Turn to the 'London Share Service' pages in which the latest share prices are listed. Right at the end you will see a footnote headed '*FT* Free Annual Reports Service'. The club symbol, ♣, indicates that the annual report is available for those companies whose entry in the share service pages carries that symbol.

There are two basic tables to refer to in the Report and Accounts of a Company; these are: (a) the consolidated (or group) balance sheet; and (b) the consolidated (or group) profit-and-loss account.

The balance sheet tells us about the capital structure of the company: what its assets are and how these assets are financed by different forms of capital.

Table 12.1 presents the balance sheet of a mythical company. Let's take a brief look at the figures.

The company has tangible assets of £20 million, which means that this is the value of its plant, machinery, building and so on. It also has investments of £2 million in other companies.

Its 'current assets' are required for the day-to-day running of the business: mainly its stocks of finished goods and work-in-progress, and its debtors (£20 million is due from customers for goods which have been sold to them).

## Table 12.1   Simplified example of a balance sheet

### CONSOLIDATED BALANCE SHEET

**£000**

**Fixed Assets**

| | | |
|---|---|---|
| Tangible assets | 20,000 | |
| Investments | 2,000 | |
| | | 22,000 |

**Current Assets**

| | | |
|---|---|---|
| Stocks | 5,000 | |
| Debtors | 20,000 | |
| Cash | 500 | |
| Creditors (falling due within one year) | (22,500) | |
| **Net Current Assets** | | 3,000 |
| **Total assets less current liabilities** | | 25,000 |
| **Creditors (falling due after more than one year)** | | (5,000) |
| **Capital and Reserves** | | 20,000 |

**Table 12.2 Simplified example of a profit-and-loss account**

---

## CONSOLIDATED PROFIT-AND-LOSS ACCOUNT

|                            | £000      |
| -------------------------- | --------- |
| Turnover                   | 60,000    |
| Operating Costs            | (54,500)  |
|                            |           |
| Operating Profit           | 5,500     |
| Net interest               | (   500)  |
|                            |           |
| Profit before taxation     | 5,000     |
| Taxation                   | (1,650)   |
|                            |           |
| Profit for the year        | 3,350     |
| Dividend                   | (1,500)   |
|                            |           |
| Retained profit for the year | 1,850   |
|                            |           |
| Earnings per share* (eps)  | 6.7p      |
| Dividends per share* (dps) | 3.0p      |

(*No of shares in issue: 50,000,000)

---

The company, itself, has trade creditors: other companies which have supplied raw materials and other goods and services which our company has bought but not yet paid for. There will also be short-term loans and overdraft facilities falling due within one year; and money which will be going out of the business to pay tax and dividends. All of these come under the 'creditors' heading, otherwise known as 'current liabilities'. Note that liabilities are conventionally written in brackets to indicate that they are negative factors in the accounts. A footnote to the accounts will tell us how much of the creditors figure is due to short-term bank and other loans; in our case, we shall assume this to be £1.5 million.

The total value of the assets of our company, less these current liabilities, amounts to £25 million. How are these assets financed?

Longer-term finance needed to run the business includes £5 million of creditors falling due after more than one year. This will comprise loans and debenture stocks with maturity dates more than one year hence – the kind of corporate bonds which we learned about in Lesson V.

The residual figure of £20 million is shown as 'capital and reserves', otherwise known as 'shareholders' funds'. This is the *book* value of the stake which the shareholders have in the company. The book value is not necessarily the same as the value which the *stock-market* places on that stake. A real-life balance sheet will sub-divide these shareholders' funds into components such as 'called up share capital', 'share premium account', 'profit-and-loss account' and 'other reserves'. We need not concern ourselves with that sub-division.

Two things which *are* of interest to us are as follows.

Dividing the shareholders' funds by the number of shares in issue will give us the net assets per ordinary share. This figure is often given at the back of the Report and Accounts as part of a five-year record of financial performance. The net asset value per share, as shown in the books, may be more or less than the value put on the shares by the stock-market: it depends how well the market feels that these assets are being used to generate current and future profits.

A figure of considerable interest is the 'gearing ratio', a

term which was defined on page 20. It is the ratio of debt to
equity. The equity is simply another name for the shareholders' funds; the debt figure is a little more difficult to work
out, because it comprises long-term loans ('creditors falling
due after more than one year') plus short-term bank loans
(which are hidden in the creditors total), less cash.

For our mythical company, net debt comprises:

| | |
|---|---|
| Long-term loans | £5   million |
| Short-term bank loans | £1.5 million |
| *less* cash | (£0.5 million) |
| | |
| | £6   million |

So our gearing, or debt/equity ratio, is £6m/£20m which
works out to be 30%.

It is gearing which is one of the factors contributing to the
level of risk. Before the company earns any profits for *you*,
the shareholders, it has to pay the interest on its debt. The
higher the level of gearing, the more sensitive will be the
shareholders' profits to any change in the general profitability of the business.

A gearing level of 30% is not particularly high. Above
100% (in other words, debt exceeding shareholders' funds),
the profits earned for the shareholders will be *very* sensitive
to changes in the business environment.

We look at this sensitivity from another angle now, as we
look at the profit-and-loss account for our mythical company, as shown in table 12.2.

Our company had a turnover (or sales revenue) of £60
million. It cost £54.5 million to pay for raw materials,
chemicals, fuel, labour, depreciation and all of the other
tangible things needed to run a business. There is also the
financial cost of interest payments on debts; this is shown as
a separate line in the accounts.

Deducting all these costs from the turnover gives us the
gross profit before taxation; and the next two lines in the
table show the effects of the tax deducted, to give us the

after-tax profit or 'earnings'. (Tax is assumed to be levied at 33%.)

Part of these earnings are paid out in the form of dividends; the remainder is retained in the business to help finance future growth. The ratio of the earnings to the amount paid out as dividends is called the dividend 'cover'.

We referred earlier to the net assets per ordinary share. From the balance sheet we see that the total of shareholders' funds is £20 million; with 50 million shares in issue, the net asset value per share is 40p. Now, our company has earned 6.7p for each ordinary share – a return of 16.75% pa on the shareholders' assets. It will come as no surprise to you to find that the shares of such a company would be valued, by the stock-market, at substantially *above* the book value of 40p.

This is a convenient time to introduce a measure called the price/earnings ratio, or P/E ratio for short. This is the ratio between the price of the company's shares and its earnings per share. Typically, shares in a company such as our mythical one might well sell at a P/E ratio of about 15. So, with earnings of 6.7p per share, the share price might be around 15 x 6.7p, or about 100p per share.

Let us now see how the factors in the profit-and-loss account contribute to risk. We will see what happens if a period of higher inflation in the costs of running the business coincides (as it often does in real life) with a downturn in sales. Suppose that sales decline by 5% and that our costs *per unit* increase by a little over 5% (such that the total cost remains the same). These are by no means unrealistic figures.

## Table 12.3   A 'before-and-after' analysis of the effect on profits of a down-turn in business

|  | £000 | |
|---|---|---|
|  | Base scenario | After down-turn in business |
| Turnover | 60,000 | 57,000 |
| Operating costs | (54,500) | (54,500) |
| Operating profit | 5,500 | 2,500 |
| Net interest | ( 500) | ( 500) |
| Profit before taxation | 5,000 | 2,000 |
| Taxation | (1,650) | ( 660) |
| Profit for the year | 3,350 | 1,340 |

Table 12.3 provides a 'before-and-after' analysis of the effect on our profits, which is quite dramatic: a relatively small decline in sales (together with a small increase in unit costs) has knocked 60% off our profits.

You can also judge the even more dramatic effect which would have occurred had our gearing been very high. Suppose that net interest had been £1.5 million instead of £0.5 million (corresponding to a gearing of nearly 100%). You should be able to calculate that the profit for the year would have been reduced from £2.68 million to £0.67 million – a reduction of 75%. See if you can work out the figures for yourself.

Conversely, of course, an *increase* in turnover or a *decrease* in unit costs (or both) will produce a pronounced *increase* in profits.

To recap, we have seen that company profits are High-Risk for at least two reasons:

(a) Profit, being a small difference between two large numbers (turnover and costs), is very sensitive to changes in the environment in which the company operates (such as the general economic climate and the entry of new competitors)

(b) Gearing

These factors are compounded, for the investor, by the vagaries of the stock-market.

## Stock-market characteristics

The stock-market effects are, perhaps, most vividly illustrated by means of two graphs. The first (figure 12.1) shows a fifteen-year history of the value of a particular stock-market index. In Lesson V, I introduced you to the FT-SE 100 index; this measures the changes in value of a 'basket' of 100 shares, corresponding roughly to the largest 100 quoted on the UK stock-market. Figure 12.1 is actually based on something called the 'All-Share Index'; as its name implies, this covers a much wider range of shares.

The general long-term trend is upwards, but there have been many downs along the way. The crash of October 1987 was a particularly sharp correction to the upwards trend.

The other graph – figure 12.2 – illustrates changes in the price/earnings ratio which was defined earlier. If stock-market operators believe that company earnings will increase in the future, they will be prepared to buy shares at a high current P/E ratio; conversely, if the market becomes concerned about future earnings, then shares will be sold until they have fallen to a much lower P/E ratio.

To make matters worse, stock-market operators do not just take a view on future corporate earnings. Many people will be buying (or selling) shares for no better reason than thinking *other* people will be buyers (or sellers) in the future, thus driving prices up (or down as the case may be). You have probably come across the words 'bulls' and 'bears': a bull is someone who buys shares on the expectation that they will go up in price; a bear is one who sells shares in the expectation that prices will go down.

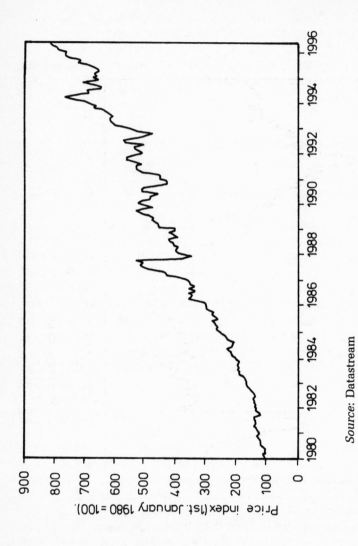

*Source:* Datastream

*Fig 12.1* Fifteen-year history of share price changes

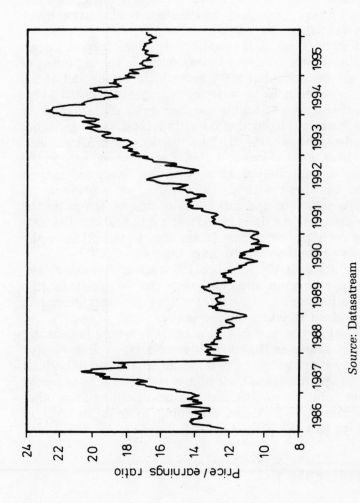

*Source:* Datastream

*Fig 12.2* Ten-year history of price/earnings ratio

The sensitivity of stock-market prices to these bulls and bears is further increased by the fact that they (just like companies) can have very high levels of gearing: they can 'bet' on future movements of the stock-market using many times their own risk capital.

All of this leads to volatility in stock-market prices. Consider a large company whose shares at the beginning of the year are quoted at 500p and which, by the end of the year, have risen by a perfectly reasonable 10% to 550p. Now, if you were to follow the share price of this company every week, it is likely that it would typically change, either way, by perhaps 20p in the week – sometimes less, sometimes more. If you add up the price movements on the 'up' weeks separately from those on the 'down' weeks, you would find that the 10% rise over the year is made up of, perhaps, 110% of ups and 100% of downs. If you do the same exercise on a daily basis, you might find that the total of the daily price movements amounts to *several times* the average price of the shares over the year.

In other words, the actions of the stock-market exaggerate, by a huge amount, any changes in the fundamentals (the real performance of companies and the real economic environment in which they operate).

You will by now, I feel sure, be quite happy to consider ordinary shares as High-Risk investments.

So, what are we going to do about it? We certainly don't want to ignore shares: their higher risks carry the potential for much higher returns than we might obtain from other investments. Instead, we are going to look at ways of *reducing* that risk.

## Spreading the risk

Our first approach will be to reduce risk by investing in a *spread* of ordinary shares. Figure 12.3 illustrates what might happen if we split our investment equally between just *two* shares, A and B. One of the shares (Company A) does very well; the other (Company B) rather badly. Our portfolio of two shares has a performance record which averages out the two individual shares.

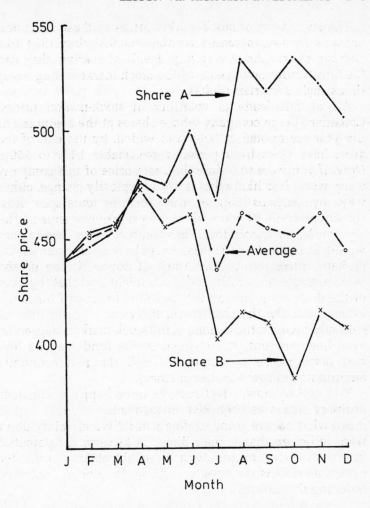

*Fig 12.3* 'Spreading the risk' with a simple portfolio of shares

In the next lesson, we shall be looking at 'collective funds' in which, typically, your money may be spread over 100 or more separate companies. Clearly, this *does* spread the risk to some extent, but I do feel that this aspect of collective funds is somewhat over-rated, for two reasons:

(a) Most of the shares in the portfolio are going to react in a very similar way to any economic shock which may lead to a stock-market crash; or even to mini-crashes and mini-booms, brought on by factors such as changes in the general level of interest rates. This point is illustrated by our simple portfolio of figure 12.3. In other words, volatility is not reduced by as much as one might hope or expect.

(b) As far as overall performance is concerned, over a period of several years we are almost guaranteeing a very *average* performance. By spreading our investment, we are (albeit unconsciously) forgoing the opportunity to focus on a few companies which might be expected to outperform the market. I'm sure that, rather than investing in our imaginary portfolio of two shares, you would have preferred to have put all of your money into Company A!

Later on I shall suggest that a spread of 20 companies is perfectly adequate for your portfolio.

## Regular savings schemes

The *real* value of collective funds is the opportunity which they offer to build up a long-term fund based on ordinary shares by means of *regular monthly savings*. The regular contributions can be quite small – as little as £25 per month.

This is where we take a look at the answers to your homework questions.

We shall look, first, at a regular savings scheme in which you acquire a fixed number of units each year for five years. The calculation is shown in table 12.4.

**Table 12.4   Regular savings plan, example (a): constant number of units acquired each year**

| Year | No of Units bought | (i) High volatility Unit price (p) | Cost (£) | (ii) Low volatility Unit price (p) | Cost (£) |
|------|------|------|------|------|------|
| 1 | 1,000 | 100 | 1,000 | 100 | 1,000 |
| 2 | 1,000 | 150 | 1,500 | 120 | 1,200 |
| 3 | 1,000 | 100 | 1,000 | 100 | 1,000 |
| 4 | 1,000 | 50 | 500 | 80 | 800 |
| 5 | 1,000 | 100 | 1,000 | 100 | 1,000 |
|   | 5,000 |   | 5,000 |   | 5,000 |

Nothing very exciting about these figures! We have reduced the level of risk by spreading the investment over time, but we have added the uncertainty of not knowing just what our financial commitment will be in future years.

**Table 12.5   Regular savings plan, example (b): constant amount of money invested each year**

| Year | Amount invested (£) | (i) High volatility Unit price (p) | No of units bought | (ii) Low volatility Unit price (p) | No of units bought |
|------|------|------|------|------|------|
| 1 | 1,000 | 100 | 1,000 | 100 | 1,000 |
| 2 | 1,000 | 150 | 667 | 120 | 830 |
| 3 | 1,000 | 100 | 1,000 | 100 | 1,000 |
| 4 | 1,000 | 50 | 2,000 | 80 | 1,250 |
| 5 | 1,000 | 100 | 1,000 | 100 | 1,000 |
|   | 5,000 |   | 5,667 |   | 5,080 |

Now see what happens with regular payment of *equal amounts of money* (table 12.5). Not only have we reduced the risk level considerably, we have also *increased the return*.

This illustrates the great advantage of this kind of regular savings plan: when the price of units is low, you benefit considerably from the fact that your money buys more units at that time; this more than outweighs the converse situation: namely, that you acquire fewer units in the periods when the price is high. This is called 'pound cost averaging', although you do not need to remember this term.

Note that the effects of this pound cost averaging are much more pronounced when the unit price is more volatile; in other words, when the unit price is subject to wilder swings of ups and downs. I hope that you correctly answered the homework Question 2!

We can use table 10.2 in the earlier homework (page 139) to quantify this effect. In fact, with the more volatile price history, the effect of pound cost averaging has been to provide us with an average 4% pa return on our investment, *even though* there was no overall increase in price over the life of the investment. In the case of the less volatile price performance, we have produced a much more modest return of $\frac{1}{2}$ % pa on our money by virtue of the averaging process.

These figures seem to be borne out in practice. When I looked at actual data for unit trusts, I found that the average annual return for regular savings schemes was generally *slightly* higher than for lump-sum investments; with the highly volatile Far Eastern Trusts, the effect was more pronounced – around 3% pa higher.

It is worth pausing for a moment to recap on where we have come so far, and to take in fully the benefits of regular savings. With such a scheme, we are happy when the unit or share price goes *up* – because the value of our accumulated investment has increased; we are also happy when the price of units or shares goes *down* – because then we acquire more units or shares for our money; and the 'price' we pay for all this peace of mind is an *increase* in the expected return on our investment. What more could we ask?

Actually, there *is* a little more to add. Homework Question 3 asked you to think of any such additional advantages.

Because you are not putting up the whole of the money in a lump-sum, it means that you have the use of that money (or, rather, of a gradually declining proportion of it) whilst you are operating the plan. You will be able to earn interest on that money whilst you are waiting to invest it; and the interest rate will be higher than the dividend which you have forgone by *not* acquiring all the units or shares at the outset.

In the case of investment trusts, there is yet another advantage of regular savings: many such trusts have extremely low charges for regular savings plans.

The full benefits of regular savings schemes are so important that I am going to firm up my sixth law by promulgating a new one:

---

*Thorneycroft's Seventh Law of Successful Investment*

**_All_ High-Risk investments should be made via regular savings schemes.**

---

The one possible advantage of lump-sum investments (homework Question 4) is that, *if* you get the timing right, then all of the money will be yielding capital appreciation from the word 'go'. To achieve this, however, would mean attempting to forecast the future direction of the stock-market, which is a dangerous practice. It would also put us firmly back into the High-Risk category. (Remember that High-Risk investments made by means of regular savings become Medium-Risk investments.)

In the next two lessons, I shall help you choose for yourself two specific regular savings investments, one via a collective fund (a unit trust or an investment trust) and the other via a personal equity plan. First though, I need to set the scene by describing these types of investment and showing how they differ from each other.

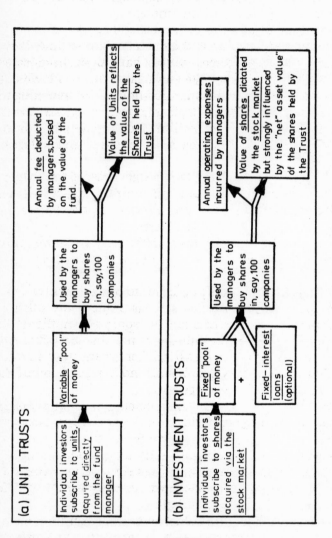

*Fig 12.4* The general characteristics of collective funds

## Unit Trusts

These are very straightforward investments – see figure 12.4.

Your investment money is combined with that of, probably, thousands of other investors to create a pool of money which (after deduction of initial charges) is then invested by the fund managers in a wide range of ordinary shares.

The value of your units goes up or down directly in line with the average value of those shares.

The fund is of a type known as 'open ended': in other words, the total number of units in issue expands (or contracts) in line with the number of new units being bought (or existing units being sold back to the managers).

Charges are quite high. The managers quote two prices: an 'offer' price at which you buy the units; and a 'bid' price at which you can sell them. The difference between the two is usually between 5% and 7%, although sometimes slightly less; very occasionally it can be as high as 8%. In addition, there is an annual management charge of around $1\frac{1}{2}$% pa.

Daily information on unit trust prices is given in the *Financial Times*. Look under the 'Managed Funds Service'; this starts off with unit trust prices and associated information.

An example of part of an entry (reproduced with the permission of the *Financial Times* from their issue of 21 September 1996) is as follows:

| | Initial Charge | Selling Price | Buying Price | + or – | Yield, Gross |
|---|---|---|---|---|---|
| **Baring Fund Managers Ltd. (1200)H** | | | | | |
| American Growth | 5 | 135.3 | 143.0 | +0.9 | 0.0 |
| American Smllr Cos | 5 | 171.7 | 184.6 | +1.6 | 0.0 |
| Eastern | 5 | 304.1 | 327.0 | +0.8 | 0.3 |
| Equity Income | 5 | 99.26 | 106.2 | +0.2 | 4.2 |

The entry also includes the name, address and telephone number of the management company. Don't worry about the '(1200)H': this just indicates the precise timing of the daily valuation of the funds.

There follows a list of the various unit trusts offered by

this management group; the names of the individual trusts are usually quite descriptive of the shares in the fund: for instance, 'American Smllr Cos' will have most of the fund invested in smaller US companies.

Against each individual trust, the first number is the initial charge (in this case 5%). On top of this management charge, the managers can also charge something for the initial costs of acquiring additional shares to add to the fund. What is really of interest to you is the *spread* between the 'selling price' (or 'offer price') and the 'buying price' (or 'bid price'); in the case of the 'American Growth Fund', for instance, this is about 5.7%; whilst for the 'Eastern Fund' it is about 7½%. If you were to buy and then sell back the units on consecutive days (assuming that the prices had not changed in the meantime), these are the amounts of your capital which would be lost in initial charges.

After the buying and selling prices comes a figure for the change in price, up or down, on the previous day. Finally, there is given the gross yield (if any) which you would receive (less tax at 20%) in the form of dividends.

The table does not indicate the level of annual charges. For many trusts, over a period of many years, these could actually be more significant than the initial charge.

## Investment trusts

These are somewhat more complicated than unit trusts – see figure 12.4 on page 180 – but it is well worth getting to know about them.

Unlike a unit trust, an investment trust is a company in its own right, with its own shares and shareholders. As such, you will find price information in the *Financial Times*, not under 'Managed Funds Service' but under 'London Share Service'. There is a section of this latter service devoted to 'Investment Trusts'. We have, earlier, mentioned split-capital trusts; these have a section to themselves in the *FT* share price pages, but they will not be relevant to us again until we come to Lesson X.

For now, we shall concentrate on the straightforward investment trusts. The managers raise capital *initially* direct from the public; after that, if you wish to acquire shares in a particular trust, you have to do so via the Stock Exchange.

The trust, like any other company, is able to raise additional loan capital, thus providing an element of gearing.

The initial pool of money is, as with unit trusts, used for the purchase of shares in a wide range of companies. Unlike unit trusts, investment trusts are 'closed-end' funds: that is, once the trust has been set up, the number of shares in issue does not change. No additional shares are created when someone else comes along wishing to buy shares; the new investor acquires them via the Stock Exchange, so that there will be a corresponding seller of the shares. (However, investment trusts can, and sometimes do, make a new issue of shares, just as any other company can, usually as a rights issue: in other words, *existing* shareholders may occasionally be invited to subscribe additional money to the trust in this way.)

You will see, in the *FT* table, a column headed 'NAV'. This stands for 'net asset value'. This is the value per share of the assets of the trust which are applicable to the ordinary shareholders (that is, after deducting assets attributable to investors with a first call on the assets, namely the holders of loan stock).

The NAV is usually a little higher than the share price. In other words, the share price normally stands at a small *discount* to the asset value. The percentage discount is given in the last column of the *FT* table. Occasionally, the share price stands at a *premium* to the net asset value; in this case, the discount would be negative, as is again clear from the *FT* table.

This 'discount to net asset value' is an important concept to appreciate. The price of shares in an investment trust could go up (or down) without any change at all in the value of the shares held by the trust, simply because this discount goes down (or up).

In recent years, the discount has tended to narrow, in other words to go down. This means that the share price performance of investment trusts has been better than one would have expected simply on the basis of the performance of the underlying holding of shares. See figure 12.5.

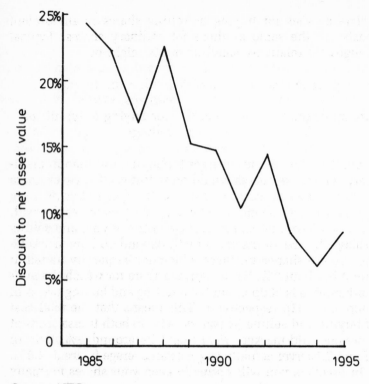

*Source*: AITC

*Figure 12.5* Average discount to net asset value of investment trusts (at year end)

When we come to compare the historical performance of investment trusts to that of unit trusts, it will be important to correct for this narrowing of the discount. The reduced discount has been a major factor in enhancing the relative performance of investment trusts *in the past*, but it is more important to try to judge what the relative performance might be *in the future;* and there is no reason to suppose that the discount will be either higher or lower in the future than it is now.

The propensity of investment trust shares to stand at a discount to the NAV has led to the introduction of 'warrants', which are issued along with the original offering of shares. These warrants will be featured in Lesson X.

The charges for buying or selling shares in investment trusts are the same as those for ordinary shares. Typical charges for relatively small amounts might be:

| | | |
|---|---|---|
| Broker's commission | 1.25% | (with a minimum of, perhaps, £20) |
| Stamp duty | 0.5% | (for buying only; nil for selling) |

So, the total obvious charges for buying and then immediately selling the shares would be about 3%. However, there is also an additional cost which is the *spread* between the buying and selling prices. The daily *FT* table gives the mid-market prices; that is, the average of the buying and selling prices. The size of the spread will depend on how 'marketable' are the shares: for those which are frequently traded, it might be about 2%. For instance, a share for which the mid-market price is 200p might have selling and buying prices of 198p and 202p respectively. This means that the total cost of buying and selling (if you were to do both transactions at the same mid-market price) might be around 5%. Data in *Money Observer* actually suggests an average figure of 4.8%.

In practice, you will normally keep your shares for many years, so that it is the *buying* costs which are most important to you. A rough guide would be to assume that the initial charges (including the difference between the buying price and the mid-market price) would be around 3% of your investment.

Annual charges are quite variable, with the larger trusts generally having the lower percentage charges. To find out what these charges are, you will need to look into the annual report of the trust. The figure is not given explicitly in the accounts, so you will need to search for it, as follows.

As a footnote to the accounts, you will find a set of figures such as 'administration charge', 'directors fees' and 'auditors remuneration'. Adding these up will give you the total annual management and administration expenses. You then look at the balance sheet and will find, at the bottom, a figure for shareholders' funds, just as with an industrial or commercial company. Dividing the expenses by the shareholders' funds and multiplying by 100, will give you a

figure for the annual charges as a percentage of the net assets
of the trust. This would typically be in the range ½% to 1%
pa.

Most investment trusts, these days, offer regular savings
plans. One advantage is that they often dispense with the
stockbroker's fee, so that this is a very cheap way of buying
the shares. Not every management company does this; for
instance, some trusts carry an initial charge on savings
schemes of perhaps 4% of the investment. You will
naturally want to steer clear of these trusts, but how do you
find the information easily? The answer is that magazines
such as *Money Observer* frequently have articles on these
savings schemes, and these articles will tell you the charges
applicable to the various savings plans.

## Unit trusts v investment trusts

You will have noticed that the charges associated with
investment trusts are lower than those for unit trusts. You
would rightly anticipate, therefore, that we should expect to
see this reflected in the relative performance statistics of the
two types of collective fund.

You may also have anticipated that the price of investment trust shares will be more volatile than the prices of
units of unit trusts. This is for two reasons:

(a) the existence of gearing with many investment trusts
(b) the fact that share prices of investment trusts do not
    faithfully reflect changes in the net asset values, but
    can and do also include changes in the discount (or
    premium) which the stock-market places on the
    shares

We have seen already that, so far as regular savings plans
are concerned, higher volatility is a plus point.

The Saturday edition of the *Financial Times* actually
provides figures for the volatility of unit trusts and investment trusts. Turn to the 'Weekend Money' section of the
paper where you will find performance tables for the
different kinds of trusts. Then take comparable sub-sectors

and compare the figures for the Sector Average under the heading 'Volatility'. For instance, on average the figures might be approximately:

| Sector | Volatility Unit trusts | Volatility Investment trusts |
|---|---|---|
| UK | $3\frac{1}{2}$ | 5 |
| North America | $3\frac{1}{2}$ | 5 |
| Japan | 6 | $7\frac{1}{2}$ |
| Far East excl Japan | 7 | $8\frac{1}{2}$ |

Don't worry about the way in which volatility is measured. The relevant feature is that the volatility of investment trust prices is, indeed, greater than that for unit trusts.

I regard investment trust savings plans as Britain's best-kept investment secret. You may think it strange to regard it in that way, when there are some 100,000 savings plans already in existence! I believe, though, that there is the potential for the number to run into millions.

It is not entirely surprising that investment trusts are less well known than unit trusts. For one thing, investment trusts are not allowed to advertise themselves (although they can advertise their savings plans). More significant, though, is the matter of commission to financial advisers: it is only natural that such advisers will recommend unit trusts (on which they receive commission) rather than investment trusts (on which they do not, except with a new issue).

If, as a result of studying the next lesson, you decide to go in for an investment trust savings plan, you will need to know how to contact the managers and where to find details of the charges. Details of the management groups are given in the monthly report of the Association of Investment Trust Companies. This information, together with details of charges, is also contained in occasional articles in *Money Observer* and an excellent magazine called, appropriately, *Investment Trusts*.

Implementing your chosen plan could not be easier. You simply fill in the application form and the bankers order form which will be supplied by the trust's managers, and away you go!

## Personal equity plans

Everyone over 18 is entitled to take out two PEPs in any one financial year, namely:

(a)  up to £6,000 in a general PEP (which can be invested in a wide range of UK and European companies)
(b)  up to £3,000 in a single company PEP (which, as its name implies, must all be in the shares of one such company)

PEPs have specific tax advantages: they are free from both income tax and capital gains tax. The income tax concession makes them especially suitable for higher-rate taxpayers; for standard-rate taxpayers, the management charges often negate the income tax benefits.

This applies particularly to managed funds, in which you leave it to a fund manager to choose the investments for you, and to change them from time to time as he sees fit. The managed PEP could actually be a unit trust or an investment trust, adapted for the PEP investor. (In the jargon of the financial services industry, this is referred to as putting the unit or investment trust in a PEP 'wrapper'.)

A much lower-cost way of building up a PEP fund for yourself is to take the self-select route; in this case, *you* choose which shares you want to include, and *you* decide if and when you want to change them.

I personally regard self-select PEPs as the ideal mechanism for building up a portfolio of ordinary shares of one's own choice. We shall see in Lesson IX how to identify appropriate companies in which to invest.

If and when you *do* decide that you would like to make a change in your portfolio, nothing could be easier. You just phone your PEP manager, who will put you through to someone in a dealing room; he in turn will take your instructions and implement them. I find that this service (provided, in my case, by one of the large High Street banks) is simple, efficient and not too costly.

There is usually a relatively small initial charge for setting up the plan and an annual charge of between $\frac{1}{2}$% and 1% pa with a maximum charge of, perhaps, £200 pa. Don't forget, also, the charges for stockbroker's commission and stamp duty for each share that you acquire.

Don't ignore the capital gains tax advantages, even if you do not currently expect to pay such tax. You might well build up a substantial PEP investment over many years, and then wish to sell all of the shares at some appropriate time, for instance to fund an annuity to provide income for your later years. It is comforting to know that, when that time comes, the full value of your fund will be available for such an annuity, with no deduction of capital gains tax.

The managed variety of PEPs can be acquired by means of a regular, monthly savings plan. However, monthly savings would be inappropriate for the self-select route which I prefer; there is usually a minimum investment which you can make in any one company in your PEP, and this is probably £1,000 or more.

Hence, a self-select PEP is more appropriately organised as a regular *annual* rather than monthly savings plan. This raises one extra question: is there a particular time of the year at which it is best to make one's annual contribution to the plan. Yes, there is: we shall see what this is in Lesson IX.

The next two lessons will help you to make specific choices of collective funds and ordinary shares. I believe that, in future years, you may well look back on these two lessons as providing some of the most significant investment information you have ever read.

That being the case, you won't mind doing quite a lot of work as a necessary precursor to these lessons! I would urge you to work very seriously through this next set of homework exercises.

# Homework VII

For your homework, I would like you to do quite a lot of research for yourself on the historical performance records of different collective funds. One objective is to help you look intelligently and critically at published performance statistics; the main purpose, though, is to prepare you for the next lesson, after which you should be able to choose one or more specific funds for investment.

You will need your copy of *Money Observer*, which gives seven-year performance data for unit trusts and investment trusts. You might also find it useful to obtain a copy of *Money Management*, which extends the timescale to ten years, and which extends the range of collective funds considerably (to include, for instance, insurance company funds and offshore funds).

This homework is also where you will need to carry out some simple mathematical calculations, so you will find a pocket calculator invaluable.

## Exercise 1

The first thing I should like you to do is to look at some quite realistic figures relating to a mythical unit trust. Its performance in five recent 12-month periods was assumed to be:

| | |
|---|---|
| Year 1 | –20% |
| Year 2 | +10% |
| Year 3 | –25% |
| Year 4 | +100% |
| Year 5 | +50% |

What I should like you to do is this. Imagine that you are the manager of this trust, and you want to illustrate the trust's performance over the last five years for advertising purposes. You are going to draw up a table like this:

---

## PERFORMANCE

| last 5 years | last 4 years | last 3 years | last 2 years | last 1 year |
|--------------|--------------|--------------|--------------|-------------|
| - - - - | - - - - | - - - - | - - - - | +50% |

---

Your job is to fill in the blank spaces.

Let me give you a start. The performance of the trust over the most recent one-year period ('year 5') is clearly +50% and I have written this in for you. Remember that, looking back at past performance, the 'last 1 year' performance figure corresponds to 'year 5' in our earlier table; the 'last 2 years' corresponds to years 4 plus 5; and so on.

Over the *two* most recent years, we need to combine the performance in year 4 with that in year 5. Assume that the price started off at 100p at the *beginning* of year 4. Then, by the *end* of year 5 it has increased first by 100% to 200p, and then by a further 50% to 300p; this makes a total *increase* of 200% over the starting point of 100p. So this figure of 200% goes into the 'last 2 years' space in the planned advert.

Now start off with a price 'index' of 100p at the beginning of year 3 and calculate the 3-year percentage increase; and repeat the exercise for the 4-year and 5-year performance figures.

You will find that the performance over the whole of the five years looks quite impressive, but that this performance is entirely due to two very good years; performance in the earlier years was very uninspiring.

## Exercise 2

You can use, for this exercise, either or both the seven-year statistics given in *Money Observer* or the ten-year figures in *Money Management*. I shall first lead you through the relevant tables in *Money Observer* before telling you what I would like you to do.

Near to the back of the magazine you will find some pages edged in blue; these relate to unit trusts. The first few pages give 'The Top 10 Performers in Each Sector' for periods of 1 month, 3 months, 6 months, 1 year, 3 years and 7 years.

You will see that 'Sector' generally means a geographical area; in addition, there are a few specialist 'business sectors', such as: Commodity & Energy, Financial & Property, Investment Trust Units and Money Market.

At the bottom of the table for each sector are 'average' figures for all the trusts in that sector, for each of the time-periods. The figures which we are going to use are these averages for the seven-year time-period. These figures indicate the values, after seven years, of an initial investment of £100, allowing for the difference between the offer and bid prices and with net income re-invested.

A few pages further on in the magazine there are equivalent tables (edged in green) for investment trusts. In this case, since there are not all that many such trusts, the tables list *all* of the trusts in each sector, not just the 'Top 10'. However, for the moment we are still going to work on the 'average' figures at the bottom of the table for each sector.

Concentrate, for the moment, on these average returns over seven years. Note that the word 'return' is used rather differently from the way in which we have used it: in this case, it means the total value, at the end of the seven years, of an initial investment of £100, after deducting charges and with net income re-invested. (The percentage deduction for charges is based on a more normal level of investment, not on £100.)

**Table 12.6   Blank table for recording performance data, by sector, on collective funds.**

'Return' over seven years from an initial investment of £100

| Unit Trusts | | Investment Trusts | |
|---|---|---|---|
| UK Growth and income | - - - - - | UK General | - - - - - |
| Europe | - - - - - | Continental Europe | - - - - - |
| North America | - - - - - | North America | - - - - - |
| Japan | - - - - - | Japan | - - - - - |
| Far East Excluding Japan | - - - - - | Far East Excluding Japan | - - - - - |
| International Balanced | - - - - - | International General | - - - - - |
| Global Emerging Markets | - - - - - | Emerging Markets | - - - - - |
| UK Gilt and Fixed Int | - - - - - | | |

We are going to pick a wide selection of geographical sectors and compare the seven-year averages of unit trusts and investment trusts. I would like you to fill in the spaces in table 12.6, taking from the magazine the average seven-year return for the sector in each case.

I have included two new sectors which did not appear in the unit trust tables until very recently, namely Emerging Markets and UK Gilt and Fixed Interest. (You may well find, when you come to carry out this homework that some of the sectors have again been redefined.)

You are no doubt familiar with the expression 'to give a hostage to fortune'; well, I guess that that is just what I am doing with this exercise.

The precise numerical results which you insert into the table will depend on the particular month's issue of *Money Observer* or *Money Management* which you use. I would expect, nevertheless, that you would come to the same general conclusions as I shall present in the next lesson, whichever issue you choose. There will be occasions, however, when – for various reasons – this may not be the case. I'm sure that there is somebody's 'law' which states that you will choose one of the issues of the magazine which gives the 'wrong' results. We shall soon see.

The figures which you enter into the table will tell you what has happened *in the past*. I would like you to consider why the figures may give an over-optimistic view of the *future* relative performance of investment trusts.


## Exercise 3

I would now like you to focus on one particular investment trust sector in your *Money Observer*; this is Far East excluding Japan.

We are going to see whether there is one trust, within this sector, which has performed *consistently* better than the others in its sector.

The *Money Observer* table includes performance data for three years as well as for seven years (and also for one year, but we shall not use those figures).

You will appreciate that the seven-year period *includes* the most recent three-year period. We have seen, from Exercise 1, that we can get a misleading picture when time-periods overlap like this: one recent good year can make it seem that performance has been good over the *whole* of the seven-year time-period.

What we have to do, then, is to adapt the data so as to obtain *separate* performance figures for two *distinct* time-periods which do not overlap; namely:

(1) *the first four years* of the seven-year period; *and*
(2) *the most recent three years* of the seven-year period

Three and four years respectively are reasonable periods over which to judge the performance of the individual trusts. We can, of course, carry out this exercise only on those trusts which have been in existence for at least seven years.

I'll now explain how we arrive at the results. Suppose the performance of a particular trust has been as follows:

|  | 1 year | 3 years | 7 years |
|---|---|---|---|
| Trust XYZ | 103.5 | 158.3 | 172.9 |

We are only interested in the 3-year and 7-year figures.

The performance of the trust for the most recent three years of the seven-year period is read directly from the column headed '3 years'; so, from the above table, we see that the 3-year performance figure for our trust at that time was 158.3: an investment of £100 three years earlier would have grown (after expenses and with net interest reinvested) to £158.30.

So far, so easy. But what about the *first* four years of the seven-year period? What we have to do is to divide the '7 years' figure by the '3 years' figure and multiply by 100.

So, in the case of our chosen trust, the calculation would be:

$$\text{First 4 years performance} = \frac{172.9}{158.3} \times 100$$
$$= 109.2$$

Incidentally, this process of division happens to eliminate the effect of charges. This does not matter since we are only comparing the *relative* performance of the different trusts. If you want to estimate the after-charges performance in the first four years, you need to reduce your answers by about 5%.

Do this in turn for each of the very few investment trusts in the sector 'Far East excluding Japan'. Ignore trusts which concentrate on individual countries (for instance, Korea-Europe Trust and New Zealand Trust).

The final step is to plot a graph of the performance in the most recent three years against the performance in the first four years.

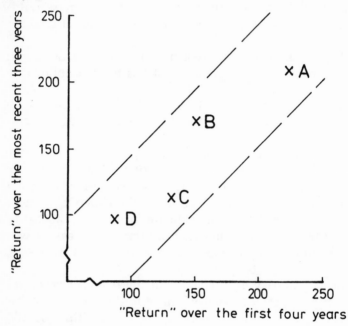

*Figure 12.6* Idealised graph showing consistent relative performances over two time-periods

What we would *hope* to see is a graph something like that of figure 12.6, in which the trusts are ranked in the same order in both time-periods. If we *were* to obtain such a result, then we would be happy to invest our money in Trust A, on the basis that it had delivered a performance *consistently* better than its rivals B, C and D.

I should warn you not to be surprised if the graph you produce is rather different from the idealised hypothetical one.

If you have worked your way conscientiously through the homework exercises, you will be in a very good position to

appreciate the important ideas which are developed in the
next lesson.

# Chapter 13
# Lesson VIII: High-Risk
# Investments – Collective Funds

The general term 'collective funds' has been used many times already to mean unit trusts and investment trusts. There are, in fact, several other types . . . and a bewildering array they are. What we shall try to do, in this lesson, is to narrow down the choice from several *thousands* of funds, so that we can choose just one.

One obvious selection method would be to choose, say, a unit trust based on an outstanding performance record publicised in its advertisements – but is this any guide to *future* performance?

Let's look at the answer to your homework Exercise 1. It should look like this:

---

### PERFORMANCE

| last 5 years | last 4 years | last 3 years | last 2 years | last 1 year |
|:---:|:---:|:---:|:---:|:---:|
| + 98% | +147.5% | +125% | +200% | +50% |

---

This looks like a very impressive five-year record, but we have seen that it is due to just two good years; anyone buying at the beginning of the five-year period and selling after three years would have made a *loss* of one-third of their investment; and it tells us nothing about *future* perform-ance.

This is one reason why many people are less than entirely

happy with their investments in collective funds. The trusts which are actively promoted (and which therefore attract much 'new' money) are, naturally, the ones which have just had one or two good years. We have seen how that recent good performance can *appear* to give a longer-term performance more consistently good than it really is; and it is *most* unlikely that the outstanding performance recently advertised will be maintained.

The analysis which will be presented in this lesson will provide extensive evidence that past performance of trusts is generally little or no guide to the future. There *may* be odd occasions when future performance correlates well with past performance, but there is no way of identifying such cases in advance.

---

*Thorneycroft's Eighth Law of Successful Investment*

**Ignore advertisements which illustrate the past performance of collective funds.**

---

Rather than ignoring such advertisements you could, if you wish, amuse yourself by using the quoted percentage increases to identify earlier years in which the performance was *negative.*

Now, if past performance figures were given, for instance, in respect of two *non-overlapping* three-year periods, that would be a different matter altogether! That would be something to be welcomed.

Incidentally, I would also ignore all new issues of specialised investment trusts. They will almost always come to the market for the first time when that specialised sector is booming – that is the time when interest is at its peak and when the new issue is likely to sell very well.

In recent years, three huge new specialised investment trusts were issued, two based on European privatisations and one on gold and other mining shares. They attracted vast amounts of money because the promotional literature could rightly point to recent excellent performance statistics for, respectively, the UK version of privatisations and the price of gold mining shares.

After a lengthy period of desultory performance following its launch, one of the fund's managers was reported by the *Sunday Telegraph* as saying: 'The problem is, the trust was launched at what turned out to be the top of the market.' Well, of course it was! The time to sell something is when people are keen to buy it; it's very difficult to market a new specialised trust at the bottom of the market as, by definition, that is the time when there is not much interest in the sector.

In short, it is best just to ignore all trusts which are being actively promoted, whether on the basis of: (a) recent excellent performance; or (b) being new issues specialising in an 'exciting' sector.

Just crossing off the trusts which are currently being advertised is not going to reduce our field of search by very much. We are going to have to look in much greater depth at the historical performance of trusts, whether or not they are the ones being currently promoted.

*Money Management* gives performance statistics for a much wider range of collective funds than just unit trusts and investment trusts. The number of funds available to choose from is quite staggering; it includes:

| | |
|---|---|
| Unit trusts | about 1500 |
| Investment trusts | about 300* |
| Insurance funds | about 1300 |
| 'Offshore' funds | about 1800 |

plus many more.

This, however, is just the tip of the iceberg: according to an article in the *Financial Times*, it has been suggested that there are some 32,000 investment products to choose from! The situation will be complicated further by the introduction of yet another new breed of collective fund, the OEIC (Open Ended Investment Company).

* The investment trust total excludes split-capital trusts, which are dealt with separately in two other lessons – Medium-Risk and Very-High-Risk.

Not all of these thousands of products are High-Risk ones; for instance, many are fixed-interest and money-market funds, which would be more appropriately classed as Low- or Medium-Risk. Nevertheless, there are several thousands in our High-Risk category.

We are setting ourselves the task of choosing just *one* fund from this number which, I'm sure you will agree, is quite a challenge.

We are going to have to be very disciplined in our approach. These are the steps which we shall follow:

1. Comparing the ten-year performance records of different types of collective funds, invested in different geographical regions.
2. Identifying additional reasons for focusing on investment trusts.
3. Identifying the best geographical area(s) on the basis of *consistency* of historical performance.
4. Identifying additional reasons for focusing on the Far East excluding Japan.
5. Choosing a specific trust on the basis of consistency of historical performance.
6. Summarising the Risk v Reward characteristics for our chosen trust.

## Ten-year performance records

Table 13.1 summarises data for a ten-year period up to the beginning of 1996, for the main geographical sectors. The numbers in brackets indicate the numbers of individual trusts which existed ten years earlier and which, therefore, contribute to the ten-year average performance figures.

**Table 13.1   Summary of ten-year performance records of collective funds**
(Average value in £ for each sector, at 1 January 1996, based on an initial investment of £1,000)

|  | Unit trusts | Insurance funds | 'Offshore' funds (SIB Recognised) | Investment trusts |
|---|---|---|---|---|
| **UK**[1] | 3,089 (76) | 2,563 (99) | 3,140 (8) | 3,783 (7) |
| **Europe**[2] | 3,034 (44) | 2,384 (25) | 2,919 (6) | 3,468 (4) |
| **North America** | 2,912 (73) | 2,254 (48) | 2,826 (12) | 3,174 (4) |
| **Japan** | 2,742 (45) | 2,122 (9) | 3,319 (12) | 3,425 (4) |
| **Far East excl Japan** | 5,366 (12) | 3,455 (6) | 5,549 (8) | 8,264 (1) |
| **International**[3] | 2,920 (50) | 2,309 (66) | 2,691 (10) | 4,191 (16) |

*Source of information: Money Management*

**Notes:**  [1] Variously designated UK Growth & Income, UK Income Growth, UK Equity General, UK General
[2] Variously designated Europe, European, Continental Europe.
[3] Variously designated International Growth, International, International Equity, International General.

**Charges:** Unit trust and insurance fund statistics are given in *Money Management* on a 'buy-to-sell' (or 'bid-to-offer') basis, so that they already include the effect of charges. Offshore funds are quoted on a 'sell-to-sell' basis and investment trusts on 'mid-market to mid-market'.

Generally speaking, an investment of £1,000 ten years earlier, in a wide variety of funds, has grown to around

£3,000. There are, however, some notable exceptions:

(a) The insurance funds have consistently underperformed the other types of investment (possibly because of the cost of the life assurance element, but probably more because insurance companies – unlike unit trusts and investment trusts – pay tax on capital gains; there is then no further tax liability for standard-rate taxpayers).

(b) The geographical sector 'Far East excluding Japan' has produced substantially better returns than the other sectors.

(c) The investment trusts have consistently outperformed the other types of investment.

We are actually going to concentrate on unit trusts and investment trusts; both offer highly appropriate regular savings schemes, and we have already decided that this is the way in which we are going to use collective funds.

For your homework, you will have produced your own table for unit trusts and investment trusts, for the various different geographical sectors, but taking just a seven-year view. Nevertheless, I expect that you will still have noticed the particularly good results from investment trusts in general and 'Far East excluding Japan' in particular.

Now, I have to tell you that it is a little premature to rule out unit trusts in favour of investment trusts. Most of the outperformance of investment trusts in recent years is due to the fact that their 'discounts to net asset value' have fallen substantially. You might wish to refer back to the previous lesson in order to refresh your memory about these discounts.

Indeed, you may well have found that, within the Far East excluding Japan sector, the unit trusts have outperformed the investment trusts. You will probably see, on closer examination, that the unit trust average is buoyed up by some really splendid returns from trusts invested specifically in Hong Kong; meanwhile, the investment trust average is depressed by a couple of very poor performers.

In fact, the Far East sector generally (with the exception of Hong Kong) has actually not performed all that well for the last two years or so, for a variety of reasons which might be expected to reverse in the future. For instance, there has been a temporary slow-down in growth rates (to levels which would still be the envy of Western countries); and the recent strength of the pound has depressed the value of overseas shares to the UK investor.

There is no particular reason to think that investment trust discounts will either increase or decrease in the future. Hence, we must be careful not to project the recent excellent performance of investment trusts generally into the future, without correcting for the recent narrowing of the average discount.

If we look at the changes over the years in the *net asset values* of investment trusts, we find that there is, in fact, very little difference between the underlying performance of unit trusts and investment trusts.

So, there will be nothing wrong with you deciding to choose a unit trust for your regular savings scheme. Personally, however, I prefer investment trusts. One very practical reason is that there are relatively *few* of them, but an amazing proliferation of unit trusts. When we come to choose a particular geographical sector, we will find that there is just a handful of investment trusts which we need to consider, so that we drastically reduce our field of search.

As mentioned above, there is no reason to suppose that investment trusts will continue to benefit from a further reduction in the discount to net asset value; nor to think that they may suffer from a widening of that discount. One factor that *can* be confidently predicted is that their *charges* will remain below those of conventional unit trusts – both the initial charges and the annual management charge.

The benefit of lower charges with investment trusts is amplified with regular savings schemes. Many such trusts dispense with the normal stockbrokers' commissions altogether, thus making them particularly attractive.

In the previous lesson, we saw how the prices of investment trust shares were more *volatile* than those of unit trusts. This, as we have seen, is a further plus point for regular savings plans.

So, are there *any* reasons for choosing a unit trust in preference to an investment trust? It could be that there is no suitable investment trust which meets your specific requirements. Examples could be: a trust that invests exclusively in the shares of gold mining companies; or one which invests exclusively in the shares of a particular country (although that is not normally something to be recommended, despite the outstanding performance of trusts invested in Hong Kong).

Could there be some simple rule for selecting a unit trust, such that one could be confident of offsetting the charges with enhanced performance? The book *Which? Way to Save and Invest* (published by Which? Ltd) presents a review of several popular theories, with the following results:

| | |
|---|---|
| 'Small funds do best' | 'not a particularly useful criterion' |
| 'Go for last year's winners' | 'past performance is not a good guide' |
| 'Go for last year's losers' | 'not a good guide for picking a unit trust' |
| 'New is best' | 'may have some initial benefit compared with others, but is not guaranteed' |
| 'Pick a management company' | 'little evidence that this is a good way to pick a unit trust' |
| 'Look for investments in small companies' | 'just a little evidence to back this up, but only over the very long-term' |

It doesn't look as if we can hope to find consistently outstanding performance by any of these selection criteria!

The unit trust industry itself has come to recognise that there is little or no evidence of consistent management performance. In fact, it is well known that – in any one year – some 80% or so of trusts fail to match up to the relevant index of stock-market performance. One consequence of this realisation is the introduction of something called 'tracker funds'. These funds simply hold a representative selection of (or all of) the shares which go to make up the index which is being tracked (for instance, the FT-SE 100 index).

In tracker funds, the managers dispense with any attempt

to beat the market and recognise that they might just as well try to *match* the market. In this way, they can keep their charges down below the normal level. The growth of tracker funds is a clear admission of the below-par historical performance of conventional trusts.

Even these tracker funds are not quite what they seem. They don't always succeed in fully tracking the share price index, especially when dividends are taken into account. These tracker funds still cost something to administer, but they are, nevertheless, a better bet than actively managed funds. (Remember Thorneycroft's Fifth Law of Successful Investment on page 145!)

In summary, when we come to make our final choice, we can anticipate that we shall prefer to select either an investment trust or a tracker unit trust.

However, we won't completely reject the conventional unit trusts just yet: we must leave ourselves the opportunity of seeing if there is a specific unit trust, within our chosen sector, with such a consistently good performance that we shall be happy to pay the charges.

Whilst we are looking at unit trusts, I want to mention in passing a particular 'business' (rather than geographical) sector, namely 'UK Gilt and Fixed Interest'. You looked at these trusts as part of Homework VII. You will probably have found that their performance over many years has not been particularly outstanding.

The reason I mention this is to refer back to Lesson V, when we talked about 'corporate bond PEPs'. These consist mainly of UK fixed-interest securities. You should see from the historical performance data why I am not particularly enthusiastic about them.

## Geographical areas

The next stage of the narrowing-down process is to decide just *where* in the world should be the focus of our attention.

It is already clear, from the ten-year performance tables, that the region described as 'Far East excluding Japan' has had the best *average* performance over that decade; the question we now have to ask is: has that performance been *consistently* good?

We have seen that the track records of individual trusts can appear to be more consistent than they really are. Does the same apply to the various geographical sectors? This is what we are going to study next.

Incidentally, I should mention just which countries are embraced by the term 'Far East excluding Japan'. Trusts which fall into this category have most of their money invested in companies located in Hong Kong, Singapore, Malaysia, Thailand, Philippines, Taiwan, South Korea and Indonesia; some may include Australia and New Zealand.

This group of countries overlaps with another category of investment trusts which has been very popular in recent years, namely 'Emerging Markets'. This category of trusts will often have a substantial part of the money invested in the Far East region; but they also include the South American countries, the Indian subcontinent, Eastern Europe and, indeed, any country which is still at a relatively early stage of economic development. We shall come back to the Emerging Market funds shortly.

First, though, let's look at the consistency of performance of the various geographical sectors. Table 13.1 gave us the average performance over ten years for the six main sectors. These are largely non-overlapping sectors, with one minor and one major exception. The minor one is that 'Europe' could include 'UK' – although, in practice, these funds have rather low percentages invested in the UK.

The major exception is the 'International' sector: these trusts are clearly made up very largely of shares each of which would fall into one of the other five sectors. We might expect, therefore, that these 'International' funds would have produced a consistently *average* performance. Oddly, this is not so; they have tended to underperform the average. I have a suspicion – and it's no more than that – that this is because it is too tempting for the investment managers to switch from country to country; in other words, to do too much active management.

I've taken three separate time-periods and calculated the average performance for each sector for each period. (The earlier two time-periods *do* overlap somewhat, I'm afraid. The statistical purist will also rightly point out that the data for the different time-periods are not strictly comparable, since only the recent time-periods include figures for newly introduced trusts; whilst this is true, it will not have introduced any bias into the calculations.) The results (for both unit trusts and investment trusts) are summarised in table 13.2.

**Table 13.2   Relative performance of geographical sectors for three time-periods**

| | | Time-period (to 1 Jan) 1986–91 (5 years) | 1989–93 (4 years) | 1993–96 (3 years) |
|---|---|---|---|---|
| **UK** | Inv Trusts | Average | Average | Poor |
| | Unit Trusts | V Good | Average | Poor |
| **Europe** | Inv Trusts | V Good | Poor | Average |
| | Unit Trusts | Average | Average | V Good |
| **N America** | Inv Trusts | V Poor | Poor | V Good |
| | Unit Trusts | V Poor | Excellent | Average |
| **Japan** | Inv Trusts | V Good | V Poor | Average |
| | Unit Trusts | Excellent | V Poor | Poor |
| **Far East excl Japan** | Inv Trusts | Excellent | Excellent | V Good |
| | Unit Trusts | V Good | Excellent | V Good |
| **International** | Inv Trusts | Poor | V Good | Poor |
| | Unit Trusts | Poor | Average | Poor |

**Key:**   Excellent   V Good   Average   Poor   V Poor

You can see from this that the average performance of the Far East excluding Japan sector is *consistently* in the 'very good' and 'excellent' rankings. Unless there are reasons for thinking that this might change in the future, we need look no further for our chosen sector.

In your homework, I asked you to look also at the Emerging Market sector. This sector had one splendid year which created a flurry of interest (as it would, of course, at the top of that particular market). However, if you look at the performance over many years, then you will find that it has not been *consistently* outstanding.

Once again, it would have been unwise to be carried away by the euphoria of one year's performance. This is a good example of another general principle, which is really a corollary to my eighth law:

---

*Thorneycroft's Ninth Law of Successful Investment*

**Ignore the latest investment 'fashion'.**

---

There might need to be an exception to my ninth law. If this book is as successful as I hope it might be, it could generate a fashion for regular savings into investment trusts from the Far East excluding Japan sector!

We shall see, next, some of the reasons for thinking that this is *not* just a short-term fashion.

## The future of the Far East excluding Japan sector

No one can say with certainty that this geographical region will continue to outperform the others in the future, but the omens look excellent. I will mention some of the factors which encourage me to continue putting money into this region, on a regular basis.

The growth in share values reflects growth in the economies of these countries. Independent forecasts indicate that the region is expected to continue to grow much faster than the 'developed' world.

The World Bank has produced a report entitled 'The East Asian Miracle' (for a brief summary, see *The Economist*, 2 October 1993) which explains why that august body sees the continuation of economic growth in the region, despite the possibility of its starting to suffer from the 'problems of success'.

As these newly developing countries become more integrated into the global economy, this may reduce their scope for inhibiting imports, for subsidising exports and for keeping interest rates low. However, it seems that these possible negative factors will be more than outweighed by some very positive ones: in particular, the emphasis on good education (especially basic primary and secondary education) and on a flexible labour market. Also, compared with other emerging markets, there is a 'competence and relative lack of corruption of civil servants'.

Colleagues who know the region well at first hand refer, not just to the good education, but also to the absence of a 'dependency culture': the people don't assume that the State will look after their every need. With people taking more responsibility for their own lives, there is not the same heavy burden of government spending which acts as such a drag on the growth potential of the developed world.

The successful countries of south-east Asia have clearly given a great deal of priority to their 'human capital'. So far as education is concerned, it's not just 'the three Rs', but an extra one for good measure – Responsibility. This contrasts with the situation in the UK, for instance, where – for a highly 'advanced' country – too many people fail to achieve reasonable standards in reading, writing and mathematics; and where so many look to the State for support.

**Table 13.3   Growth rates and public consumption for various countries**

| | Average annual growth in real GDP (1985–93) | Public consumption as a % of total GDP |
|---|---|---|
| China | 9.2% | 9.0% |
| Thailand | 9.1% | 10.1% |
| South Korea | 8.9% | 10.8% |
| Singapore | 7.8% | 9.3% |
| Malaysia | 7.4% | 12.6% |
| Hong Kong | 6.8% | 8.1% |
| Taiwan | 6.7% | 15.7% |
| Indonesia | 6.4% | 9.9% |
| Japan | 3.5% | 9.6% |
| Philippines | 3.1% | 8.1% |
| Spain | 3.0% | 17.2% |
| Germany | 2.8% | 18.0% |
| USA | 2.3% | 17.5% |
| France | 2.1% | 19.3% |
| UK | 2.0% | 21.9% |
| Italy | 2.0% | 17.9% |
| Switzerland | 1.6% | 14.5% |
| Sweden | 0.8% | 27.7% |

(GDP = Gross Domestic Product, a measure of the total output of an economy)

*Source*: *The Economist Pocket World in Figures*, 1996 edition

Table 13.3 vividly illustrates the advantages enjoyed by the Far East, in terms of economic growth rates and low public spending. (The public spending figures do not include transfer payments from one group of people to another: for instance, from taxpayers to the unemployed and pensioners; they just indicate what the public sector actually spends.)

My own interpretation of the future prospects for investment in south-east Asia is, that it will continue to be a key area of opportunity so long as it continues to put 'economically correct' policies and actions before 'politically correct' ones.

One of the lessons of Japan's successful period was this: it can take decades, not just years, for the Western countries to learn the messages. The Western car industry was on the point of collapse before it finally embraced Japanese production methods and working practices.

One can reasonably predict that it will be many years, and one or more economic disasters hence, before the Western governments (re-)learn the lessons of economic competitiveness.

Until that time, I will certainly be directing a substantial part of our regular savings towards the Far East.

An additional factor which is likely to have a major impact on the region is the growth of China. I wonder how many of you can cast your minds back some thirty or forty years, to the time when Japanese goods were starting to infiltrate the British market. One can sense a very similar process going on right now, except that this time it is China which is supplying the products. Just go round to one of the shops which specialises in children's toys, for example, and have a look to see where they are made.

We all know, now, what has happened to Japan in the last thirty or forty years: it has become one of the great world economic powers. Now, however, it is faced with a real problem, namely a rapidly ageing population. The growth 'mantle' for the future looks set to pass to China and the rapidly emerging economies of the Far East – the so-called Tiger economies. China, in particular, has (to an extreme extent, brought about by its official one-child-per-family policy) the kind of population distribution which has historically been associated with rapid economic growth: namely, a large increase in the population of young workers, coupled with a reduction in the birth rate.

This contrasts starkly with Europe and Japan's rapidly ageing populations. A particular problem for the developed world is the so-called 'pensions time-bomb': how will a declining proportion of workers support an increasing number of retired people?

I remember reading, many years ago, an article which was ahead of its time in anticipating this forthcoming problem. This article actually came up with two alternative recommendations for protecting the future value of your capital. These were:

(a) invest in countries with a large proportion of young workers (that is, countries for which pensions are not a major problem)
(b) invest in whatever other people of your own age group are *not* investing in

Both of these make sense. The first idea points directly to the Far East; the second one reflects our intention to avoid today's fashions. It actually takes my ninth law a stage further: don't just avoid fashions, but positively seek out the unfashionable.

Now, it is one thing to observe what other people *are* investing in (for instance, many retired people tend to choose bank and building society investments which – on this analysis – seem doomed to offer poor real returns whilst the number of retirees continues to increase); it's not quite so easy to consider what they are *not* investing in. In my own case, I have invested a proportion of regular savings into a trust of gold mining shares whilst they have been generally out of fashion. Maybe you can think of other ideas for yourself.

Choosing the Far East as the home for some of our regular savings is much more clear cut. We must be aware that the growth of China into a major world economy is likely to be much less orderly than was that of Japan; there will, no doubt, be many hiccups along the way. This will be true, also, of other emerging countries in the region; for instance, the takeover of Hong Kong by China will have quite unpredictable consequences.

Luckily, we have already established that our way into the region will be via a regular savings plan. We won't be too worried by the inevitable periodic setbacks for these countries; indeed, these setbacks will provide opportunities to pick up more shares for our money, by virtue of the pound-cost-averaging process.

## Choosing a specific trust

Within the Far East excluding Japan sector, we now need to see if we can identify a specific trust which has consistently outperformed its rivals over distinct time-periods. This is where we look at homework Exercise 3.

In figure 13.1, I have plotted graphs of the performance of individual investment trusts for two non-overlapping periods:

(a) the four years up to 1 January 1993
(b) the three years up to 1 January 1996

The figures on the graphs indicate the value, at the end of each period, of an initial investment of £100 made at the beginning of the period.

For your homework, you should have prepared a similar graph just for the 'Far East excluding Japan' sector. In figure 13.1, I have given you a rather wider set of results.

These results are very disappointing. They show no evidence at all of *consistent* performance. Indeed, if anything, the opposite is the case: trusts which performed well in the first period were the ones which performed worst in the second period.

In figure 13.2, I've had a look at unit trusts on the same basis, to see if we can find one or two outstandingly consistent performers. The answer is just the same.

The unit trust data are actually rather strange. There was a huge variation in performance in the earlier period, whereas (with one exception) there is a remarkable degree of uniformity in the more recent performance figures.

On figure 13.2 I have also indicated the performance data for the three investment trusts which have been in existence since 1 January 1989. I have corrected the 'raw' data on share price performance, to allow for the changes in the discount to net asset value. As we saw earlier, this is a fairer way to compare the two types of trust.

The investment trusts, on average, were the winners in the first time-period – but not by all that much; in the more recent time-period, there seems to have been no difference in average performance.

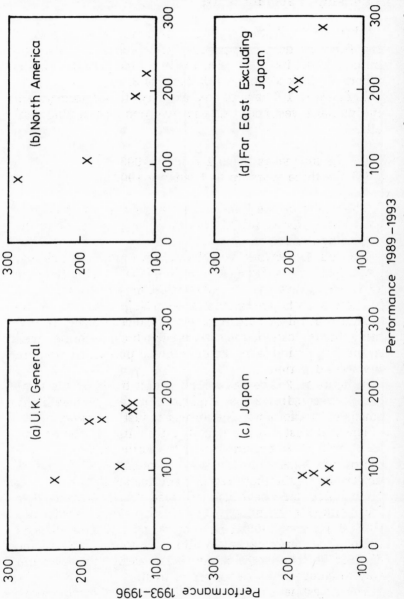

*Figure 13.1* Performance data for individual investment trusts for two non-overlapping time periods

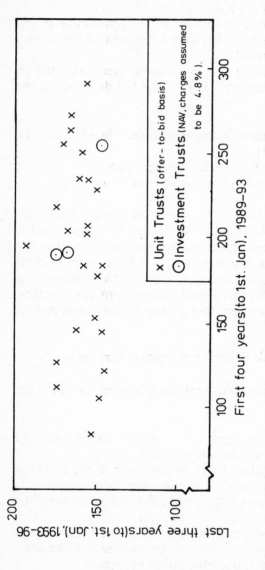

*Figure 13.2* Unit trust performance, 'Far East excluding Japan', for two non-overlapping time periods

From this analysis, we should be happy to choose an investment trust, for the reasons discussed earlier. The other option which we identified was to select a tracker unit trust, but that route would only really be appropriate if our geographical analysis had led us to focus on a single country (UK, America or Japan).

Since we have found that we cannot select our trust on performance, the best plan is to make the decision on the basis of:

(a) low management charges (as calculated from the annual report)
(b) low costs for the regular savings plan
(c) a highly reputable management company

We have had to base our analysis on trusts which have been in existence for at least seven years. You don't need to limit yourself to those trusts when it comes to choosing one to invest in; some newer trusts also have good savings schemes. Also, every year or so, it's worth repeating the analysis presented in this lesson, to see if any specific trust *has* emerged with a consistently good performance record.

## Summary of Risk v Reward characteristics

The conclusions from our analysis of collective funds are four-fold:

(1) Of the various types of collective funds, we will concentrate on investment trusts
(2) We shall acquire shares in such a trust via a regular monthly savings plan spread over many years
(3) We shall choose a trust from the 'Far East excluding Japan' sector
(4) We shall select a specific trust, not on the basis of past performance, but mainly on its low levels of management charges and savings plan charges

We have started from a choice of several *thousands* of collective funds and, in a logical way, have narrowed it down to the one which we shall choose. To see just how good a decision this is likely to be, let us again work our way through the Risk v Reward graph – see figure 13.3.

Our starting point for a High-Risk investment is point A in the diagram, with an 'expected' real rate of return of about 7% pa. Because we are spreading the risk (partly because the trust has a wide spread of ordinary shares, but mainly because of our regular savings plan), the risk level is reduced to Medium – point B on the graph.

There is a cost for this, namely the charges associated with buying the shares (very small for a regular savings plan) and the annual management charge. These charges might reduce the return by about 1% pa – point C.

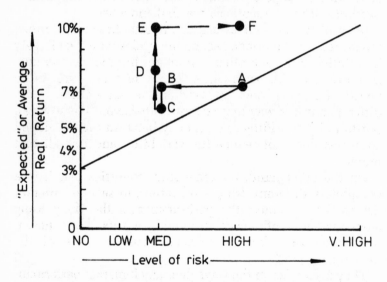

*Figure 13.3* The Risk v Reward graph applied to a regular savings plan invested in the Far East

Far more than offsetting this cost is the enhanced return we shall obtain by the process of pound-cost-averaging; this might be about 2% pa – point D. The volatility of the Far East markets will help to ensure that we *do* derive this benefit from our regular savings plan.

By choosing a Far East fund, we should increase our expected return even further, perhaps (conservatively) by a further 2% pa – point E. However, do we also increase the risk somewhat by choosing that part of the world? In other words, do we move back to point F on the diagram?

So long as the investment is just one part of our complete portfolio of shares, the answer is No, as I will now explain.

Generally speaking, of course, higher investment returns *are* associated with a higher degree of risk. And there *are* risks associated with the region: for instance, much of its future growth and prosperity will be greatly influenced by what happens in China – and only a very bold person would bet on its uninterrupted stability and economic growth.

However, we need to distinguish between the risk associated with a *single* investment and that associated with a *portfolio* of investments, as we shall now see.

Most of the developed markets (North America, Europe, Japan) tend to experience economic cycles which go largely in parallel with each other. Although, in practice, the ups-and-downs of the American economy may be a year or so ahead of Europe, nevertheless there is not all *that* much difference in the way these countries behave. Diversifying a portfolio by spreading one's money between the developed countries does not reduce the variability and risk all that much.

On the other hand, the 'emerging' countries march to a completely different drum – or, rather, to several different drums. For instance, the performance of the Hong Kong stock-market is influenced far more by events in or concerning China than by the normal business cycle of the developed world.

They also differ in the ways their stock-market performances vary through the year. I shall be talking in the next lesson about the best time of the year to buy shares. In general, stock-markets tend to fall in October (thus providing a buying opportunity) when there is a seasonal demand for money ahead of Christmas. However, the Hong Kong stock-market seems to be influenced more by the timing of the horse-racing season!

So, the inclusion of some emerging market investments, such as the Far East, in our portfolio can actually *reduce* the overall risk of the portfolio – as well as offering the possibility of higher investment returns. Very much a case of the best of both worlds.

We can illustrate this by drawing a Risk v Reward graph for *portfolios* of investments with different proportions of emerging market shares – see figure 13.4.

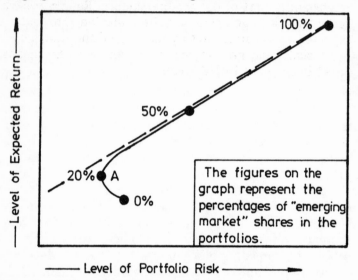

*Figure 13.4* Risk v Reward for different *portfolios* of investments containing increasing proportions of 'emerging markets' shares
© *The Economist*, London (25 September 1993)

As the proportion of 'emerging market' shares increases, we would expect both risk and reward to increase, as shown by the dotted line. In practice, up to the point marked A on the graph, an increasing proportion of the higher-risk, higher-reward investments can actually *reduce* the risk level of the overall portfolio!

An American study of the effects of adding an increasing proportion of emerging market investments, to a portfolio of North American equities, indicated that point A was around 20%. In other words, if about one-fifth of the portfolio were invested in emerging markets, then the general level of portfolio risk would be reduced. (See, for instance, 'Survey of Third World Finance' in *The Economist,* 25 September 1993.)

Actually, I would judge the emerging markets of the Far

East to be much less risky than others (such as the South American countries). Given our regular savings strategy, I would suggest that it makes sense to allocate around 30% of one's High-Risk regular savings to these markets.

This gives us a very good start to deciding on a 'home' for a substantial part of our regular savings. Referring back to figure 13.3, it is going to be quite a challenge to better the expected return indicated by point E on the diagram!

We shall look now to see if we can do so by means of direct investment in UK shares.

## Homework VIII

We are going to look next at investing directly in ordinary shares. It would be useful if you were to go over Lesson VII again, to ensure that you are happy with the description of company accounts; also with personal equity plans. You should also spend a little time studying the share price pages of the *Financial Times*.

*Money Observer* has a regular feature entitled 'Top Companies Update'. This gives ten-year performance records for the major UK companies; it is worthwhile familiarising yourself with the content.

The main object of the next lesson is to help you select, for yourself, a few ordinary shares that might be expected to provide you with long-term growth in the value of your investments. The homework exercises are intended to provide a somewhat light-hearted look at alternative ways of picking 'winners'.

### Exercise 1

Just for fun, I would like you to consider the following four ways of selecting shares:

(a) by sticking a pin at random into the share price pages of the *Financial Times*
(b) by letting a baboon do the job for you (as with an experiment supposedly carried out in Sweden)
(c) by letting intelligent schoolchildren make the selection
(d) by leaving it to experts

The question is: which (if any) of the above methods would you expect to produce a portfolio of shares which would beat the 'All Share Index'?

## Exercise 2

I would like you to do a little research for yourself on the historical performance of experts' 'tips'.

A good place to start is the magazine *Investors Chronicle*. In the middle of each week's issue you will find a section headed 'Popular Shares'. These pages summarise current recommendations from different stockbrokers on those shares which are most widely held by private investors.

What I should like you to do is to see how these recommendations fare over the ensuing six months and twelve months.

There are various ways in which you could do this, some of which mean going along to a library to look up back issues of the magazine.

In the first place, you could just go back twelve months, note the recommendations, and then refer to the *Financial Times* six months and twelve months later (that is, six months ago and the current issue, respectively).

For simplicity, divide the recommendations into three groups according to whether they could be interpreted as 'positive', 'neutral' or 'negative':

Group 1   *('positive')* includes summary recommendations such as 'Buy', 'Long-term Buy', 'Outperform'.

Group 2   *('neutral')* is generally characterised by the rec-ommendation 'Hold': sometimes by 'Weak Hold' or 'Strong Hold'.

Group 3   *('negative')* includes such summary recommen-dations as 'Sell', 'Over-valued', 'Underperform' and 'Take Profits'.

I'm sure that you get the idea. Each recommendation includes (in brackets) the mid-market price at the time the recommendation was made; this would actually be some days before the publication date of the magazine, but this doesn't matter.

For each group, calculate the average change in the share price over the ensuing six and twelve months.

A slightly different approach would be to start with a

table in *Money Observer* headed 'Performance Analysis of All Listed UK Equities'. For each equity (ordinary share) the table indicates the % change over periods of 1 month, 6 months and 1 year. Using this table will avoid having to look up the prices in the *Financial Times*. (We shall ignore the '1 month' figure in the *Money Observer* table.)

Now refer to the back numbers of *Investors Chronicle*, six months and twelve months ago, and again categorise the recommendations into the three groups: 'positive', 'neutral' and 'negative'. See how each of these groups has performed, on average, over the subsequent six and twelve months, using the figures in the *Money Observer* table.

If you do not have access to back numbers of *Investors Chronicle*, then you could simply start by referring to the *current* issue, and then waiting for six or twelve months to do the calculations.

This exercise is another of my 'hostages to fortune'. You may well choose six- and twelve-month periods which end up with the 'wrong' results so far as the next lesson is concerned. Never mind; in the process, you will have usefully familiarised yourself with much published information.

## Exercise 3

One of the factors which we shall consider in the next lesson is that of *timing:* are there particular times of the year which are best for buying and selling shares?

The following homework question is probably only appropriate for those of you who *already* invest from time to time in either ordinary shares or collective funds. The question is this: have you noticed any particular times of the year when:

(a) your interest in investment is at a peak?
(b) your interest is at a very low ebb?

You may not be aware that you are likely to experience such seasonal variations in your enthusiasm for investment, but nevertheless have a think about the question.

# Chapter 14
# Lesson IX: High-Risk Investments – Choosing Shares for Long-Term Growth

We have seen that the Far East is the most promising region for future investment; accordingly, I have suggested that, perhaps, 30% of your regular savings should be allocated to that region.

We don't need to know anything about the individual companies in that region: we are leaving that to the managers of a collective fund.

We *can* hope to know (or to be able to find out) about UK companies, so it is to the UK that we shall naturally turn for direct investment in ordinary shares. By being very selective about the shares we choose, we shall hope at least to match the performance of our Far East fund. The *means* by which we shall invest in UK shares is, I suggest, via a 'self-select' personal equity plan. These plans were introduced in Lesson VII and are very easy to set up and operate, as we have seen.

In principle, we shall create our own 'investment trust' by selecting two or three shares each year to add to our PEP. The main focus of this lesson will be on the selection of appropriate shares.

We can invest on a regular basis into an actual investment trust for as little as £25 per month. For ordinary shares, I suggest that the minimum realistic investment in any one share would be about £1,500 . . . so we are unlikely to be doing this on a monthly basis.

For those of you who *can* contemplate this monthly outlay (and who are married), then this figure of £1,500 per month also represents the *maximum* which you can invest in personal equity plans. The annual limits for each person over 18 are:

General PEP          £6,000
Single company PEP   £3,000

so that two of you *could* invest £18,000 per year between you, or £1,500 per month.

For the majority of people, though, I guess that regular savings with self-select PEPs will mean *once per year* rather than once per month. I would suggest that a realistic minimum annual investment would be £3,000 (which would give you the opportunity of acquiring shares in two companies each year). Unless and until you can put away that amount each year, it would be more appropriate to stick with the regular monthly savings scheme of a Far Eastern investment trust plus possibly a UK tracker fund; the latter can be held within a PEP. (Some tracker PEPs have high charges for regular monthly payments; make sure that you avoid these.)

If we are investing just once per year, we shall need to address the question: is there a best time of year to make our annual contributions to the plan? This question will be answered at the end of the lesson.

To start with, though, we shall look at some selection methods for choosing our shares.

## 'Expert' opinion – some historical evidence

We shall start by looking at the shares which the experts have been advising in recent years. The way in which I have tackled your homework Exercise 2 is as follows.

I took three issues of *Money Observer*, spaced six months apart, and referred to the pages edged in orange entitled 'Performance Analysis of All Listed UK Equities'. For instance, in the January 1996 issue, this table tells us that the share prices and performance statistics were based on the middle-market prices on the morning of 7 December 1995.

I then went back for both 6 months and 12 months prior to that date and looked up the centre pages of *Investors Chronicle* – the section headed 'Popular Shares'. These pages tell you what a selection of stockbrokers were saying, shortly before publication date, on about twenty of the most popular shares; the entries also indicate the market prices at which the recommendations were made.

The stockbrokers' views obviously relate to some time before the publication date of the magazine. However, as an indication of the value *to us* of the recommendations, it is correct to start the clock ticking from the day we can buy the magazine.

Some people may have access to stockbrokers' reports before the magazine is published. So I have also looked at the recommendations made in the *following* week's magazine (by a different selection of stockbrokers), on the assumption that the recommendations were actually made one to two weeks prior to *that* publication date . . . not that this really makes any difference.

This gives me *two* sets of tips, published one week apart, to relate to the *Money Observer* performance tables for six and twelve months later. I've averaged the results for these two sets of tips, as otherwise there would be too few entries in some of the categories, especially the 'hold' and 'sell' categories.

Now, *Investors Chronicle* also publishes a weekly column on 'Brokers' Tips', which is a selection of tips on a much wider range of shares. I repeated the exercise for these tips.

The results of the analysis are presented in table 14.1. They relate to 242 separate share tips.

**Table 14.1   Analysis of performance of share tips over the ensuing six- and twelve-month periods**

| 6 months commencing | 'Popular Shares' 'Buy' | 'Hold' | 'Sell' | 'Brokers' Tips' 'Buy' | 'Hold' | 'Sell' | FT-SE All Share Index |
|---|---|---|---|---|---|---|---|
| June 94 | +4% | +8% | +4% | −3% | −16% | 0% | +2% |
| Dec 94 | +6% | +9% | +8% | +6% | +4% | +11% | +9% |
| June 95 | +1% | +5% | +5% | −1% | −2% | +17% | +8% |
| | +4% | +7% | +6% | +1% | −5% | +9% | +6% |

| 12 months commencing | 'Buy' | 'Hold' | 'Sell' | 'Buy' | 'Hold' | 'Sell' | |
|---|---|---|---|---|---|---|---|
| Dec 93 | −7% | 0% | +4% | −5% | −15% | −9% | −5% |
| June 94 | +10% | +18% | +11% | +8% | −11% | +15% | +11% |
| Dec 94 | +6% | +25% | +15% | +19% | +20% | +10% | +19% |
| | +3% | +14% | +10% | +7% | −2% | +5% | +8% |

You will see that there is no evidence of consistently good performance by the stockbrokers. If we combine the 'Popular Shares' and 'Brokers' Tips', we obtain the following results:

|  | Recommendation | | | |
|---|---|---|---|---|
|  | 'Buy' | 'Hold' | 'Sell' | All Share Index |
| over the next 6 months | +2% | +1% | +7$\frac{1}{2}$% | +6% |
| over the next 12 months | +5% | +6% | +8% | +8% |
| Average | +4% | +4% | +8% | +7% |

Five companies no longer appeared, either six or twelve months later, in the *Money Observer* tables – they had disappeared as a result of being taken over. The recommendations made in respect of these companies were: one 'buy', three 'hold' and one 'sell'. These shares will have performed well, leading up to takeovers, but clearly their omission has not been a factor depressing the 'Buy' group relative to the other groups.

Rather than taking notice of the 'Buy' recommendations, we would do just as well by sticking a pin at random into the share price pages of the *Financial Times*!

I was not able to record all of the tips made in one particular back number of *Investors Chronicle*; someone had ripped out that page of the magazine, presumably with a view to investing some money in the tips. He obviously had faith in the tips; no doubt he has since regretted his action.

A recent article ('Tip-toe guide through the top share tipsters', *Investors Chronicle*, 27 September 1996) indicates that *some* of the people producing subscription tipsheets (and also some newspapers) have, some of the time, offered their readers some excellent tips, as measured by short-term performance. I have no personal experience of any of these tipsheets.

Meanwhile, coming back to the stockbrokers' tips, I wonder if you found similar results, based on different starting dates for the performance evaluations?

If you played hookey and missed out on this homework exercise, I do encourage you to go back and do it for yourself. It should convince you, more than any words of mine, not to expect above-average performance from stockbrokers' tips.

I'm not saying that there are not *some* stockbrokers who have consistently good track records in respect of UK equities; it's just that I haven't yet found them!

What I find more than a little puzzling is that, presumably, there are other people out there in the financial world who are actually paying good money for this 'advice'.

There *is* one well-known name in the United States who *does* command universal respect for his long and outstanding track record. This is Warren Buffett, who has become one of the two richest men in America by virtue of his ability to pick winners for his Berkshire Hathaway Trust.

It is estimated that he has achieved an average annual investment return of nearly 25% pa for forty years. He acquires substantial stakes in a very few companies and stays with those companies for many years.

The process which we shall discuss in a minute is, I believe, entirely consistent with the Buffett philosophy. In particular:

(a) Limiting oneself to a relatively small number of shares; I suggest that your PEP should never contain more than 20 shares.

(b) Only buying shares which you intend to keep for many years. (Don't go in for active management.)

(c) Selecting the shares according to specific criteria, which can be summarised by saying that the companies have strong 'strategic positions' (which I shall define later).

My own experience of following these guidelines so far (after several years' contributions to the plan) is to achieve an average nominal return on a self-select PEP of nearly 20% pa; that represents a *real* return of about 15% pa (double our target return for High-Risk investments). So, you will see that you do not have to be a Warren Buffett to achieve very useful results from your portfolio. For various reasons, I don't expect to be able to keep up this performance for forty years – but there is no reason why you should not try to do so, so long as you are able to start early enough in life.

## Selection criteria

In the Introduction, I mentioned briefly something called the PIMS programme (see page 6). PIMS stands for 'Profit Impact of Market Strategy' although it might, more appropriately, be called 'Profit Impact of *Business* Strategy' as it is not limited to considering 'market' factors. It is widely acknowledged as the world's best database on how businesses perform in real life and I must say that I have been greatly influenced by its insights.

A few years ago, a very popular business book entitled A *Passion for Excellence* said of PIMS that it 'has at its command the most extensive strategic information database in the world'.

You will probably be interested in the origins of this database. It started many years ago in the General Electric Company in America. They noticed that some of their individual businesses consistently produced good results (as measured by the return-on-investment), whereas others consistently produced poor results, no matter how much management effort was devoted to them.

They decided to see, by statistical analysis, whether there were some general features of the individual businesses which were consistently associated with either good or poor performance. It turned out that the answer was Yes.

Later, the project was taken up by the Harvard Business School, who developed the database to incorporate real-life evidence from many different companies and for several separate businesses within each company. The database subsequently moved to an organisation called the Strategic Planning Institute.

Today, the database incorporates information on over 3,000 different businesses, with several years of historical data on each, and with a wide global spread.

It can be used in two principle ways:

(a) to provide general messages which apply, *on average* to all businesses
(b) to look in detail at a specific business, by extracting a relatively few 'look-alikes' from the database and using these to highlight detailed business strategies which have, historically, proved to be winning ones for those 'look-alikes'

We shall, of necessity, use only the first of these approaches. An excellent book on the subject, which will give you much more detail, is *The PIMS Principles – Linking*

*Strategy to Performance* by Robert D Buzzell and Bradley T Gale, (The Free Press, 1987).

Incidentally, if you work for a company which you think could benefit from joining the programme, you can obtain details from PIMS Associates, 7th Floor, Moor House, 119 London Wall, London, EC2Y 5ET (tel 0171 628 1155).

What I am going to do is to approach the selection process in two stages:

(a) identifying the factors which are associated with consistently good *business performance* (in terms of return-on-capital)

(b) seeing whether these factors need to be modified in order to achieve the objective of *increasing shareholder value.*

## Factors associated with good business performance

If you cast your mind back to Lesson VII, you will remember the way in which we outlined the basic financial reports of a company, namely its balance sheet and its profit-and-loss account. You will also recall that I felt it unnecessary for you to study them in very great detail; I indicated that the factors which *really* determine future business performance are, in the main, not to be found in the published accounts.

The key factors which *do* have a pronounced impact on future performance – that is, which contribute to the 'strategic position' of a company, are as follows.

### Market share

Businesses with a high share of their market generate *much* better returns than those with a low share. The PIMS approach actually works on a figure called 'Relative Market Share'; this is the market share of our business divided by those of the largest three competitors combined.

Let me illustrate this with an example. Consider the market for two completely different kinds of products. For instance, product/market X could be food sold in supermarkets and product/market Y could be petrol sold to private motorists. The top four competitors in each product/market might have the following market shares (the figures are imaginary):

| Product/Market X ('Supermarkets') | | Product/Market Y ('Petrol') | |
|---|---|---|---|
| Competitor $A_1$ | 12% | Competitor $A_2$ | 24% |
| Competitor $B_1$ | 10% | Competitor $B_2$ | 20% |
| Competitor $C_1$ | 8% | Competitor $C_2$ | 16% |
| Competitor $D_1$ | 6% | Competitor $D_2$ | 12% |

Product/market Y is a much more 'concentrated' one than product/market X; that is, there are only a few competitors. That is actually another beneficial factor, but the major effect on expected future performance is determined by *relative* market share. Both competitor $A_1$, in its market, and competitor $A_2$, in its market, have relative market shares of 50%.

Similarly, competitors $D_1$ and $D_2$ both have relative market shares of only 20%.

Let us now put into perspective the effect of these relative market shares on return-on-investment (ROI).

All other things being equal, businesses with very high market shares might have ROIs of around 30%, whereas those with very low shares might have ROIs of around 10%. Quite a difference!

## Quality

Perhaps the most important insight from the PIMS database is the enormous impact of quality on business performance.

Now, you would think that 'quality', by definition, was unquantifiable; hence it is going to be difficult to represent it in a mathematical equation. PIMS does actually derive a measure of quality which, whilst fascinating to work through in practice, would be an unnecessary digression for us to consider. Incidentally, as with market share, it is *relative* quality which is important.

Companies whose products (and service) are perceived by the customer to be of high quality significantly outperform their lower-quality competitors. Superficially, the effect is of a similar order to that of market share. It is worth noting, however, that one of the reasons for a company to have acquired a high market share in the first place is likely to have been that it was offering good value for money; so the 'quality' factor contributes both directly *and* indirectly to expected future performance.

The impact of quality on performance always seems rather comforting! It establishes that 'profits' are the *reward* for providing people and firms with the goods and services which they want, and by doing so in a way which provides value for money.

The following three 'anecdotes' will reinforce the quality message.

The retailer Marks & Spencer has a deserved, long-standing reputation for quality in both its products and in the service which it offers its customers. This is reflected in the steady growth of its profits and share price over very many years – but this example also illustrates the difference between quality and relative quality. Several years ago, M & S was unrivalled amongst the High Street department stores: its relative quality was thus very high indeed. In more recent years, its relative quality will have fallen somewhat, but this is no reflection on the company itself; it is just that the other department stores have learned some lessons from M & S and have started to catch up.

Do you subscribe to the Consumers' Association magazine *Which?*, I wonder? If so, you will know that they most often highlight, as their 'best buys', the products which are as good as the competitors' but *cheaper.* How do the shares of 'best buy' companies perform on the stock-market? A study carried out several years ago, I recall, came up with a particularly interesting result. Those companies which offered 'best buy' products by virtue of being cheaper than competitors did *not* have good stock-market records. The shares of companies that *did* perform well were those which offered products which *Which?* recommended, *even though* they were not the cheapest: they were charging somewhat more than competitors, but were offering *very* much better quality.

The opposite effect (selling low-quality products) is epitomised by the example of the former Ratner's chain of jewellers. At a CBI Conference, Gerald Ratner reportedly described his own company's products as 'crap'. The audience loved it, but it was no laughing matter for his shareholders, the value of whose shares faithfully reflected the value of the products!

## Differentiation

Suppose you have two major competitors in a business, both of them offering excellent quality in both products and service. Their *'relative* quality' scores will both be quite average.

They can, however, score 'brownie points' if they *differentiate* themselves from each other in some way: one of the companies may score highly on one particular aspect of quality, whilst its rival scores well on another aspect.

You might like to consider, for yourself, the example which I have used as a practical illustration for students. Think of all the major supermarket chains: Sainsbury, Tesco, Asda, Safeway, Marks & Spencer and so on. Some will tend to outperform the others on the basis of market share and quality (which is also something you could judge), but one or two may also have succeeded in *differentiating* themselves in some way from their rivals. This should contribute to an enhanced return-on-investment.

## Innovation

Another strong plus point is innovation. One way in which companies can develop a competitive advantage is via product and process patents and by generally being more innovative than their rivals.

In the PIMS database, innovation is measured as the proportion of sales revenue which arises from new products (again, relative to the competitors). Highly innovative companies gain market share; moreover, innovation is about the only way in which companies with an already *very* high share of their market can maintain or increase that share.

Innovation is most usually associated with spending on research and development, but it doesn't have to be. You might find it useful to repeat the earlier exercise on supermarket chains, but this time consider which you would regard as the most innovative.

## Capital investment

High levels of fixed capital investment have a surprisingly large *negative* effect on profitability. I suspect that this is because, in a recession, 'capital intensive' businesses compete fiercely on price in an attempt to keep their expensive capital equipment fully utilised.

A high level of capital investment *can* be a positive factor under certain circumstances: if the company is coming out of a recession with a high level of unused or under-utilised equipment, it will be able to expand its sales considerably before needing to consider further investment.

## Employee productivity

Not surprisingly, businesses which have a high level of value-added per employee will outperform similar companies with low employee productivity. Experience suggests that companies with a good image for quality are also the companies with loyal and hard-working employees. So we won't try to evaluate 'productivity' separately.

## Market growth rate

Businesses operating in the higher-growth markets tend to have somewhat higher returns-on-investment, but this effect is nothing like so pronounced as with the factors already mentioned.

## Other factors

There are several 'second-order' factors which affect performance, but it will pay us to concentrate on the most important ones which we have already discussed.

## Factors associated with increasing shareholder value

Businesses with the positive characteristics listed above (that is, with strong 'strategic positions') are the ones most likely to produce excellent results in terms of return-on-investment. How does this translate into performance for the shareholder?

There is, actually, a technical difficulty in carrying out this translation: a company often comprises *several* businesses, not all of which may have the desired characteristics. Also, even if they have, the company's shares may well be priced at such a high price/earnings ratio (see Lesson VII) that the shares are very expensive to buy in relation to future profits.

Luckily, PIMS has tackled this question and comes up with some clear answers.

Basically, the factors which are good for return-on-investment are *also* those which are good for growth in shareholder value. However, there is one very important difference.

In respect of ROI, we saw that market growth rate has only a modest impact on future performance; in terms of shareholder value, it has a *major* impact. Operating in high-growth markets is a key factor which points to likely future appreciation in value to shareholders. This effect is particularly beneficial if a growth in sales leads to a reduction in the ratio of marketing costs to sales revenue.

There are, again, one or two other factors that are relevant which, for simplicity, we shall need to ignore. For instance, the stock-market puts a high value on spending on research and development.

## Summary of key factors

In order to keep things relatively simple, I suggest that it is best to concentrate on just a few key factors. Look for companies with the following characteristics:

- They operate in a *fast-growing market* or markets.
- They have a *high (or increasing) share of their market(s)* – they are number 1 or number 2 in a market where there are not many competitors.
- They have, at least for most of their businesses, *a reputation for quality* (or are in the process of moving 'up market' in terms of quality); if they are clearly 'differentiated' in some way from their competitors, so much the better.
- They have *a reputation for innovation.*
- For companies operating in 'cyclical' businesses (that is, those capital-intensive companies whose fortunes are very dependent upon the state of the business cycle), you could additionally look for companies coming out of recession with *considerable unused capacity.*

Any company which meets at least three (preferably the first four) of these characteristics should be one for your short-list.

You will, I'm sure, be asking yourself: 'Where am I going to get all this information?'

The historical growth in sales revenue is a good starting point. A high growth in sales would suggest either or both:

- that the company is operating in high-growth markets
- that it is gaining market share

Data on historical sales growth can be obtained from several sources, for instance:

- for all UK companies, there is a five-year history in the *Company Guide*, which is updated quarterly
- for nearly 900 top companies, a similar five-year history is contained in the *Financial Times*/Extel publication *Major UK Companies Handbook,* updated half-yearly

- for the top 50 or so companies, there is a ten-year history for a few companies each month in *Money Observer*

This *Money Observer* 'Top Companies Update' also gives clues as to market share. For instance, you may read, at the top of the entry for a particular company, that it is 'a world leader in . . .', 'the UK's largest . . .' or some other expression which will indicate its leading market position.

As far as quality is concerned, an excellent source of information is an annual survey entitled 'Britain's most admired companies', published around December by *Management Today*. (This survey has not been published *every* year; it did not appear in 1991 and 1993, although I hope that it is now a regular annual feature.) Some 250 of Britain's largest companies are asked to rate their *competitors* (not themselves) on various factors such as management quality, financial soundness . . . and several others including product/service quality and capacity to innovate.

These 'most admired companies' would provide you with an excellent start to assembling a short-list of suitable candidates for your PEP.

In parallel with this, you should read as much information as you can which gives background information on companies. The best source is probably *Investors Chronicle*.

Don't forget to use the evidence of your own eyes when it comes to companies selling products or services direct to you, the final consumer. In such cases, *you* are your own best judge as to the quality of a company's products or services, and sometimes even as to how its sales are going.

On one occasion, I had bought the shares of a supplier of ladies' clothing which had impressed me (a mere man) by the quality of its products. Over the subsequent weeks, it registered on me that no one actually seemed to be *buying* these clothes. The realisation dawned in time to sell the shares just a week before they fell in value by one-third as a result of some very poor results.

This is an appropriate moment to refer to the first homework question. Only one of the four selection methods, listed in Exercise 1, generally produces above-average results: not a pin, not the baboon, nor even the experts (as we have seen) . . . but *children!* When children have been asked to select shares, they naturally base their choice on the products which they themselves are buying, or which they see their parents and friends buying. Do keep your eyes open for what is happening in the High Street.

Also, you should spend a little time each week reading up about UK companies in newspapers and magazines. As a result, you will gradually build up a short-list of companies from which to make your annual PEP selection. I suggest that this short-list could eventually grow to about forty companies. From time to time you will delete some companies and add others, but keep the total to around forty.

Each year you will want to choose just two or three from this list. However long your short-list, I further suggest that at no time should the number actually appearing in your PEP exceed twenty. This will mean, as your PEP grows, that you will occasionally need to sell one or two shares to make room for other companies which better match our criteria. By restricting yourself to a maximum of twenty, you will ensure that you have to think very carefully about the relative merits of each candidate.

You can usefully give high priority to short-listed companies which are currently out of fashion with the professionals. We have seen that expert opinion is of little value in identifying winners. Even the best companies go through periods when they are out of favour with the market. When such companies have been out of favour for some while, they are often good 'buys'.

How can you judge that they *are* out of favour? One way is to look at the statistics published in the *Financial Times* share price pages. Such companies will have lower price/ earnings (P/E) ratios and higher dividend yields than they have generally had in the not-too-distant past. Also, their share prices will have fallen over the last twelve months – see the table 'Performance analysis of all listed UK equities' in *Money Observer*.

At any point in time, there are usually one or two whole *sectors* of the market which are out of favour. One of the tables in *Money Observer* is headed 'How the sectors have performed'. This tells you the average performance of the various business sectors over the last 1 month, 6 months and 1 year.

Look at the 12-month figures and you will spot one or two sectors which have significantly underperformed in relation to the market as a whole. If one of your short-listed shares is in one of these sectors, it is worth noting it as a possible 'buy'. There have been plenty of examples in recent years of out-of-fashion sectors which have yielded some very good 'pickings'; for instance: building materials, breweries, pharmaceuticals and food retailers. You can find more information on the performance of stock-market sectors in the *Financial Times*. The relevant table is headed 'FT-SE Actuaries Share Indices'.

Don't acquire shares in a company *just because* it is in one of the underperforming sectors. Make sure that it matches up to at least some of the key characteristics which we listed earlier. I make one final check on a company before going ahead to add it to the PEP:

---

*Thorneycroft's Tenth Law of Successful Investment*
**The ultimate criterion for selecting an ordinary share is that you would be proud to be an owner of the company.**

---

Don't worry if, for the first year or two, your chosen shares don't outperform the market averages. Meanwhile, you will be building up your own invaluable database on good companies, which will stand you in very good stead over the long term.

One additional advantage of 'good' companies is their ability to withstand the worst of a recessionary period. The strength of your portfolio should be most evident at such times of recession.

## When to buy

We now have to decide on a time of year for making our annual contribution to the PEP.

In my earlier book, I presented an analysis of seasonal patterns in a wide range of economic and financial factors, including stock-market performance. For each month of the year, from January to December, I showed the *average* variation from a trend line – see figure 14.1 for an example.

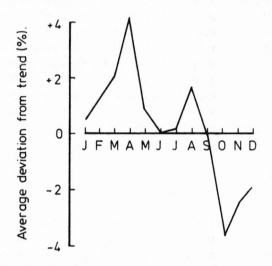

*Figure 14.1* Example of seasonal pattern detected in UK share prices (1976–84)

Many series of economic and financial data have a seasonal pattern which is rather like a distorted letter M; indeed, I call this underlying seasonality 'the M-Factor'. Characteristically, the value (for instance, of share prices) exhibits a pronounced seasonal peak in the spring (around April) and a less pronounced peak around August or September; there is a minor trough in mid-year and a major minimum around October.

The October effect was first identified a very long time ago by a British economist, W Stanley Jevons. In 1866, he published a paper entitled 'Frequent Autumnal Pressure in the Money Market and the Action of the Bank of England'. If you think about the two great stock-market crashes, you will recall that both the Wall Street crash of 1929 and the global equity market crash of 1987 occurred in October. (The long-drawn-out decline in share prices in 1972/74 included periods of panic selling in late autumn of 1973 and 1974.)

The October (or autumn) effect tends to be most pronounced in odd-numbered years. This is not as strange as it may appear at first sight. It seems to be connected with the electoral cycle in the United States: the even years are those in which they are holding either Presidential elections or mid-term elections of senators. For some reason there does not seem to be the same degree of seasonal monetary pressure in these years as there is in the odd-numbered years . . . or so it would appear.

Much of my research into seasonal patterns was focused on measures of business, consumer and investor *confidence.* These exhibit seasonal effects which are both pronounced and consistent. Confidence (as with 'hard' economic data) tends to be at its peak in the spring and at a minimum in the autumn.

How does this fit in with your answer to the questions in homework Exercise 3?

The normal peak of optimism in the spring is accompanied not only by rising share prices, but also by a pronounced peak in the number of share transactions taking place. This is clearly a time to avoid buying shares (but a reasonable time to sell, if you have to); don't be persuaded to jump on to the bandwagon.

I anticipate that you will not normally give much thought to making new investments in the period leading up to Christmas. It is the fact of Christmas which, I believe, is a major influence behind the 'autumnal pressure in the money market' (although, at the time Jevons wrote his paper, it is likely that similar seasonal effects in the agricultural sector were more important). When everyone else is more concerned about the forthcoming Christmas festivities, this is the time to buy!

To be more specific, a good time to choose is a week or two before the Chancellor's budget. Markets tend not to like uncertainty, and there is always some uncertainty, at that time, about the Chancellor's intentions. (Incidentally, in my earlier book on seasonal patterns I came to the specific conclusion that the UK economy would benefit if the budget was moved from spring to autumn. I often wonder whether some correspondence with the Treasury at that time had any influence on the decision to change the budget date; maybe someone will tell me?)

The suggestion, then, is that you fix a date in your diary, for early to mid-November, on which to make your annual subscription to your PEP. I find it useful to start thinking about the choice of companies a couple of months in advance of that date, to give me time to read up the latest information on the short-list of companies, especially in relation to the key factors for success.

If you follow this plan of campaign, you should gradually build up a portfolio of excellent UK companies, whose shares will provide you with long-term and tax-free growth in both dividends and capital value.

# Homework IX

This is the last occasion on which I shall be pressing you to do some work!

The next lesson features a class of investments called 'warrants'. A warrant is a piece of paper which gives you the *right* (but not the obligation) to buy a particular share at some predetermined price, up to some final 'exercise' date. If you do not exercise your right by that date, the warrant lapses and it becomes valueless (clearly a Very-High-Risk investment!).

Warrants have been issued by many investment trusts; also by a few companies.

They are 'tradeable securities' in their own right: in other words, warrants are bought and sold on the stock-market independently of the shares which they represent.

I am going to ask you to think about the value which you would put on a typical warrant.

The example concerns a new investment trust. When it is first issued, investors are given a package comprising five ordinary shares and one warrant; so, if you subscribe at the launch for 1,000 ordinary shares, you will also be given 200 'free' warrants as well. When dealings in the shares commence, the ordinary shares and the warrants are treated as two quite separate investments: subsequently, you can deal (as either a buyer or a seller) in the ordinary shares or in the warrants quite separately.

Each warrant gives you the right (in five years' time) to subscribe 100p for one ordinary share in the company.

To keep things simple, I am going to make two assumptions about the company:

(a) the market price of its shares today is 100p
(b) it pays no dividends (nor is it expected to do so for the next five years)

## Question 1

What value would you place on one warrant:

- (a) if you expect the share price to remain at 100p in five years' time
- (b) if you expect the share price to double to 200p over the next five years?

## Question 2

We will now remove the second of the simplifying assumptions, namely the one about no dividend payments. What would be your answers to Question 1 if the company was going to pay a dividend (after tax) of 3% pa?

# Chapter 15
# Lesson X: Very-High-Risk Investments

The whole idea of a 'Very-High-Risk' investment is, in principle, inimical to our get-rich-slowly approach. There are just a few such investments which I should like to mention out of general interest; and just one (warrants) which could well form part of a regular savings strategy.

## Share 'perks'

As a prelude to mentioning share 'perks' I ought, first, to mention something called 'ethical investing'. Some people dislike the idea of owning shares in companies which produce things like tobacco or alcoholic drinks; or which invest in certain parts of the world regarded as having poor human rights records.

Ethical investors deliberately avoid such companies. I don't really think that you reduce your potential return by ignoring such UK companies, even if they were to meet the key characteristics identified in the previous lesson; there are plenty of other companies to choose from with good strategic positions.

*Excluding* a set of companies in this way is one thing; specifically *including* some for reasons other than their strategic position is quite another.

Many people are attracted to the shares of certain companies because of the perks which go with such share ownership. To choose a share on this basis adds to the risks inherent in buying ordinary shares, and therefore qualifies them for our Very-High-Risk category. Of course, if the company *also* has a strong strategic position, as well as offering perks, then you can get the best of both worlds. At least, you could if you bought the shares *outside* your personal equity plan. Shares held within a PEP do not qualify for perks.

So, just what are these perks that I have been referring to? One of the most popular is that offered by P&O. Holders of 200 or more of their 'deferred shares' are entitled to discounts on ferry crossings, for instance 20% discount on the Portsmouth–Bilbao route.

People who invested, at the outset, in Eurotunnel received travel privileges dependent upon their level of investment.

Still on the subject of travel, British Airways offer holders of 200 shares a 10% discount for themselves and three family members travelling together.

Coming back to earth, relatively small discounts are offered by a wide range of companies – jewellers, hotel groups, brewers, and many more.

You can obtain a £1,000 discount off a McCarthy & Stone retirement home by owning 500 shares in the company.

There are various sources of information on these share perks; for instance:

- *Money Observer* (see, for example, the issue of October 1995)
- Hargreaves Lansdown (tel 0117 988 9880), who produce a booklet on the subject
- occasional articles in other financial magazines and in newspapers

## Capital shares of split-capital investment trusts

You were introduced to split-capital investment trusts in Lesson V. Let me remind you of the concept.

The simplest case is that of an investment trust which is sub-divided into two separate classes of shares:

- *Income Shares* (which receive all of the income received by the trust, but usually none of the capital appreciation)
- *Capital Shares* (which receive none of the income but all of the capital gain when the trust is wound up at some specified future date)

We saw, in that earlier lesson, that the two classes of shares have different risk characteristics. Whereas a conventional investment trust is a High-Risk investment, the split-capital trusts can be considered as:

- *Income shares* – Medium-Risk
- *Capital shares* – Very-High-Risk

Suppose that a management company created a new split-capital investment trust with the following initial capital:

> £10m of Income shares *plus*
> £10m of Capital shares

The trust is wound up after 10 years, by which time we suppose that the investments held by the trust have doubled in value from £20m to £40m. On winding up, in a simple case, the assets would be allocated thus:

- £10m to the holders of the income shares (who will have received all of the income of the trust during its lifetime)
- £30m to the holders of the capital shares

You will see that the capital shares are highly geared investments: the ups-and-downs in the value of these shares will exaggerate the movements in the average value of the investment trust's shareholdings.

Over the last ten years, the FT-SE All Share Index has risen substantially, so it should have been a good period to hold capital shares. Allowing for net re-invested income, a notional investment of £1,000 in the FT-SE All Share Index would have grown to around £3,700. Set against this figure, the performance of capital shares has been rather disappointing, as the following figures show:

> *Value after 10 years of £1,000*
> *initial investment, net income re-invested*

| | |
|---|---|
| Income shares | about £3,200 |
| Capital shares | about £3,600 |

The additional return from the capital shares hardly compensates for the substantially higher risk.

There is a new breed of split-capital trusts which incorporates the zero dividend preference shares (zeros) which were also discussed in Lesson V. You will recall that these zeros are potentially of considerable interest to higher-rate taxpayers.

Some of these newer trusts have quite complicated capital structures. Descriptions of the various types of shares (such as 'highly geared ordinary shares') can be found in the monthly report of the Association of Investment Trust Companies. Some of them are geared to an extreme extent by the high proportion of zeros, and I don't really think that they are relevant to us (apart from the zeros themselves, that is).

If you wish to invest in one of the Medium-Risk *income* shares, it is best to define your requirements clearly, so as not to allow the new breed of split-capital trusts to confuse the issue. When asking your bank or a stockbroker to recommend a specific trust for you, it is best to clearly specify that you are looking for the income shares of a *conventional* split-capital trust (with just income and capital shares and no zero dividend preference shares).

## Warrants

You will recall, from the homework, that a warrant gives the owner the right (but not the obligation) to buy ordinary shares at a fixed price at various dates in the future, up to a final 'expiry' date. If the warrants are not 'exercised' by that date (that is, if they are not converted into ordinary shares), they then cease to have any value.

As Very-High-Risk investments, you may wonder why I am featuring them, given our 'get-rich-slowly' policy. Well, for one thing, many of you may have acquired such warrants 'accidentally', when subscribing to new issues of investment trusts which may, for example, have been brought to the market in packages of shares plus warrants, with one warrant for every five ordinary shares.

More importantly, though, I will go on to suggest an

intriguing warrant-based possibility for inclusion in your portfolio, in which the level of risk is greatly reduced. First, though, let me tell you where you can find out relevant information on warrants.

The current prices of warrants are to be found in the usual *Financial Times* pages 'London Share Service'. Look under the sub-group 'Investment Trusts'. As you look down the list of trusts, you will quickly come across many of them with separate prices quoted for their warrants.

The concept of warrants has been most widely developed with investment trusts, but there are also some industrial and commercial companies which have issued them. A good example is the firm BTR (in the sector: Diversified Industrials).

Coming back to investment trust warrants, there is a separate section on warrants in the monthly information service of the Association of Investment Trust Companies. Their table tells you, *inter alia,* the terms under which the warrants can be converted into ordinary shares; also the last date for so exercising the warrants.

You may already have some warrants and may be wondering what to do with them.

Let's suppose that you had subscribed for shares in a particular trust, and had acquired 10,000 ordinary shares plus 2,000 warrants. The warrants carry the right to be converted into additional ordinary shares – at fixed times during the next five years – at 100p per ordinary share, whatever the stock-market price of the shares might be at that time.

One year after issue, we might find that the stock market-prices were:

- ordinary shares    105p
- warrants          20p

I understand that many private investors have already converted such warrants into ordinary shares by paying the 100p conversion price. What *should* they have done? Well, clearly, if they really wanted to acquire more ordinary shares, it would have been better to *sell* the 2,000 warrants in the market for 20p each and, separately, to *buy* 2,000 ordinary shares at 105p each. Compared with converting the warrants, it is true that the ordinary shares have cost us an extra 5p per share, but this is more than made up for by the cash which we would receive by selling the warrants on the stock-market, even after paying dealing charges.

Had we initially acquired just 1,000 ordinary shares (and consequently 200 warrants), then of course the charges involved in buying and selling small amounts would alter the picture. Incidentally, acquiring more ordinary shares by converting the warrants does *not* incur any charges . . . just the exercise price, which is usually (but not always) 100p per share.

In the above example, I've just picked out of the air a warrant price of 20p. We turn next to look at just how much a warrant is really worth. This was your first homework question. The share price of *that* company was assumed to be 100p.

We start off on the basis that we really *want* to have 1,000 shares in the company (whether it be an investment trust or any other company issuing warrants). Remember that, for the moment, the company does not pay any dividends.

First, consider what kind of return (net of tax and ignoring the deduction for inflation) you could obtain from one of our Low-Risk investments, the ones having fixed nominal capital and a fixed interest rate. We want one which gives us a guaranteed cash sum in five years' time; so it could be any one of:

- National Savings fixed-interest certificates
- National Savings capital bonds
- Building society term accounts (with interest re-invested)
- Building society 'escalator' bonds (again with interest re-invested)
- Insurance companies' guaranteed growth bonds

Suppose that you can obtain a total net return (*not*, note, a total net *real* return) of almost 6% pa. This means that, at the end of five years, an initial investment of £1,000 would have grown to £1,330. Put another way, an investment of £750 would have grown to £1,000 after five years.

I should like to suggest to you that you should be *indifferent* as to which of the following routes you took to acquire the 1,000 shares in the company. (For simplicity, I am ignoring dealing charges.)

(a) You acquire 1,000 ordinary shares at 100p each for a total of £1,000

(b) You acquire 1,000 warrants at a price of 25p each (costing £250) and invest the remainder of your £1,000 (ie £750) in a five-year bond yielding almost 6% pa

At the end of five years, your Low-Risk investment will have turned the £750 into £1,000. You can then use this £1,000 to convert your warrants (at the 'exercise' price of 100p per share) into 1,000 ordinary shares.

So, at the end of five years, you have got 1,000 ordinary shares, whichever route you took. On that basis, the value of a warrant to you is 25p.

I have found that most people, when presented with the homework question, come up with a much lower figure for the value of the warrants ... most frequently 10p, but sometimes up to 15p. It comes as a surprise to find that a warrant could be worth over 20p.

Now, I suggested that you should be indifferent to the two ways of acquiring the 1,000 shares. In fact, you are actually somewhat *better* off by choosing the warrant route. This is because the share price of our company may *fall* over the five years. If, at the end of five years, the share price has actually fallen to 80p, then we can save ourselves some money. We let the warrants lapse, and write off the investment in them; at the same time, we now need only £800 of our accumulated growth fund to acquire the shares; we can pocket the remaining £200. So, we end up with 1,000 shares *plus* £200 in cash.

We can look at a few variations on this calculation, to show just how variable can be the value of a warrant. If (perhaps because our investor now does not pay tax) we find that we can obtain 8% pa on a five-year bond, then the warrant is actually worth considerably more. We now have to invest only £680 in a five-year bond to produce £1,000 after five years. This leaves us with £320 to invest in 1,000 warrants, so we could pay as much as 32p each.

So far, we have assumed that the company pays no dividend. If the company *does* pay an after-tax dividend of 3% pa (homework Question 2), then the warrant is worth very much *less*. If we acquire the 1,000 shares via the warrant route, then – for the comparison to be a fair one – we need to set aside £30 per year from our capital to pay ourselves an annual 'dividend'. Over five years, we should need to allocate nearly £150 for this 'dividend'. (Not quite the full £150, strictly speaking, because some of this money would be earning interest in the early years; but we can assume, for simplicity, that this is offset by the fact that the company may increase its actual dividend over the five-year period.)

In this example, you should be indifferent to the following two routes:

(a)  As before, you acquire 1,000 ordinary shares at 100p each, for an outlay of £1,000.

(b)  You still need to put aside £750 which, invested at almost 6% pa for five years, will produce the £1,000 needed to exercise the warrants. *In addition*, you need to put aside £150 to compensate for the dividends forgone. This leaves just £100 for buying 1,000 warrants.

In this case, the value to you of the warrants is only 10p each.

Have you noticed something a little odd in the way I have arrived at the answers to the homework questions? You will see that I have done so without having to make any projection as to the likely future value of the ordinary shares. It does not matter whether, in five years' time, the shares are 100p, 200p . . . or anything else (so long as they haven't actually gone down in value).

This is because I have treated you as an *investor,* who is definitely interested in acquiring shares in the company. This distinguishes you from a *speculator,* who is only interested in making a profit on the warrants; he has no intention of actually converting them into ordinary shares.

We are going to look, next, at how the value of the warrants appears to the speculator. No, don't panic! I'm not going to throw overboard our 'get-rich-slowly' policy – but it is useful to look at warrants through the eyes of the speculator, as part of the process leading up to identifying a specific investment idea.

This time we *shall* have to consider the possible future price of the shares.

We assume that, nearly five years ago, you bought 1,000 warrants at 25p each, with every intention of converting them tomorrow, the last possible day for exercising them, into 1,000 ordinary shares. With just one day to go to the final exercise date, you see that the ordinary shares have risen in price from 100p to 200p. What is the market price of the warrant at this point in time?

Remember that each warrant gives you the option to acquire one ordinary share for an additional outlay of 100p. Logically, therefore, the warrants should now be priced at 100p. This is again arrived at by considering two options between which an investor should be indifferent (a *new* investor in this case, just buying the shares or warrants for the first time):

(a) The new investor acquires 1,000 ordinary shares at 200p each, for a total outlay of £2,000

(b) At 100p per warrant, he could acquire 1,000 warrants for £1,000 and then, the next day, spend another £1,000 to convert the warrants into ordinary shares

You are just about to convert *your* warrants into ordinary shares, when you are overtaken by a fit of speculative mania! You think to yourself: 'If I sell my warrants on the stock-market today, I shall receive 100p each, which means that I will have *quadrupled* my investment in five years! Why bother with ordinary shares when I can do so much better with warrants?'

You are suddenly in danger of becoming a speculator in warrants, rather than an (indirect) investor in ordinary shares . . . forgetting that the warrants could have become worthless!

In your saner days, as an investor, you worked out the value of a warrant to you by reference to the 6% pa which you would obtain on a Low-Risk investment. Our speculator, though, is not interested in such modest returns. He will aim, I suggest, for a return of *at least* 10% pa above inflation – in line with the assumption we made in Lesson I about the 'expected' return on Very-High-Risk investments. Adding in something for inflation, he is thinking more in terms of, perhaps, 15% or even 20% pa nominal return on his investment.

**Table 15.1  Evaluation of warrants by a mythical speculator**

| | | | At the end of five years | |
| --- | --- | --- | --- | --- |
| **Ordinary shares** | | | **Warrants (assuming no dividend)** | |
| **Average annual growth rate** | **Share price (p)** | **Warrant price (p)** | **Starting price of warrants to give capital growth of:** | |
| | | | **(a) 15% pa** | **(b) 20% pa** |
| 5% | 127 | 27 | 13.4p | 10.9p |
| 10% | 161 | 61 | 30.3p | 24.5p |
| 15% | 201 | 101 | (50.2p) | 40.6p |
| 20% | 249 | 149 | (74.1p) | (59.9p) |

If our speculator had been around five years ago, when the company was first floated on the stock-market, he *would* have had to speculate on the likely growth in the price of the ordinary shares. To produce a nominal return of 15% or 20% pa, he might have performed the kind of calculations shown in table 15.1.

He will have chosen the warrants of this company because he thinks that the company's shares will perform well. So he might, quite realistically, be prepared to pay somewhere between 13p and 40p for each warrant, depending on his assumptions and objectives.

Note that I have put some of the answers in table 15.1 in brackets. If the 'target' rate of return is 15% pa, and it is projected that the ordinary shares will rise at that rate, even our speculator should prefer to pay 100p for the ordinary shares rather than 50.2p for the warrants.

Interestingly, *on average,* it looks as if the speculator would value the warrants, initially, at more-or-less the same level (about 25p) as the investor.

So, it looks as if these warrants at about 25p each are an interesting prospect to quite a variety of potential buyers, ranging from the solid investor to the out-and-out speculator, and with all shades of risk-aversion in between. Sometimes the warrant will be worth rather more to the speculator than to the investor; sometimes it will be the other way round.

One consequence of this is that there should always be an 'active' market in these warrants, at least in the warrants of the most reputable companies. All kinds of people will be doing their sums on the value, to them, of the various warrants, and deciding to buy (or sell) if the warrant price deviates from their evaluation. Holding a portfolio of warrants is, I suspect, one of the very rare cases in which there is something to be said for active management; this is because 'management' can be reduced, to some extent at least, to a mathematical formula.

The next step is to look at the way in which warrant prices react to changes in the ordinary share price. The calculations are summarised in table 15.2. The starting points for the calculations are those which we have used already; namely, a share price of 100p and a warrant price of 25p.

## Table 15.2   Effect on warrants of different changes in the price of the ordinary shares

**Starting prices:**

| | Share price 100p | Warrant price 25p |
| --- | --- | --- |

**After five years:**

| % change in share price | Share price | Warrant price | % change in warrant price |
| --- | --- | --- | --- |
| A  −100% | nil | nil | −100% |
| B  −50% | 50p | nil | −100% |
| C  nil | 100p | nil | −100% |
| D  +50% | 150p | 50p | +100% |
| E  +100% | 200p | 100p | +400% |
| F  +150% | 250p | 150p | +600% |
| G  +200% | 300p | 200p | +800% |
| H  +250% | 350p | 250p | +1,000% |
| J   +300% | 400p | 300p | +1,200% |

Changes in the warrant price are clearly *very* highly geared: the effects of the share price movements are magnified up to four-fold, so that warrant prices can be expected to be very volatile.

Warrants are also clearly much more risky than ordinary shares; if the ordinary share price does not increase at all over the period up to 'maturity', then the warrants become valueless and the whole of the stake money is lost.

You can anticipate, from table 15.2, that you only need one winner to offset the losses from several losers. Suppose that each row in table 15.2 represents the actual performance of the shares of one of nine companies, A to J inclusive. Company A has collapsed completely, B has had a very poor run, whereas G, H and J have at least trebled in value.

The averages of the various performance statistics illustrated in table 15.2 are:

% change in share price      + 100%
% change in warrant price    + 422%

If we take just the first five companies, A to E inclusive, the averages are:

% change in share price      nil
% change in warrant price    + 40%

It is intriguing to note that a *spread* of warrants has produced a positive return even when the average price of the ordinary shares has remained static. This is the natural outcome of the way in which warrants work.

You will already have anticipated that we are going to reduce drastically the risk associated with warrants by buying them on a regular monthly basis. Some time ago, I contacted the managers of a Far Eastern investment trust to ask if their monthly savings plan applied to the warrants. The answer was No, for a rather odd reason. The managers considered warrants too risky to offer on a regular monthly basis — yet they were quite happy to issue the warrants in the first place, which would then be bought and sold in lump-sums, which is *far* more risky.

You are probably ahead of me in anticipating the conclusion which I am leading up to.

It seems to me that warrants offer a very interesting investment, so long as:

- the investment is spread over many separate warrants
- the fund is actively managed to search out differences between warrant prices and their intrinsic value
- money is invested on a regular monthly basis, to benefit from the high level of volatility

In other words, what we have are the classic reasons for choosing a regular savings plan of a collective fund; but, in this case, the fund will be invested in warrants rather than ordinary shares.

There are just a very few such collective funds available including, so far as I know, only one investment trust. I hope that others will come along (with low-cost savings schemes) to expand the market.

Those that do exist have been on offer for only a few years, during which time warrants have been rather out of fashion (which is a hopeful sign for the future!). More surprisingly, the prices of these funds have not actually been very volatile, but this may be just a short-term phenomenon.

Putting perhaps 5% or 10% of your regular monthly savings into such a fund *could* provide the icing on your investment cake.

You have come to the end of the course, but not of the book. At least there is no more homework for you to do!

The final section of the book will help you to revise what you have learned during the course. In Chapter 16, I will suggest a way of looking at a complete investment plan. The development of this plan will serve to remind you of the various individual investments. I will also suggest how you might usefully narrow down the range of investments on which to concentrate.

Finally, in Chapter 17, I shall draw together some of the general themes which run through the course.

# Part C
# Summary

# Chapter 16
# An Investment Strategy

Having now completed the basic course, your feeling is probably one of bemusement at the enormous range of opportunities, so a little revision is probably in order. At the same time, we shall seek to narrow down the range of options somewhat, especially for our regular savings.

In the process, I think that it will help if I show you how to construct an investment plan for yourself. The details of your plan will depend on your personal circumstances: your age; whether you are in work or, perhaps, retired; your income and tax positions; your existing capital; whether or not you need an immediate boost to your income; your attitude to risk; and your investment objectives. But the general *structure* of the plan which I shall outline is one which anyone can adapt to their personal circumstances.

The combination of the general plan, plus the short-list of specific investment options, is what I call a long-term investment 'strategy'.

Figure 16.1 gives the broad outlines of the plan, indicating the specific course lessons appropriate to each entry.

It is useful to think of your money as being allocated between three broad groups:

- Working accounts
- Lump-sums
- Regular savings

It is also useful to think of the development of the plan, over time, in terms of Three Ages of Investment:

*First Age:* young people starting out on working life, who can't really save much, other than as a by-product of paying off their mortgage.

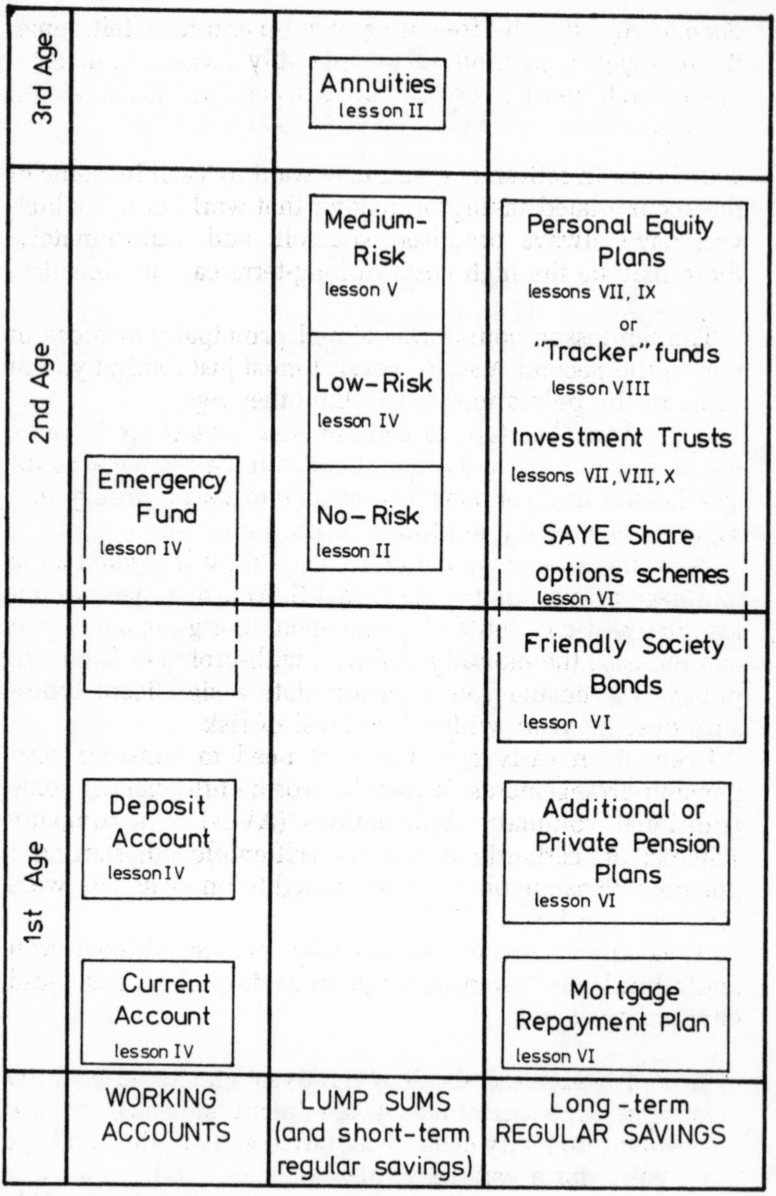

| 3rd Age | | Annuities<br>lesson II | |
| 2nd Age | | Medium-<br>Risk<br>lesson V<br><br>Low-Risk<br>lesson IV<br><br>No-Risk<br>lesson II | Personal Equity<br>Plans<br>lessons VII, IX<br>or<br>"Tracker" funds<br>lesson VIII<br><br>Investment Trusts<br>lessons VII, VIII, X<br><br>SAYE Share<br>options schemes<br>lesson VI |
| | Emergency<br>Fund<br>lesson IV | | |
| 1st Age | | | Friendly Society<br>Bonds<br>lesson VI |
| | Deposit<br>Account<br>lesson IV | | Additional or<br>Private Pension<br>Plans<br>lesson VI |
| | Current<br>Account<br>lesson IV | | Mortgage<br>Repayment Plan<br>lesson VI |
| | WORKING<br>ACCOUNTS | LUMP SUMS<br>(and short-term<br>regular savings) | Long-term<br>REGULAR SAVINGS |

*Figure 16.1* Structure of an investment plan

*Second Age:* the children are grown up and have left home; the mortgage is paid off; there's possibly a legacy to invest – this is the time when one can hope to accumulate significant savings.

*Third Age:* in retirement, you may want to 'cash in' some of the accumulated savings to pay for that world cruise which you have always promised yourself; and, unfortunately, there may be the high costs of long-term care to consider.

The ten-lesson course was aimed principally at those of you in the Second Age. However, I must just remind you of some of the points relevant to the other Ages.

Right from the start, as soon as you have some income, you will need a current account and, later, a deposit account (see Lesson III). You may also be able to start building up a separate emergency fund (see, again, Lesson III).

Your major financial commitment is most likely to be the mortgage on your house (Lesson VI). You may need to opt for the lower-cost route of a repayment mortgage; but, if you can increase the monthly outlay, a with-profits endowment policy will enable you to accumulate a significant lump-sum over 25 years with a low level of risk.

Even at an early age, you will need to consider your pension arrangements. It may be worthwhile making some additional voluntary contributions (AVCs) to a company scheme; or, certainly if you are self-employed, starting a personal pension plan. Some thoughts on pensions were also given in Lesson VI.

As soon as there is any monthly income left over, you could think about starting a regular savings plan. You could choose between:

(a) A friendly society plan – Lesson VI. (Because of the very high percentage taken in initial charges, these plans do really need to be started early in life and kept going for a *very* long time.)
(b) Regular savings into an investment trust – Lesson VIII

Jumping to the Third Age, you will have (all being well) a reasonable income from your pension, from your lump-sums and also from your accumulated regular savings plans. Nevertheless, you may wish to (or need to) augment this income. To do so, you may well wish to convert some of the accumulated High-Risk savings into lower-risk, lump-sum investments yielding a higher rate of interest (thereby forgoing the possibility of future capital gain).

It is in this Third Age that corporate bonds (Lesson V) eventually have a possible role to play. By that stage of life, you may have accumulated substantial investments in your PEP. Up to now, you should have let the dividend interest roll up within the PEP, to maximise the amount which is sheltered from tax. Late in life one worthwhile option is to convert, within your PEP, your holding of shares or units into corporate bonds . . . and then also to start withdrawing the annual interest to give a tax-free boost to your income.

From age 75 onwards, a conventional annuity is feasible; with the benefit of index-linking, though, it is now possible to entertain the possibility of an annuity much earlier – see Lesson II. There are many variations of annuities, especially for married couples, so it is as well to seek independent advice on the alternatives.

It is particularly when you are in the Second Age that you have a vast array of options to choose from.

A key feature of our plan is to draw a clear distinction between:

(a) *Lump-sum investments* which should be chosen from the *'investing-for-income'* products discussed in Lessons II to V inclusive
(b) *Regular savings schemes* which should be chosen from the *'investing-for-profit'* products discussed in Lessons VI to X inclusive

Whenever you are fortunate to receive a substantial lump-sum (for instance, on maturity of an endowment policy or as a result of a legacy), I suggest that you should resist the temptation to allocate part of it to a High-Risk investment, other than as the first instalment of a savings plan. By saving on a regular basis, you convert a High-Risk investment into no worse than a Medium-Risk one . . . *and* increase your expected rate of return at the same time.

With so many different investments to choose from, it is useful to narrow down the list to just a few broad categories. I would suggest that you can develop an excellent plan based on the following range of options.

*For lump-sums*

| | |
|---|---|
| ● National Savings products | Lessons II, IV |
| ● Banks and building societies – term, notice and escalator accounts; and PIBS | Lesson IV |
| ● Gilts (especially index-linked and short-dated) | Lessons II, IV |
| ● Investment trusts (income shares of split-capital trusts, and zero dividend preference shares) | Lesson V |

Single-premium insurance bonds (which actually appear in Lesson VI) look set to lose some of their former appeal to higher rate taxpayers.

*For regular savings*

| | |
|---|---|
| ● Investment trusts (especially Far East) | Lessons VII, VIII, X |
| ● Self-select personal equity plans (or a tracker PEP | Lessons VII, IX Lesson VIII) |
| ● SAYE share option schemes | Lesson VI |
| ● Friendly society bonds | Lesson VI |

There is an intermediate category, namely that of regular savings for a limited period with the specific objective of *spending* the money, at the end of the period, on a major capital item such as a car or house improvements. In this case, you don't want to take much risk with your regular savings plan. For such *short-term* regular savings, it is best to choose one of the options from the 'investing-for-income' category. If your time horizon is not less than five years, then a TESSA would be worth considering.

If you concentrate on these options, and learn all you can about them, you should be able to meet any investment objective. It will then be unnecessary to worry about the plethora of other investments on offer. One of the reasons for omitting conventional unit trusts from the list (apart from their charges) is that there are simply too many of them, and it's far too much effort to make a selection from them.

One of the main functions of lump-sum investments is to provide 'feeder' money for regular savings plans. Looked at in this way, it is quite reasonable to consider lump-sum investments which give a high return at the expense of a diminution in the real value of the capital; even, indeed, a diminution in the nominal value of the capital. In this way, you will increase the rate at which you can feed your regular savings schemes which, over the long term, are likely to give higher rates of return.

With this in mind, your lump-sum allocation could include some 'annuity-type' investments, in which the capital is eroded in order to generate higher income. Examples of this could be:

- Conventional gilts with a high current yield, but a capital loss on maturity – Lessons IV and V
- Income shares of split-capital investment trusts – Lesson V

Annuity-type products convert capital into income and hence increase the liability for income tax. They are, thus, really appropriate only for any non-taxpayers in the family.

Genuine annuities do not penalise taxpayers in this way: *part* of the income is treated as a repayment of one's own capital, and that part is not liable for income tax. You can obtain a high monthly feeder income for ten years by taking out a *temporary* annuity for that length of time.

Whichever lump-sum investments appeal to you, it is important to use our step-by-step calculation process, in order to calculate the Total Net Real Return on the various options. These returns then need to be compared with the benchmark returns for the particular level of risk. Don't forget that the ultimate benchmark is the return which you could obtain on index-linked gilts.

Don't choose an annuity type of investment *just* for its higher return if it doesn't also pass the benchmark test.

Beware of the possibility of being pushed into a higher tax bracket by high-yielding investments.

The *structure* of the plan, illustrated in figure 16.1, is something that should be permanent. Within that structure, however, you will need to keep an eye on the specific components. This is particularly true of the lump-sum investments. Interest rates on the different products change from time to time; hence there will be occasions when you need to make a switch from one product to another. (Make sure that you don't incur undue penalties by so doing.)

With regular savings, on the other hand, you should expect to continue with the same components year after year. (You may, of course, be able to increase the *level* of the regular contributions from time to time.)

The clear separation which we have made, between lump-sums and regular savings, has an important side-effect. As a result of this policy you will, over time, gradually be increasing the proportion of your total capital which is invested in High-Risk products. This fits in well with your changing risk profile as your capital expands: in the early years, with only limited capital, you will want to keep it all in relatively safe investments; as your pool of money grows, you will be comfortable with an increasing proportion of High-Risk investments, at least up to retirement.

I hope that this short refresher will have helped to remind you of the key investment opportunities which you learned about in the course. I also hope that it will have helped to focus your attention on just a few of the vast array of investment opportunities.

Right at the beginning of the book I quoted the words of Warren Buffett on being a successful investor: 'What is needed is a sound intellectual framework for making decisions and the ability to keep emotions from corroding that framework.' In this chapter, we have set out a framework for our investment decisions. In the final chapter, I shall be commenting, amongst other things, on some of the 'emotional' factors which all too often cloud the decision-making process.

# Chapter 17
# Concluding Remarks

In this last chapter, I am going to remind you of some of the general themes running through the course. In the process, I shall stray somewhat from the factual analysis presented in the course, and allow myself the opportunity to express some personal opinions and suggestions.

## Three investment enemies

The value to us of an investment can be seriously eroded by three factors: tax, inflation and management charges. I would like to put all of these together, for a notional investment, just to remind you of the cumulative effect.

Suppose that an investment manager achieves an excellent gross return of 13% pa on an investment portfolio, and that his fund pays income and capital gains tax at a 23% rate. His charges to investors (including an initial fee of 5%) reduce the return to the investor by an average of 2% pa. Inflation is assumed to be 4% pa.

This is what our calculation would look like:

*To the investment manager*

| | |
|---|---|
| Gross return (income + capital gain) | 13% |
| *minus* Tax (at 23%) | –3% |
| = Net Return | 10% |

*To the investor*

| | |
|---|---|
| *minus* Management charges | –2% |
| = Net Return | 8% |
| *minus* Inflation | –4% |
| = **Total Net Real Return** | **4% pa** |

Each £100 of the gross return made on the investments is

thus shared out as follows:

| | |
|---|---|
| Tax | 23% |
| Management charges | 15% |
| Inflation | 31% |
| Investor | 31% |
| | **100%** |

If all three enemies are at work, as in the above example, the investor is left with a very poor deal (and the rates which I have selected for tax, charges and inflation are not excessive).

Not all of these enemies will be eroding all of our investments: some products are tax-free; others don't involve any management charges; and some are index-linked against inflation.

Nevertheless, the general message is clear: *always* evaluate and compare investments on an after-tax, after-charges and after-inflation basis.

## Regular savings

A prominent theme of the course is the value of regular savings schemes for a particular category of investments; namely, the High-Risk 'investing-for-profit' category.

We *substantially* reduce the risks by subscribing on a regular monthly (or annual) basis. This introduces a very significant 'comfort factor': if the investment goes up in value, we are happy with the thought of the capital appreciation of our accumulated savings; if the investment goes down in value, we are happy in the knowledge that we shall acquire more units (or shares) at that time.

We not only feel comfortable with the volatile performance of High-Risk investments; we also *profit* from it, because of the higher rates of return resulting from pound cost averaging.

This relaxed view is in stark contrast to the behaviour of conventional stock-market operators.

It is a well-known phenomenon that stock-market investors typically go through alternate phases of greed and fear. When the market is rising, investors rush in to jump on the bandwagon, as their greed instinct is fed by the belief that there are easy gains to be made. Greed sometimes reaches manic proportions right at the top of a market.

Conversely, when a market has been falling for some time, it is usually very near the end of that fall that fear takes over; there can be violent attacks of panic selling at and near the bottom of the market.

It is comforting to have immunised ourselves against such manic-depressive behaviour.

Even excluding these extremes, I find the attitude of most stock-market investors to be a little puzzling. Investors always seem to view rising prices as a positive phenomenon; falling prices are viewed as negative. In the long run, we certainly hope that the *trend* is upwards, as company profitability increases, but to worry about short-term downs always seems to me to be a little odd: it's rather like hoping that Marks & Spencer will double the prices of all their clothes, just so that the clothes already in our wardrobes will be worth twice as much.

Buying shares – like buying clothes – is a continuous process, and not something that happens just once in a lifetime.

Our regular savings philosophy accepts this reality and exploits the psychology of the stock-market.


## The 'Preclusion Principle'

This is the name I give to another general principle which has probably not yet really struck you.

It is often the case that the making of one investment *precludes* others from consideration. So, however tempting an investment looks, always ask yourself whether it would preclude others.

Some specific examples of this are as follows:

(a) You are allowed only one general personal equity plan

each year. If you take out a managed PEP, whether it be a corporate bond PEP or any other kind, then you are precluding yourself from the option of choosing a self-select PEP.

(b) Similarly, if you decide to take out one of the new 'PEP mortgages', you are precluding the opportunity of starting a straightforward PEP *for a very long time.*

(c) Furthermore, if you choose *any* High-Risk investment for your mortgage repayment or your pension plan, then you are (or *should* be) precluding yourself from allocating *additional* money to other High-Risk investments, which may give you a higher return; otherwise you would be exposing yourself to too high an average level of risk.

(d) If you allocate part of your regular annual savings to a TESSA, then you are again precluding yourself from using that money for some other (higher-risk, higher-return) regular savings plan.

(e) Everyone has a limited tax-free allowance. Using up the whole of that allowance with very high-yielding, taxable investments means that you are precluding the opportunity of investing a much higher sum tax-free (in, for instance, index-linked gilts, where much of the return will be in the form of a tax-free capital gain).

In its most general form, the Preclusion Principle means that *any* one investment precludes you from assigning that money to *any other* investment. So it is very important that you undertake the Total Net Real Return calculations, especially on Low-Risk investments, to make sure that you have chosen the right one(s).

This is a most valuable discipline. For just the same reason, I suggested that you limit your self-select personal equity plan to no more than 20 shares; this again imposes a great discipline, and ensures that you don't leave any poor performers in the portfolio.

## Ethical investing

I mentioned ethical investing in Lesson X in relation to UK equities. Many people prefer to avoid investing in certain types of companies (for instance tobacco and alcoholic drinks). I suggested that this need not limit your potential for long-term growth.

There *is*, however, one aspect of ethical investing which certainly *could* limit your potential returns. This concerns any inhibitions you may have about investing in the Far East.

Understandable concern has been expressed, for instance, at the record of China in respect of human rights; you may have other concerns about countries in that region.

I can well understand that quite an effort of will may be required to keep emotions at bay in such cases. I must say that I do not find this a personal problem: I am just as horrified by the well-publicised failure of the UK to satisfy the right of every responsible child to a good understanding of reading, writing and arithmetic . . . and I am quite happy to invest some of my capital and regular savings in the UK.

## Quality

You were encouraged, during the course, to ignore the latest fashions. The spirit of the age in the Western world is to emphasise equality rather than quality; one is not supposed to discriminate (or, in our terms, 'differentiate') between anything.

For our investment plan, on the other hand, we must always seek out quality and differentiation if we are to be successful.

These concepts were most strongly evident in our selection of ordinary shares. We also need to look at the quality of investment returns with our lump-sum investments, in terms of what they mean to us after allowing for tax, charges and inflation; and we shall need to differentiate between returns in the form of taxable income and those in the form of tax-free capital gains.

We may also need to differentiate between the quality of

different providers of investment products, in terms of the future stability and reliability of the organisations concerned. *Never* be tempted to opt for an extra ½% or 1% of additional interest if it means depositing your money with some organisation which may be judged to be less than 100% safe and secure.

## An idea for an 'added-value' investment product

I've been thinking about those 'safe and secure' financial institutions, and wondering if I could dream up a new investment product which *would* justify the kind of charges which they normally like to levy. The result of this deliberation is the Thorneycroft Bond, which is presented here as a challenge to the financial industry.

It combines two key components of our plan into one package:

(1) a No-Risk lump-sum investment, the (index-linked) yield from which feeds, on a regular monthly basis . . .
(2) a low-cost unit trust (for instance, a tracker fund or a Far Eastern trust)

In more detail . . .

The lump-sum would buy a ten-year, *index-linked* temporary 'protected' annuity. A 4% pa index-linked yield plus the gradual repayment of capital over the ten years would give a total income of 12% pa initially, increasing each month by the rate of inflation.

This income would feed monthly into the unit trust, which would have an offer-to-bid spread of no more than 5%; and the annual management charge would be no more than 1% pa (For this bond, a unit trust is actually more appropriate than an investment trust).

There would be a six-monthly progress report, indicating:

- the residual value of the lump-sum
- the accumulated value of the units
- the 'surrender value' in case an investor wishes to cash

in the policy early (a penalty of 10% in the first year,
decreasing by 1% per year would seem reasonable)

At the end of ten years, the investor could either retain the
accumulated units or receive a lump-sum equal to the value
of those units.
The benefits would be . . .

## To the investor

- Complete security of the annual income.
- The ability to use a *temporary* index-linked annuity
  (something which seems hard to find).
- A high 'feed rate' into what should prove to be a very
  good investment. (It's actually quite difficult for taxpayers to find a good No- or Very-Low-Risk investment
  which can provide a high regular monthly income to
  'feed' a savings plan.)
- Fixed regular payments in *real* terms, rather than just in
  nominal terms.
- A Low-Risk investment with good prospects for growth.
- A simple package: a £10,000 lump-sum would acquire,
  initially, £100 of units each month; this amount would
  rise each month in line with inflation.

## To the manager

- Any investment manager worth his salt should be able to
  project a real, after-tax return averaging at least 6% pa.
  On that basis, he would make – on average – at least a
  2% profit margin each year on the residual value of the
  lump-sum.
- The manager *earns* his money because he is shouldering
  the risk, which he is better able to do than is the investor
  (especially since he would be receiving money for
  investment on a continuous basis).
- His margin would be a highly 'geared' return on his
  investment performance; there would be a great incen-
  tive to achieve (and to justifiably profit from) superior
  performance. This would be a *very* much better reward

system than the usual one based simply on a percentage of the asset value of a fund.

● The manager could offer a range of bonds. For instance, some which I should like to see would be based on:

- A UK tracker fund ('PEP-able' for those who don't wish to manage their own self-select PEP)
- Emerging markets, especially the Far East
- Gold mining shares
- Warrants

All are appropriate candidates for regular savings schemes funded by risk-free annuities.

Indeed, for money which can be left untouched for ten years, one could have a perfectly reasonable, simple investment strategy in which *substantially all* of one's lump-sum and regular savings were combined in the form of these four bonds (with capital allocated between them, perhaps, in the ratio 5:3:1:1). So long, that is, as the financial institutions providing these bonds were absolutely safe-and-secure.

Any takers?

Or is there no one out there who has sufficient confidence in their investment skills?

## Thorneycroft's last theorem

I have been rather critical, not only of management charges, but also of the track records of experts and professionals . . . or, rather, I have tried to portray those track records accurately.

The professionals themselves are actually quite sanguine about their own abilities. A City saying is: 'When it comes to market forecasts, there are only two types of expert: those who don't know and those who don't know that they don't know.'

I have also mentioned the moods of mania and panic which occasionally grip the stock-market.

Can you cast your mind back to the stock-market crash of October 1987? I remember that, in the weeks leading up to the crash, the pundits were actively spewing out 'buy' recommendations, accompanied by all kinds of reasons why that particular stock-market boom was different from its predecessors. After the crash, oddly, there seemed to be many more 'sell' recommendations. This is rather strange: you would think that, if something has suddenly become 30% cheaper, it would actually be a better buy.

None the less, professionals and individuals were rushing in to buy before the crash rather than after it.

Before telling you what this preamble is leading up to, I need to digress for a moment to tell you about 'Fermat's Last Theorem'. Pierre de Fermat was a famous French mathematician whose last theorem was scribbled, without proof, in the margin of one of his works. Following his death in 1666, mathematicians struggled for over 300 years to seek to prove this theorem*.

It was finally proved quite recently by the mathematician Andrew Wiles. The story of his lifetime of dedicated effort to prove the theorem is a great inspiration.

So, I finally wish to introduce you to:

---

### *Thorneycroft's Last Theorem*

**Two groups of people are usually wrong – the experts and the majority**

---

This theorem (or, more precisely, conjecture) relates specifically to the world of investment. I suspect that it is widely applicable in other walks of life, at least to the experts but, perhaps, not so much to the majority of the general public.

Perhaps this theorem is a good subject for research for the *next* 300 years! (Maybe a useful, practical application of Chaos theory?) Meanwhile, I would suggest that you pursue your investment plan as if it *were* correct.

* Fermat's Last Theorem states that equations of the form $x^n + y^n = z^n$, where x, y, z and n are integers (whole numbers), have no solutions if n is greater than 2. And you thought that investment was complicated!

Finally, it only remains for me to wish you well with your investments.
Good luck!

# Index